CherokeeEntertains

ii

The object of the Service League of Cherokee County, Georgia, is to encourage interest in the needs of the community and to train its members for efficient service in any charitable work undertaken by the League.

The proceeds from the sale of **Cherokee Entertains** will be used to support the charitable work sponsored by the League.

First Printing - September 1985
Second Printing - April 1986
Third Printing - September 1989
Fourth Printing - May 1991
Fifth Printing - July 1994

To order additional copies of

Cherokee Entertains

please use the forms provided in the back of the book or write to:

Cherokee Entertains
P.O. Box 1132
Canton, Georgia 30114

Library of Congress Card Number 85-51158

ISBN 0-9614610-1-2

Printed in the USA by

WIMMER
The Wimmer Companies, Inc.
Memphis • Dallas

Introduction

Whether handed down from one generation to the next or conceived in moments of culinary creativity, recipes are a legacy of the South. Southern recipes are meant to be shared, treasured and exchanged, but most of all to be enjoyed with family and friends.

The year 1985 marked the 50th anniversary of the Service League of Cherokee County, Georgia. Through the volunteer efforts of its members, the Service League has provided food, clothing, school supplies and medical assistance to many deserving families with children. **League Legacy**, the original name for our current **Cherokee Entertains**, was conceived and created to celebrate 50 years of this community service.

Many hours have gone into the selecting and testing of the recipes included in this cookbook. The Cookbook Committee has attempted to provide recipes of interest to all tastes by including unique, new and all-time favorites. Each recipe has been carefully edited for consistency and accuracy.

Cherokee Entertains is dedicated to all those who have served as members of the Service League over the past 50 years for the love, time and devotion each has given. It is also dedicated to our community for the continued support given to the League's activities.

We hope this collection of recipes will become favorites with you–a legacy to be treasured and enjoyed for many years to come.

Cherokee Rose–the Georgia State Flower

Legend tells us that the name was derived from the Indian tribe which widely distributed the plant, but little is written about the Cherokee Rose. The simple but exquisite Cherokee Rose grows throughout Georgia, officially becoming the state flower in 1916, but as early as the late 1700's it was found in Georgia gardens and was used to fence off large plantations. Today it often provides protection and a nesting place for Georgia's official bird, the Brown Thrasher.

Cookbook Committee

Cookbook Chairmen & Co-Chairmen

Wanda Roach, 1985-1986
Frances Gober, 1986-1987
Ollie White, 1987-1988
Ollie White & Dianne Murphy, 1988-1989
Dianne Murphy & Paula DeLuca,
1989-1990
Dale Roper & Janis Farr, 1990-1991
Donna Beavers & Debbie Weissenberg,
1991-1992
Debbie Weissenberg, 1992-1993
Nancy Kinsey & Pam Carnes, 1993-1994
Pam Carnes & Patti Skelton, 1994-1995

Current Cookbook Committee 1994-1995

Pam Carnes - Chairman
Patti Skelton - Co-Chairman
Paula Doss
Connie Garrison
Kay Halpin
Karen Hawley
Nancy Kinsey
Lynda McFarland
Veda Moss
Charlotte Sparks
Tracy Weaver

Original Cookbook Committee 1985-1986

Chairman

Wanda Roach

Committee Chairmen

Joan Anderson
Frances Gober
Margaret Logan
Shirley Pahl
Emma Ridenhour

Committee Members

Jeannie Adams
Ann Benzel
Judy Bishop
Cissy Cloud
Deanie Fincher
Deborah Fincher
Pat Gold
Debra Goodwin
Linda Hasty
Elly Hobgood
Rebecca Johnston
Susan Padgett
Madelin Phelps
Helen Spears
Lila Stevens
Carolyn Weaver
Marjean Morris, typist
Betty McDaniel, typist

Artist

Joan McFather

The Cookbook Committee wishes to express grateful appreciation to our ARTIST, Brenda Tustian. More about Brenda on page 339.

The Committee wishes to thank everyone who submitted their recipes for the cookbook. We regret we were unable to use all recipes due to similarity and lack of space.

Table of Contents

SERVICE LEAGUE OF CHEROKEE COUNTY
ACTIVE MEMBERS
1994-1995

Beth Allison
Jennifer Bagwell
Linda Bell
Sally Bradshaw
Leslie Bryan
Jan Buchanan
Katie Buckner
Pam Carnes
Pam Chandler
Trudy Christopher
Leticia Cline
Cathy Conway
Janie Cuzzort
Paula DeLuca
Paula Doss

Susan Dreschel
Joan Duff
Teresa Foster
Kebra Galt
Connie Garrison
Lisa Garrison
Christie Geiger
Kim Groves
Kay Halpin
Karen Hawley
Debbie Haygood
Marlene Hefner
Ivy Hilliard
Paula Holtzclaw
Nancy Kinsey

Alicia Looper
Joan Lumpkin
Ellen McElyea
Lynda McFarland
Jamie Morgan
Veda Moss
Dianne Murphy
Janice Newbold
Lynn Payne
Sharon Peters
Betty Roach
Carla Roach
Lynn Satterfield
Earlene Shadburn
Sandy Simmons

Patti Skelton
Vicki Smith
Charlotte Sparks
Dana Swords
Michelle Thacker
Susan Thacker
Rena Weatherby
Tracy Weaver
Debbie Weissenberg
Ollie White
Michelle Whitmire
Candy Wilbanks
Dawn Wilbanks
Mary Wuestefeld
Kathy Yarbrough

HONORARY MEMBERS

Sara Jones*
Helen Vandiviere*
Sue Garlington*
Mary Darnell*
Nina Jones
Era Foster*
Evelena Haworth*
Bill Daniel*
Marie Pressly
Grace Hyatt
Betty Coker
Peggy Jones
Frances Jones*
Hattie Mae Price*
Martha Fincher*
Marjorie McCanless
Sally Boring
Elizabeth Garrett
Lynn Jones*
Frances Owen
Clarice Bagwell
Elizabeth Andrews*
Selene Hendrix
Tissie Jones

Katherine Fincher
Virginia Jones
Patricia Alexander
Ann Cullens
Rachael Palmer
Virginia Spears
Martha Jane Haney
Sarah Buffington
Ruth Denney
Mary Sparks
Lane Towers
Lillian Thomason
Sara Lathem
Frances Pulliam
Beth Raines
Ann Weeks
Ann Bradshaw
Charlotte Gray
Sybil Turner
Peggy Moore
Betty Barrett
Hazel Price
Elaine Swift
Carolyn Vancil*

Dot Anderson
Martha Brigham
Barbara Manous
Eugenia Reid*
Sue Ellen Turner
Ann Rutledge
Ann Hopkins
Pat Stewart
Jo Ellen Wilson
Raye Snell
Ann Fincher
Barbara Helton
Mary Johnston
Joan McFather
Linda Merrell
Barbara Gentry
Patty Mann
Linda Schwamlein
Peggy Rutledge
Margaret Logan
Joan Anderson
Shirley Pahl
Helen Spears
Cissy Cloud

Linda Hasty
Jeannie Adams
Debra Fincher
Wanda Roach
Margie Bagwell*
Frances Gober
Judy McClure
Susan Padgett-
  Harrison
Julia Dennis
Carole Haley
Lila Stevens
Judy Bishop
Deanie Fincher
Pat Gold
Debra Goodwin
Rebecca Johnston
Mandy Mills
Ann Benzel
Christi Kook
Madelin Phelps
Anne Harris
Joy Owen
Carolyn Weaver

*Deceased

Appetizers

Stuffed Pasta Shells

Oven: 350° - 30 minutes   **Yield:** 25-30 servings

1 (8-ounce) package large
    shell macaroni
2 eggs, beaten
2 cups Ricotta cheese
½ cup green peppers,
    finely chopped
¼ cup onion, finely
    chopped
¼ cup snipped parsley
¼ cup milk or light cream
½ teaspoon lemon peel,
    finely shredded

½ teaspoon mace
½ teaspoon salt
1 (15½-ounce) can
    salmon, drained and
    bones removed
1 cup fine dry bread
    crumbs
2 tablespoons butter,
    melted
1 cup Parmesan cheese,
    grated

Cook macaroni uncovered in large amount of boiling salted water for about 20 minutes; drain. Rinse with cold water; drain. Set aside. Combine eggs, Ricotta, green pepper, onion, parsley, milk, lemon peel, mace and salt. Beat in salmon. Pipe or spoon into cooked shells. Place shells filled side up in 13x9-inch baking dish. (This may be prepared 24 hours before serving, at this point.) Before serving, add 2 tablespoons water to dish. Bake covered in 350° oven for 30 minutes. In saucepan, combine crumbs and butter; cook and stir until browned. Cool. Stir in Parmesan. Sprinkle over shells. Bake uncovered 5 minutes more. Serve hot.
Can be served as a luncheon dish.

Gaye Mothershed

Hot Cheese Canapés

Oven: Broil 2-4 minutes   **Yield:** 4 dozen

1 (8-ounce) package small
    dinner rolls
1½ cups Cheddar cheese,
    grated
1 cup ripe olives,
    chopped

½ cup mayonnaise
½ cup green onions,
    chopped
½ teaspoon chili powder
½ teaspoon salt

Split rolls in half. Combine remaining ingredients. Spread mixture on each half of rolls. Place under broiler for 2-4 minutes until hot and bubbly.
Do ahead. Freezes well.

Virginia Spears

Chutneyed Snow Peas

Yield: 50

1 (8-ounce) package cream
   cheese
3 tablespoons mango
   chutney or other
   chutney
1 teaspoon lemon juice
   Dash of garlic salt

¼ pound sliced bacon,
   cooked well and drained
1½ quarts water
1 teaspoon salt
6 ounces fresh snow peas
   (about 50)

In food processor with fitted steel blade, combine cream cheese, chutney, lemon juice, garlic salt and bacon. Process until smooth. (Can be made ahead. Transfer to a small bowl; cover and refrigerate up to 3 days. Let stand at room temperature 2 hours before using.) In a large saucepan, bring water and salt to a boil over high heat; add snow peas. Cook 30 seconds; drain and rinse under cold water. (Can be covered and refrigerated up to 24 hours.) With pastry bag or small spoon, fill each snow pea with cream cheese mixture. Cover and refrigerate until serving time.
Delicious.

Helen Spears

Jalapeño Cocktail Pie

Oven: 350° - 30 minutes **Yield:** 3 dozen

2 or 3 Jalapeño peppers,
   seeded and chopped
1 pound sharp Cheddar
   cheese, shredded

6 eggs, beaten

Sprinkle peppers in a well-greased 9-inch square pan; cover with cheese. Pour eggs over cheese. Bake at 350° for 30 minutes or until firm. Cool and cut into 1-inch squares.
Easy, do ahead. A hit at parties.

Martha Nichols

Ham and Cheese Sandwiches

Oven: 250°   Yield: 8 dozen

1 cup margarine, softened
2 tablespoons poppy seeds
3-4 tablespoons prepared
    mustard
1 small onion, grated
1 tablespoon Worcestershire
  Salt and pepper to taste

4 (8-ounce) packages small
  dinner rolls, frozen
1 pound baked ham,
  finely chopped
½ pound Swiss cheese,
  grated

Combine margarine, poppy seeds, mustard, onion, Worcestershire, salt and pepper. Spread on both sides of split frozen rolls. Sprinkle with ham and cheese. Press together firmly in original tray. Cover with foil tightly; refreeze. Remove from freezer ½ to 1 hour before serving. Heat at 250° until hot.

Judy Bishop

Rumaki

Yield: 8 servings

1 pound chicken livers,
  halved
4 tablespoons soy sauce
4 tablespoons brown sugar

1 (8-ounce) can water
  chestnuts, drained
12 to 14 bacon slices,
   cut in thirds

Dip liver halves in combined soy sauce and brown sugar. Slice water chestnuts in half. Hold each piece of liver and water chestnut and wrap bacon slice around both pieces. Secure both ends with a toothpick. Broil until bacon is crisp.

Frances Gober

Chicken Log

Yield: 1 (9-inch) log

2 (8-ounce) packages cream
  cheese, softened
1 tablespoon steak sauce
½ teaspoon curry powder
1½ cups cooked chicken,
   minced

⅓ cup celery, finely chopped
2 tablespoons parsley, minced
½ cup almonds, toasted
  and chopped

Combine cream cheese, steak sauce and curry powder. Beat with electric mixer until smooth. Stir in chicken, celery and parsley. Shape into a 9-inch log. Roll log in toasted almonds. Wrap in waxed paper. Chill 4-5 hours. Serve with crackers.

Florence Cauble

Chicken Curry Cream Cheese Ball

Yield: 1 large ball

1 (8-ounce) package cream
  cheese, softened
1 cup cooked chicken,
  finely chopped
¾ cup almonds, toasted
  and finely chopped

⅓ cup mayonnaise
2 tablespoons chutney,
  chopped
1 tablespoon curry powder
¼ teaspoon salt
  Chopped parsley

Mix cream cheese, chicken, almonds, mayonnaise, chutney, curry and salt. Chill several hours. Shape into ball. Roll in parsley. Serve with crackers.

Cissy Cloud

Oriental Meatballs

Oven: 450° - 8-10 minutes

Yield: 4½ dozen

1½ pounds ground beef
  chuck
¾ cup water chestnuts,
  finely chopped
2 tablespoons onion, grated
¼ cup dry bread crumbs
1 egg
  Salt and pepper to taste

¼ cup soy sauce
½ cup pineapple juice
½ cup dry sherry
2 tablespoons brown sugar
¼ teaspoon ginger
1 tablespoon cornstarch
½ cup chicken broth

Mix together beef, water chestnuts, onion, crumbs, egg, salt and pepper to taste. Form into balls about 1-inch in diameter. Place slightly apart on greased cookie sheet. Bake uncovered at 450° for 8-10 minutes or until lightly browned. (Cover and chill if made ahead.) Stir together soy sauce, pineapple juice, sherry, sugar and ginger in a wide saucepan. Add meatballs; simmer 15 minutes. Stir cornstarch into chicken broth to dissolve. Stir into meatball mixture. Simmer until slightly thickened. Keep meatballs warm in chafing dish.
Worth the effort.

Judy Bishop

Tangy-Sweet Meatballs

Oven: 350° - 30 minutes

Yield: 5 dozen

1 pound ground beef
1 pound ground pork
2 cups soft bread
  crumbs
2 eggs, slightly beaten
½ cup onion, finely
  chopped

1 tablespoon minced parsley
1 teaspoon salt
2 tablespoons margarine,
  melted
1 (10-ounce) jar apricot
  preserves
½ cup barbecue sauce

Combine first seven ingredients, mixing well. Shape into 1-inch balls and brown in margarine. Drain meatballs on paper towels. Place in a 13x9-inch baking dish. Combine preserves and barbecue sauce; mix well. Pour over meatballs. Bake at 350° for 30 minutes. Serve in chafing dish with sauce.

Ann Ruppel

Ham Asparagus Roll Ups

Yield: 48 servings

1 (8-ounce) package cream
cheese, softened
1 tablespoon mayonnaise
2 teaspoons Worcestershire
Dash of dry mustard
(optional)

3 (8-ounce) packages sliced
ham
1 (15-ounce) can asparagus
spears, extra long

Cream together cream cheese, mayonnaise, Worcestershire and dry mustard.
Spread 2 teaspoons of creamed mixture on dried ham slice. Roll asparagus
spear in ham. Slice into desired size. Secure with toothpick.

Judy Bishop

Mushroom Squares

Oven: 400° - 7 minutes   **Yield:** 20 squares

5 slices sandwich bread
Butter
4 ounces mushroom stems
and pieces, drained and
chopped
4 slices bacon, cooked
and crumbled

¼ cup Swiss cheese, shredded
2 tablespoons mayonnaise
1 tablespoon dried parsley
flakes
Dash of salt

Trim crusts from bread; cut into quarters. Butter bread and place on a baking
sheet buttered side down. Mix the remaining ingredients; spoon a small amount
on bread squares. (May be prepared a day ahead, covered and refrigerated.)
Bake at 400° for 7 minutes.

Wanda Roach

Marinated Mushrooms

Yield: 1 pound

⅔ cup dry white wine
⅔ cup white wine vinegar
½ cup salad oil
½ cup onions, finely
chopped
4 tablespoons parsley,
freshly chopped

1 clove garlic, crushed
2 bay leaves
2 teaspoons salt
½ teaspoon dried fresh
thyme
Dash of pepper
1 pound fresh mushrooms

Combine all ingredients except mushrooms in a saucepan; bring to a boil. Add
mushrooms. Simmer 10-12 minutes, uncovered. Ladle into a warm jar. Cool
and store in refrigerator at least 12 hours before serving.
Will keep in refrigerator up to 3 weeks.

Frances Gober

Hot Mushroom Turnovers

Oven: 450° - 12-14 minutes   **Yield:** 3½ dozen

Turnovers

 1 (8-ounce) package cream
    cheese, softened
 1½ cups all-purpose flour

 ½ cup butter or margarine,
    softened

In large bowl with mixer at medium speed, beat cream cheese, flour and butter or margarine until smooth. Shape into ball; wrap. Refrigerate 1 hour or longer.

Filling

 3 tablespoons butter
    or margarine
 2 tablespoons all-purpose
    flour
 1 large onion, minced
 ½ pound mushrooms,
    minced

 ¼ cup sour cream
 1 teaspoon salt
 ¼ teaspoon thyme leaves
 1 egg, beaten

Melt butter or margarine; cook mushrooms and onions until tender. Stir in sour cream, salt, thyme leaves and flour; set aside. On floured surface with floured rolling pin, roll half of dough ⅛-inch thick. With floured 2¾-inch round cookie cutter, cut out as many circles as possible. Repeat. Place a teaspoon of mushroom mixture onto one half of each dough circle. Brush sides of circle with egg; fold dough over filling. Firmly press edges together to seal with a fork; prick tops. Place on ungreased cookie sheet; brush with remaining egg. Bake at 450° for 12-14 minutes until golden.
Can be done ahead and frozen unbaked, then cooked.

Cissy Cloud

Spinach Balls

Oven: 325° - 15-20 minutes   **Yield:** 11 dozen

 2 (10-ounce) packages frozen
    chopped spinach
 3 cups herb-seasoned
    stuffing mix
 1 large onion, finely
    chopped
 6 eggs, well beaten

 ¾ cup margarine, melted
 ½ cup Parmesan cheese,
    grated
 1 tablespoon pepper
 1½ teaspoons garlic salt
 ½ teaspoon thyme

Cook spinach according to package directions; drain well and squeeze to remove excess moisture. Combine spinach and remaining ingredients, mixing well. Shape spinach mixture into ¾-inch balls; place on lightly greased cookie sheets. Bake at 325° for 15-20 minutes.
Can be frozen before baking. Place on cookie sheets and freeze until firm. When frozen, remove and store in plastic bags. Thaw slightly and bake.

Margaret Logan

Spinach Tarts

Oven: 350° - 30-35 minutes   **Yield:** 2½ dozen

Cream Cheese Pastry Shells

1 (3-ounce) package cream
  cheese, softened
½ cup margarine, softened

1½ cups all-purpose
  flour

Combine cream cheese with margarine. Cream; add flour, mixing well. Shape into 1-inch balls. Place in tiny muffin pans. Shape into shell.

Spinach Filling

1 (10-ounce) package frozen
  chopped spinach, thawed
  and drained
1 egg, beaten
¼ teaspoon salt
⅛ teaspoon pepper
2 tablespoons onion,
  chopped

1 cup Romano or Parmesan
  cheese, grated
¼ cup butter, melted
2 tablespoons Parmesan
  cheese, grated
Diced pimiento (optional)

Place spinach on paper towels; drain thoroughly. Combine spinach with egg, salt, pepper, onion, cheese and butter. Mix well. Fill each pastry shell with teaspoon of spinach mixture. Sprinkle with cheese. Bake at 350° for 30-35 minutes. Garnish with pimiento.

Linda Hasty

Spinach Cheese Puffs

Oven: 350° - 30 minutes   **Yield:** 30 servings

1 medium onion, finely
  chopped
¼ cup olive oil
1 (10-ounce) package frozen
  chopped spinach, thawed
½ pound Feta cheese,
  crumbled

1 (3-ounce) package cream
  cheese, softened
3 eggs, beaten
¼ cup dry bread crumbs
½ pound Phyllo dough
½ cup butter, melted

Sauté onion in oil for about 5 minutes. Add spinach; simmer until most of moisture has evaporated. Add Feta cheese to cream cheese, blending well. Add eggs, mixing well. Toss bread crumbs into spinach-onion mixture; add to cheese mixture. Stir until well blended. Place 6 or 7 sheets of Phyllo dough in a buttered 11x14x2-inch pan, brushing each sheet with melted butter. (Keep sheets not being used covered with a damp cloth.) Add spinach mixture. Place 7 or 8 sheets of Phyllo dough on filling, buttering each sheet. Bake at 350° for 30 minutes or until golden brown. Cut into small squares or triangles.
Can be cut into larger squares for a luncheon dish.

June Phillips

Canapé Crackers

Oven: 450° - 5 minutes   **Yield:** 5 dozen

2 cups Bisquick
⅓ cup butter, softened
1 (8-ounce) package cream
   cheese, softened

1 envelope sour cream
   sauce mix
1 teaspoon dill weed
   or poppy seeds

Blend Bisquick, butter, cream cheese and sauce mix. Work with hands to make a soft dough. Divide dough in half. Roll each half about ⅛ inch thick on floured board. Cut with floured 2-inch cutter. Sprinkle with dill weed or poppy seeds. Bake on ungreased baking sheet at 450° for 5 minutes or until light brown. Cool. Spread each with your favorite sandwich spread.

Carole Haley

Olive Cheese Balls

Oven: 350° - 20 minutes   **Yield:** 4 dozen

2 cups Cheddar cheese,
   shredded
½ cup butter, softened
1 cup all-purpose flour

1 teaspoon paprika
48 large pimiento-
   stuffed olives

Combine all ingredients except olives. Shape 1 tablespoon of cheese mixture around each olive. Bake at 350° for 20 minutes or until lightly browned.

Judy Bishop

1, 2, 3 Cheese Straws

Oven: 350° - 12-15 minutes   **Yield:** 3 dozen

1 pound sharp Cheddar
   cheese, grated and
   softened
1 cup margarine, softened

3 cups all-purpose flour
   Several dashes of red
   cayenne pepper

Cream together cheese and margarine. Add flour and pepper. Mix thoroughly. Force through cookie press, using the star design, onto greased cookie sheet. Make into long strips and break into shorter ones later. Bake at 350° for 12-15 minutes until lightly browned. Do not overcook.

Jeweldine Chambers

Cheddar Cheese Pennies

Oven: 400° - 12-15 minutes   **Yield:** 2 dozen

½ pound Cheddar cheese,
   grated
1 cup all-purpose flour

½ cup margarine, softened
1 teaspoon dry mustard

Combine all ingredients until a ball forms. Roll dough into 1-inch balls; place 2 inches apart on an ungreased cookie sheet. Bake at 400° for 12-15 minutes. Serve hot.

Cindy Holcomb

Cheese Wafers

Oven: 375° - 10 minutes   **Yield:** 8 dozen

8 ounces sharp Cheddar
   cheese, grated
1 cup margarine, softened
2 cups all-purpose flour
   (measure, then sift)

⅛ teaspoon red cayenne
   pepper
Dash of salt
2 cups oven-toasted
   rice cereal

Combine cheese, margarine, flour, pepper and salt. Mix well. Add rice cereal. Shape into small walnut-sized balls. Place on ungreased cookie sheet. Flatten with a fork. Bake at 375° for 10 minutes or until lightly browned.

Geneva Johnson

Pic-A-Pepper Spread

1 (8-ounce) package cream
   cheese

½ (5-ounce) bottle
   Pic-A-Pepper sauce

Place cream cheese on tray. Cover with Pic-A-Pepper sauce. Serve with Triscuits or other crackers.
Variation: Cover with ½ bottle Mayor Grey's Chutney.

Nathan Brandon

Cheese Ball I

Yield: 1 large ball

1 pound Cheddar cheese,
   grated
2 (8-ounce) packages cream
   cheese, softened

1 cup pecans, chopped,
   divided
2 cloves garlic, minced
1-2 tablespoons steak sauce

Mix cheeses, ½ cup pecans, garlic and steak sauce. Shape into a ball; roll in remaining pecans. Refrigerate. Serve with crackers.

Pam Gaddis

Cheese Ball II

Yield: 1 large ball

½ pound medium sharp
   Cheddar cheese, grated
1 (8-ounce) package cream
   cheese, softened
½ pound pimiento cheese
   spread

2 or 3 cloves garlic,
   minced
¾ cup pecans, chopped
   Chili powder

Combine cheeses and pimiento cheese spread; add minced garlic. Shape into ball. Roll in chopped pecans. Sprinkle with chili powder. Chill. Serve with crackers.

Debbie Perry

Melba's Boursin Cheese

Yield: 3 cups

1 cup butter, softened
2 (8-ounce) packages cream
   cheese, softened
2 cloves garlic, pressed
½ teaspoon oregano
¼ teaspoon basil

¼ teaspoon dill weed
¼ teaspoon marjoram
¼ teaspoon freshly ground
   black pepper
¼ teaspoon thyme

Mix all ingredients thoroughly with mixer. Place in decorative containers. Refrigerate to blend flavors. Serve at room temperature with crackers.
Best if made 2 days ahead. Keeps several days in refrigerator. Makes a nice gift.

Elly Hobgood

Cheese Puffs

Oven: 400° - 10-12 minutes

Yield: 8 dozen

1 (16-ounce) loaf unsliced
   sandwich bread
1 (3-ounce) package cream
   cheese
1 (8-ounce) package sharp
   Cheddar cheese

1 cup margarine
4 egg whites,
   stiffly beaten

Trim off and discard bread crust; cut bread into ¾-inch cubes. Set aside. Combine cheese and margarine in top of double-boiler; cook over boiling water until cheese is melted and mixture is smooth. Stir often. Remove from heat. Fold small amount of hot cheese into egg whites; then fold in remaining cheese. Using a fork, dip each cube into cheese, coating on all sides. Set 1 inch apart on greased baking sheet; cover and refrigerate overnight. (Can freeze at this point on trays; then remove to plastic bags.) Bake uncovered at 400° for 10-12 minutes until golden brown. Serve immediately. (Bake frozen cubes at 400° for 12-15 minutes.)

Joan McFather

Tex Mex Dip

Yield: 8 servings

3 medium ripe avocados
2 tablespoons lemon juice
½ teaspoon salt
¼ teaspoon pepper
1 cup sour cream
½ cup mayonnaise
1 package Taco
  seasoning mix
2 (10½-ounce) cans plain
  or Jalapeño bean dip

1 bunch green onions,
  chopped
3 medium tomatoes, cored,
  seeded and chopped
2 (3½-ounce) cans pitted
  ripe olives, chopped
1 (8-ounce) package sharp
  Cheddar cheese, shredded

Peel, pit and mash avocados in bowl with lemon juice, salt and pepper. Mix in separate bowl sour cream, mayonnaise and Taco seasoning mix. To assemble: Spread bean dip in large dish; top with avocado mixture; top with sour cream taco mixture; sprinkle with onion, tomato, olives, and cheese. Serve with corn chips.

Bertice Muddiman

Pico de Gallo

Yield: Approximately 1 quart

10 medium tomatoes,
  chopped
2 small onions, chopped
6 Jalapeño peppers, finely
  chopped
2 medium green peppers,
  chopped

2 cloves of garlic,
  minced
½ teaspoon salt
½ to 1 teaspoon Cilantro
  (optional)

Mix all ingredients together. Refrigerate until ready to use. Serve with tostados or chips.
Can use more or less Jalapeño peppers to taste.

Janis Farr

Angels on Horseback

Oven: Broil - 12-15 minutes   **Yield:** 30

1 (12-ounce) can oysters,
  fresh or frozen
10 slices bacon,
  cut in thirds

2 tablespoons parsley,
  chopped
½ teaspoon salt
Paprika

Drain oysters. Place an oyster on each piece of bacon. Sprinkle with parsley and seasonings. Wrap bacon around oysters and secure with toothpick. Place on broiler pan. Broil about 4 inches from heat 8-10 minutes or until bacon is crisp. Turn. Broil 4-5 minutes longer until bacon is crisp.

Cookbook Committee

Hot Crabmeat Pastries

Oven: 425° - 12-15 minutes   **Yield:** 24 pastries

Dough

½ cup butter, softened   1½ cups all-purpose flour
1 (3-ounce) package cream
  cheese, softened

Mix butter, cream cheese and flour. Put small amount of dough in 1-inch muffin tins. Prick bottoms. Bake at 425° for 12-15 minutes.

Filling

1 (6½-ounce) can crabmeat,   ¾ cup cream
  drained   ¼ cup sherry
2 tablespoons onion,   4 tablespoons chili sauce
  finely chopped   1 teaspoon Worcestershire
1 very small clove garlic   ⅛ teaspoon Tabasco
3 tablespoons butter   1 teaspoon Accent
4 tablespoons all-purpose   Salt to taste
  flour

Brown onion and garlic in butter. Blend in flour. Add remaining ingredients. Cook, stirring constantly until thick.

Topping

2 ounces mild Cheddar   ½ teaspoon paprika
  cheese, grated   ½ teaspoon dry mustard
1 (3-ounce) package cream   ½ teaspoon baking powder
  cheese, softened   ½ teaspoon Worcestershire
3 tablespoons butter   1 egg white, stiffly
1 egg yolk   beaten
1 tablespoon cream
  Salt to taste

Blend all ingredients except egg white. When thoroughly mixed, fold in egg white. Fill shells to rim with filling. Pile on topping. Broil until puffed and brown, about 4 minutes.
Very delicious and worth the effort.

Wanda Roach

Miniature Cream Puffs

Oven: 375° - 30 minutes   **Yield:** 4 dozen

1 **cup water**
½ **cup margarine**
¼ **teaspoon salt**

1 **cup all-purpose flour**
4 **eggs**

In a saucepan, heat water and margarine to boiling and margarine is melted. Reduce heat and add salt and flour while stirring with wire whisk. Stir approximately 1 minute, or until mixture forms a ball. Remove from heat. Beat in the eggs one at a time with whisk until mixture is smooth. Place rounded teaspoons of the dough on an ungreased baking sheet (non-stick surface). Bake at 375° for 25 minutes, or until golden brown. Remove from oven; quickly cut slit in side of each puff to allow steam to escape. Return to oven for 5 minutes. Cool on wire rack. Fill with chicken salad, ham salad, etc. Puffs can be made a day ahead. Store in covered container in cool place until filled. Refrigerate after filling. *This dough can be used for making larger puffs to be filled with pudding or whipped cream, sprinkled with confectioners' sugar, and used as a dessert.*

Margaret Logan

Scallop Kabobs

Yield: 8 servings

12 **strips sliced bacon**
16 **large sea scallops,**
      halved
16 **water chestnuts,**
      halved
16 **(5 to 6-inch) bamboo**
      skewers
⅓ **cup soy sauce**

⅓ **cup white wine**
      vinegar
      Dash Worcestershire
1 **clove garlic, minced**
1 **teaspoon ginger**

Partially cook bacon until light brown; cut into pieces the same size as scallops. Alternate bacon, scallops and water chestnuts on skewers. Arrange in shallow dish. Combine other ingredients in processor; mix well. Pour over kabobs. Cover and marinate 2-3 hours. Grill kabobs over low coals, about 6 minutes per side. *Delicious.*

Helen Spears

Oysters Keithsburg

Oven: Broil   **Yield:** 24 servings

1 pound bacon, uncooked,
   chopped fine
1 cup green peppers,
   chopped
1 (4-ounce) can pimientos,
   drained and chopped

1 teaspoon salt
½ teaspoon pepper
1 tablespoon paprika
1 quart oysters or
   2 dozen fresh oysters
Rock salt

Mix first 6 ingredients well; set aside. Line broiler pans with aluminum foil and fill with rock salt. Place cleaned oyster shells filled with oysters on rock salt bed (rock salt simply supports oyster shell). Put one heaping spoonful of bacon mixture on each oyster. Cook under broiler until golden brown on top. Save oyster shells for next time. Serve with cocktail forks.
Good with either fresh or shucked oysters.

Skip Spears

Smoked Salmon Spread

Yield: 3½ cups

1 (15½-ounce) can salmon,
   drained
1 (8-ounce) package cream
   cheese, softened
2 tablespoons lemon juice
3½ teaspoons onion, grated

2½ teaspoons horseradish
¾ teaspoon salt
¼ teaspoon liquid smoke
   Dash of Worcestershire
   Several dashes cayenne
   pepper

Debone salmon. Mix all ingredients. Chill. Serve with crackers.

Frances Gober

Shrimp Mold

1½ envelopes unflavored gelatin
½ cup boiling water
1 (8-ounce) package cream
   cheese, softened
1 cup mayonnaise
2 teaspoons onion, grated

1 cup celery, finely
   chopped (optional)
1 tablespoon lemon juice
   Salt and pepper to taste
   Accent to taste
2 cups (1 pound) shrimp,
   finely chopped

Soften gelatin in boiling water. Mix cream cheese, mayonnaise, onion, celery, lemon juice and seasonings. Add gelatin and shrimp. Pour in a greased mold. Chill until firm. Better if chilled overnight. Serve with crackers.

Pat Gold

Shrimp Butter

Yield: 2½ cups

1 pound shrimp, cooked
1 (8-ounce) package cream
  cheese, softened
¾ cup soft butter
  (no substitute)

Juice of 1 lemon
4 tablespoons mayonnaise
1 tablespoon onion, minced

Chop shrimp by hand or in food processor. Save a few to use as garnish. Mix all other ingredients until smooth. Add shrimp last. Pack in a greased mold. Chill for several hours. Unmold and serve with crackers.

Cookbook Committee

Shrimp Spread

2 teaspoons sugar
2 teaspoons water
2 teaspoons vinegar
1 pinch salt
2 eggs, beaten
1 (8-ounce) package cream
  cheese, softened

3 heaping tablespoons sour
  cream
1 medium onion, grated
2 (6-ounce) cans shrimp

Combine sugar, water, vinegar, salt and eggs. Cook over low heat, stirring constantly until thick. Pour over cream cheese; add sour cream. Mix with electric mixer, beating about 1 minute. Add onion and shrimp. Beat until shrimp is shredded. Place in freezer for about 1 hour. Serve with party crackers, rye or pumpernickel.

Betty McDaniel

Crab Paté

Yield: 12 servings

1 (10¾-ounce) can cream of
  mushroom soup, undiluted
1 envelope unflavored gelatin
3 tablespoons cold water
¾ cup mayonnaise
1 (6½-ounce) can crab meat
1 small bunch green onions,
  finely chopped

1 cup celery, very
  finely chopped
Garlic salt to taste
Tabasco to taste
Parsley sprigs

Heat soup in saucepan over low heat. Dissolve gelatin in cold water and then add to soup; stir well. Add next 4 ingredients along with garlic salt and Tabasco sauce to taste. Pour into a greased 1-quart mold. Chill overnight. Unmold and garnish with parsley.

Deborah Fincher

Hot Tuna Puffs

Oven: Broil

Yield: 2 dozen

1 (6½-ounce) can tuna
¼ cup mayonnaise or
  salad dressing
1 tablespoon catsup
1 tablespoon vinegar

Dash of salt
Dash of cayenne pepper
2-3 drops Worcestershire
24 Melba toast rounds
Parsley sprigs

Drain tuna and flake finely. Mix with mayonnaise, catsup, vinegar, salt, pepper and Worcestershire. Spoon mixture on the toast rounds. Place on a cookie sheet in a preheated broiler, about 3-4 inches from heat for 1-2 minutes, or until lightly browned. Garnish each with a tiny sprig of parsley
Easy and quick. Ingredients always available for last minute guests.

Joan Anderson

Crab Supreme on Toast Points

Yield: 4-6 servings

4 tablespoons butter
4 tablespoons all-purpose
  flour
1½ cups half and half
2 cups baked crab

½ cup mushrooms
½ cup pimiento-stuffed
  olives, chopped
3 pimientos, chopped
Toast points

Melt butter in saucepan. Add flour; then add remaining ingredients. Cook until hot. Serve over toast points.

Julia Ellis

Hot Crab Triangles

Oven: 400° - 10-12 minutes

Yield: 48

1 (8-ounce) package cream
  cheese, softened
½ teaspoon dry mustard
1 tablespoon milk
¼ teaspoon salt
  Dash of cayenne
1 (6-ounce) can white
  crab meat, drained
  and flaked

2 tablespoons green onion,
  minced
2 tablespoons blanched
  almonds, chopped
12 slices white bread,
  crusts trimmed
Paprika

Beat cheese until fluffy. Combine mustard and milk; add to cheese with next 5 ingredients. Mix well. Spread on bread slices. Cut each slice into 4 triangles. Sprinkle with paprika. Bake at 400° for 10-12 minutes or until browned.

Joan McFather

Shrimp Dip

Yield: 4 cups

1 (8-ounce) package cream
   cheese, softened
¾ cup mayonnaise
3 tablespoons catsup
Juice of 1 lemon

1 pound shrimp, cooked
Salt to taste
1 stalk celery, finely
   chopped
1 medium onion, grated

Combine cream cheese, mayonnaise, catsup and lemon juice; blend until smooth. Stir in remaining ingredients. Cover and refrigerate overnight. Serve with crackers or corn chips.
Always a hit at parties.

Mary Sparks

Clam Dip

Yield: 2½ cups

1 (8-ounce) package cream
   cheese, softened
1 tablespoon mayonnaise
½ teaspoon onion, grated
1 teaspoon lemon juice

½ teaspoon garlic salt
⅛ teaspoon Worcestershire
   Dash of Tabasco
1 (6½-ounce) can minced
   clams, drained

Mix the cream cheese, mayonnaise, onion, lemon juice, garlic salt, Worcestershire and Tabasco. Add the clams. Chill. Serve with chips or crackers.

Jane Wofford

Hot Crab Dip

Oven: 400°   **Yield:** 12-16 servings

2 (8-ounce) packages cream
   cheese, softened
¼ to ½ cup milk or
   half and half
1 pound fresh crabmeat or
   2 (6½-ounce) cans
   crabmeat, drained

½ cup onion, minced
1 tablespoon horseradish
Salt to taste
Tabasco to taste
Worcestershire to taste
½ cup almonds, toasted

Combine all ingredients except almonds in a 2-quart baking dish. Sprinkle with almonds just before baking. Bake at 400° until hot and bubbly. Serve with crackers.

Sarah Buffington

Hot Seafood Dip

Yield: 30 servings

3 (8-ounce) packages cream
    cheese
6 tablespoons butter
2 (6-ounce) packages frozen
    crab meat or 2 (6½-ounce)
    cans crab meat
1 (8-ounce) can tiny
    cooked shrimp

2 or 3 (6½-ounce) cans minced
    clams, reserve juice
Worcestershire to taste
Tabasco to taste
Lemon juice to taste

Melt cream cheese and butter in top of double boiler. Thaw and drain crab meat and shrimp. Drain minced clams; reserve clam juice to add later if dip is too thick. Combine cream cheese mixture and seafoods. Add Worcestershire, Tabasco and lemon juice to taste. Serve hot in a chafing dish with large corn chips.

Linda Hasty

Tuna Ball

Yield: 4-6 servings

1 (8-ounce) package cream
    cheese, softened
1 (6½-ounce) can tuna,
    drained
¼ teaspoon Tabasco

1 small onion, minced
Salt and pepper to taste
Pecans, chopped
Parsley

Mix ingredients with mixer at low speed. Shape into ball or log. Roll in chopped pecans and parsley. Chill. Serve with crackers.

Pam Gaddis

Petite Broccoli Quiches

Oven: 400° - 25 minutes

Yield: 24 quiches

1 (3-ounce) package cream
    cheese, softened
½ cup butter
1 cup all-purpose flour
½ (5-ounce) package frozen
    chopped broccoli, thawed

1 cup Swiss cheese, grated
½ cup half and half
3 eggs
1 teaspoon salt
1 teaspoon monosodium
    glutamate

Combine cream cheese, butter and flour. Blend well. Chill dough. Shape into 24 1-inch balls. Place in ungreased tiny muffin tins. Drain broccoli well. Into each cup, spoon about 1 teaspoon broccoli. Top with some cheese. In a small bowl, mix half and half, eggs, salt and monosodium glutamate. Spoon 1 to 2 teaspoons egg mixture into each cup. Bake at 400° for 25 minutes.

Wanda Roach

Mystery Dip

Oven: 350° - 30 minutes   **Yield:** 2 cups

1 (8-ounce) package cream
    cheese, softened
1 (2½-ounce) jar dried
    beef, chopped
2 tablespoons milk
2 tablespoons onion,
    minced

¼ teaspoon salt
½ teaspoon garlic salt
½ cup green onion,
    chopped
½ cup sour cream
½ cup pecans, chopped
2 tablespoons butter

Mix all ingredients except pecans and butter. Melt butter and toast pecans.
Place all ingredients in a small casserole dish; top with toasted pecans. Bake at
350° for 30 minutes. Serve with corn chips or crackers.

Brenda Satterfield

Hot Mushroom Dip

Yield: 2½ cups

4 slices bacon
½ pound fresh mushrooms,
    sliced
1 medium onion, finely
    chopped
1 garlic clove, minced
2 tablespoons all-purpose
    flour

¼ teaspoon salt
⅛ teaspoon pepper
1 (8-ounce) package cream
    cheese, cut into
    small pieces
2 teaspoons Worcestershire
2 teaspoons soy sauce
½ cup sour cream

Fry bacon in a large skillet over medium heat until crisp. Drain, reserving 2
tablespoons drippings in skillet. Crumble bacon and set aside. Add mushrooms,
onions and garlic to reserved drippings. Cook over medium heat until tender
and most of mushroom liquid has evaporated, about 6-8 minutes. Mix in flour,
salt and pepper. Add cream cheese, Worcestershire and soy sauce. Reduce
heat to low and stir until cheese is melted. Remove from heat. Stir in sour cream
and bacon. Serve immediately with crackers.
A crowd pleaser.

Wanda Roach

Honey-Curry Dip

Yield: 1½ cups

1 (8-ounce) carton sour
    cream
½ cup mayonnaise

⅓ cup honey
3 tablespoons curry

Mix well. Store in refrigerator. Serve with assorted vegetables.
Sounds like a lot of curry, but it takes it.

Kathi Goddard

Broccoli Dip

Yield: 10-12 servings

½ cup butter
¾ pound Velveeta cheese
Dash of garlic salt
Dash of minced onion
1 (10-ounce) package frozen
chopped broccoli,
cooked and drained

1 (10¾-ounce) can cream
of mushroom soup
1 (4-ounce) can of mushrooms
Slivered almonds (optional)
3 stalks celery, finely
chopped

Melt butter and cheese; add garlic salt, minced onion and broccoli. Add mushroom soup, mushrooms, almonds and celery. Serve warm in chafing dish with chips, corn chips or vegetables.

Deanie Fincher

Spinach Dip with Variation

Yield: 8-10 servings

1 cup mayonnaise
1 cup sour cream or
1 cup plain yogurt
1 (8-ounce) can water
chestnuts, minced

1 (10-ounce) package frozen
spinach, thawed and
drained well
1 (1⅝-ounce) package Knorr
Swiss dry vegetable
soup mix

Mix mayonnaise, sour cream, water chestnuts, spinach and soup mix. Make several hours ahead or day before to blend flavors. Serve with party slices or hollow a loaf of pumpernickel and fill with dip. Serve with the bread pieces scooped from the inside of the loaf in a basket on the side or serve with crackers or large corn chips.
Variation: Add 1 small chopped onion, ¼ cup chopped parsley, 1 teaspoon dill weed, 1 teaspoon salad seasoning, pinch of garlic powder.
Unusual combination which makes a habit forming dip.

Elly Hobgood

Fake Clam Dip

Yield: 20 servings

1 (6-ounce) can marinated
artichoke hearts,
coarsely chopped
1 (8-ounce) package cream
cheese, softened
6 slices bacon, cooked
and crumbled

1 (.4-ounce) package regular
Ranch dressing mix
Garlic salt to taste
Seasoning salt to taste

Mix ingredients together and allow flavors to blend at least 12 hours or overnight. Serve with crackers.

Deborah Fincher

Mexican Salad Dip

Yield: 8 servings

1 (12-ounce) can tomatoes, drained and chopped
1 (4-ounce) can pitted ripe olives, drained and chopped
8 green onions with tops, sliced
2 (4-ounce) cans chopped green chilies

2 tablespoons olive oil
2 tablespoons red wine vinegar
1 teaspoon garlic salt
3 tablespoons Jalapeño relish or Salsa

Mix together. Chill several hours. Serve with corn chips.
Adjust the hotness of dish by the kind of Salsa used (mild, medium, or hot.)

Kathleen Harbin

Buffalo Wings

Yield: 24 servings

24 chicken wings
½ cup butter
2 tablespoons vinegar

6 tablespoons hot sauce
Oil for deep frying

Cut chicken wings up at joints. Discard the tiny third joint tips. Heat cooking oil to 375°. Deep fry the chicken wings 10-12 at a time, for about 7 minutes. Keep them warm on a cookie sheet in a 350° oven. Combine butter, vinegar and hot sauce in a saucepan over medium heat. Stir until butter melts. Drain chicken on paper towels; heap the wings on a platter and pour sauce over them.

Cheryl Ellis

Sausage Swirls

Oven: 400° - 18-20 minutes

Yield: 80 swirls

2 (8-ounce) cans crescent dinner rolls

2 tablespoons hot mustard
1 pound hot pork sausage

Separate rolls into 4 rectangles. Spread with mustard; then spread a thin layer of sausage. Roll and chill until ready to serve. Thinly slice each roll into 10 swirls. Place on an ungreased pan. Bake at 400° for 18-20 minutes. Serve hot.

Pat Gold

Beef Balls

Oven: 350° - 15 minutes   **Yield:** 3½ dozen

1 cup stuffing bread mix	½ teaspoon salt
1 (8-ounce) jar mild taco sauce	1 (8-ounce) can tomato sauce
1 pound ground beef	2 tablespoons parsley, chopped
1 small onion, finely chopped	

Combine stuffing mix and ½ of taco sauce in a large bowl. Let stand until liquid is absorbed. Add beef, onions and salt to stuffing mixture. Mix lightly until well blended. Shape into 1-inch balls; place on a lightly greased jelly roll pan. Bake at 350° for 15 minutes or until lightly browned. Combine remaining taco sauce and tomato sauce in a small saucepan; heat until boiling. Spoon meatballs into a dish. Pour sauce over the top. Sprinkle with parsley. (Meatballs can be made ahead and refrigerated; cook just before serving.

Cindy Holcomb

Easy Bourbon Hotdogs

Yield: 16 servings

¾ cup bourbon	1 tablespoon minced onion
1½ cups catsup	1 pound hot dogs, cut into 1-inch slices
½ cup brown sugar	

Mix all ingredients. Simmer on very low heat for 1 hour. Serve hot in chafing dish.

Becky Bailey

Tasty Little Pizza Snacks

Oven: 425° - 8-10 minutes   **Yield:** 11 dozen

1 pound Italian sausage	1 teaspoon garlic salt
1 pound hot pork sausage (bulk)	1 pound processed American cheese, cut into small pieces
1 cup onion, chopped	
½ cup green pepper, chopped	1 pound Mozzarella cheese, cut into small pieces
1 tablespoon oregano	3 (8-ounce) loaves party rye bread
1 tablespoon fennel seeds	

Remove casing from Italian sausage; crumble into large skillet. Add hot sausage, onion and green pepper; cook until browned. Drain well. Return meat mixture to skillet; add seasonings. Heat gently over low heat. Stir in cheese until melted. Remove from heat. Spread a scant tablespoon of mixture on each bread slice. Place slices in a single layer on large baking sheet and freeze. When slices are frozen, place in plastic bags and store in freezer until needed. To serve, thaw and place on lightly greased baking sheets. Bake at 425° for 8-10 minutes.

Debbie Perry

Toasted Pecans

Oven: 200° - 60 minutes

12 cups pecan halves   **Salt**
½ cup margarine, melted

Place pecans in 17x12-inch pan. Toast in a 200° oven for 30 minutes. Add margarine. Sprinkle with salt generously, stirring often. Toast pecans 30 minutes more until all margarine has been absorbed and pecans are crisp.

Jackie Swords

Glazed Pecans

Yield: 2-2½ cups

1 cup sugar
½ cup water
1 teaspoon cinnamon

¼ teaspoon allspice
1 teaspoon vanilla extract
2-2½ cups pecan halves

Combine all ingredients except pecans and vanilla. Cook over medium heat 5 minutes. Add pecans. Cook an additional 5 minutes. Remove from heat. Add vanilla. Place pecans on waxed paper to cool.
Makes a good gift.

Deborah Fincher

Cream Cheese Nut Puffs

Oven: Broil - 1 minute   **Yield:** 1½ dozen

1 (3-ounce) package cream
    cheese, softened
2½ tablespoons mayonnaise
1 tablespoon chives

2½ tablespoons macadamia
    nuts, chopped
Pinch of salt
Crackers

Beat cream cheese and mayonnaise until blended. Add remaining ingredients. Spread small amount on crackers. Broil 1 minute or until lightly browned.

Brenda Lawson

Grapes in Sour Cream

Yield: 4 servings

2 pounds green seedless
    grapes, washed, drained
    and dried

1 (8-ounce) carton sour
    cream
4 tablespoons brown sugar

Using sherberts or individual serving dishes, layer grapes; then layer the sour cream. Sprinkle lightly with brown sugar. Refrigerate at least 2 hours before serving. Pass extra brown sugar, if desired.

Sue Cannon

Caviar Mold

First Layer

2 tablespoons unflavored
   gelatin
½ cup cold water
6 hard-cooked eggs,
   chopped small
½ cup mayonnaise

¼ cup parsley, chopped
2 green onions, minced
1 teaspoon salt
2 dashes of Tabasco
Pepper to taste

Soften gelatin in water; heat until dissolved. Combine remaining ingredients; add gelatin. Place in a greased 9-inch springform pan. Chill until set.

Second Layer

2 tablespoons unflavored
   gelatin
½ cup cold water
2 avocados, mashed
2 green onions, minced

2 tablespoons lemon juice
1 teaspoon salt
1 teaspoon pepper
1 teaspoon Tabasco

Soften gelatin in water; heat until dissolved. Combine remaining ingredients; add gelatin. Place on first layer. Chill until set.

Third Layer

2 tablespoons unflavored
   gelatin
½ cup cold water
1½ cups sour cream

½ cup onion, minced
Salt and white pepper
   to taste

Soften gelatin in water; heat until dissolved. Combine remaining ingredients; add gelatin. Place on avocado mixture. Chill until set.
Drain 1-2 (3½-ounce) jars lump fish caviar. Release sides of springform pan. Place mold on serving tray. Spread caviar over top. Serve with pumpernickel bread.

Beverly Brandenburg
Pine Crest Restaurant
Canton, Georgia

Mushrooms in Sherry Sauce

4 tablespoons butter
2 (8-ounce) cans mushrooms,
   drained and chopped
2 medium onions, chopped
Seasoned salt

1 (10¾-ounce) can cream of
   mushroom soup
¼ cup dry sherry
Melba rounds

Melt butter; sauté onions until tender. Add mushrooms and remaining ingredients. Heat, but do not boil. Serve warm in a chafing dish with melba rounds. *Can be made ahead; any leftover can be used as a sauce for steak or broiled chicken.*

Beverly Brandenburg
Pine Crest Restaurant
Canton, Georgia

Wontons

½ pound ground pork
1 (4½-ounce) can shrimp, drained
1 (4-ounce) can ham
6 water chestnuts, finely chopped
2 green onions with tops, chopped

1 tablespoon soy sauce
1 teaspoon cornstarch
½ teaspoon salt
1 pound wonton wrappers
Vegetable oil for frying

Stir-fry pork in wok or skillet until brown; drain. Stir in remaining ingredients, except wrappers. Place 1 teaspoon filling on center of wonton wrapper. Moisten edges with water. Fold each wrapper to form triangle; press edges to seal. Pull corners of triangle down and overlap slightly. Heat oil to 360°; fry 6-8 wontons at a time until golden brown.
These may be frozen before frying.

Beverly Brandenburg
Pine Crest Restaurant
Canton, Georgia

Shrimp Toast Appetizers

Yield: 32 triangles

8 slices white bread, crusts removed
1 (4½-ounce) can shrimp, drained and chopped
1 egg
1 tablespoon cornstarch
1 tablespoon water chestnuts, finely chopped
1 tablespoon green onion, thinly sliced

2 teaspoons soy sauce
1 teaspoon ginger root, grated
1 teaspoon dry sherry
1 teaspoon sugar
¼ teaspoon salt
Vegetable oil for deep frying

Lay the bread slices in a single layer on a cookie sheet; let stand 1 hour. Turn bread slices over; let stand 1 hour more. (If bread has been opened more than a day, this step is unnecessary.) Combine shrimp and egg; beat at low speed for ½ minute, scraping sides of bowl constantly. Add cornstarch, water chestnuts, green onion, soy sauce, ginger root, sherry, sugar and salt. Beat until well blended. Spread about 2 tablespoons shrimp mixture on each slice of bread. Cut each slice into 4 triangles. Heat oil in wok to 365°. Fry a few at a time until golden brown. Remove with a slotted spoon; drain on paper towels. Keep warm in a 250° oven. Serve immediately.
Can be prepared ahead of time and refrigerated before frying.

Elly Hobgood

Antipasto

Yield: 6 servings

1 (9-ounce) package frozen
   artichoke hearts
1 cup Italian dressing,
   divided
1 small head cauliflower

3 cups water
1 tablespoon lemon juice
½ teaspoon salt

Choose from the following as desired:

Provolone cheese or other Italian cheese, cut into small strips
Sliced pepperoni
Sliced salami
Proscuitto
Pimiento-stuffed olives
Ripe olives
Anchovies
Cherry tomatoes

Cook artichokes according to package directions; drain thoroughly; cool. Pour
½ cup Italian dressing over artichokes. Chill at least 2 hours. Break cauliflower
into bite-size pieces. Bring water to a boil in a saucepan; add lemon juice, salt
and cauliflower. Simmer for 7 minutes; drain and cool. Pour remaining ½ cup of
dressing over cauliflower; chill for 2 hours. Arrange artichoke hearts and
cauliflower on lettuce-lined tray. Add remaining cheese, meat, anchovies and
olives as desired. Garnish with cherry tomatoes.

Ollie White

Turkey in Lettuce Leaves

6 tablespoons butter
2 cups onion, finely
   chopped
¾ cup green pepper,
   finely chopped
1 (4-ounce) can green
   chilies, drained and
   chopped

½ teaspoon pepper
4 cups turkey, cooked
   and shredded
1 teaspoon salt
⅓ cup cognac
¼ cup parsley, chopped
   Lettuce leaves

Sauté onions and peppers in butter until wilted. Add green chilies, pepper and
turkey. Cover; simmer 5 minutes. Add remaining seasonings and cognac. Place
in serving bowl. Arrange lettuce leaves around bowl. Better if made a couple of
days ahead; bring to room temperature before serving.
*The person eating takes a lettuce leaf and places a small amount of turkey on it;
wraps it and eats.*

Beverly Brandenburg
Pine Crest Restaurant
Canton, Georgia

Beverages

Pitcher Bloody Marys

Yield: 1¾ quarts

1 (46-ounce) can tomato
  juice
1 cup vodka
2 tablespoons Worcestershire
½ teaspoon hot sauce

¼ teaspoon pepper
⅛ teaspoon celery salt
Juice of 2 lemons
Celery sticks

Combine first 7 ingredients. Stir well. Serve over ice. Garnish with celery sticks.

Linda Hasty

Whiskey Sours

Yield: 6 servings

1 (6-ounce) can frozen
  lemonade concentrate
1 juice can whiskey
  or bourbon
1 juice can water
1 juice can ice, or more

Cherries for
  garnish
Orange slices for
  garnish

Combine lemonade, bourbon, water and ice. Shake well. Strain and pour in whiskey sour glasses. Garnish with cherries and orange slices.

Betty McDaniel

Strawberry Daiquiris

Yield: 8 cups

1 (6-ounce) can frozen
  lemonade concentrate
1 juice can rum
  Crushed ice to fill
  blender

1 (10-ounce) package frozen
  strawberries
  Strawberries for garnish

Put lemonade, rum, crushed ice and frozen strawberries in blender container; process until smooth. Garnish each glass with a fresh strawberry.

Frances Gober

Wine Spritzers

Yield: 8-10 servings

1 (25.4-ounce) bottle white
  wine
1 (33.8-ounce) bottle club
  soda

Lemon slices
Lime slices

Combine wine and club soda. Mix gently. Pour over ice-filled glasses. Garnish with slices of fruit.

Cissy Cloud

Brandy Alexander

Yield: 1 serving

1½ ounces brandy
¾ ounce crème de cacao

2 scoops vanilla ice cream
Nutmeg

Combine all ingredients in blender until smooth. Sprinkle nutmeg on top. Serve immediately.

Pat Stewart

Mint Julep

Yield: 1 serving

½ teaspoon sugar
3 tablespoons water
5 mint leaves

1½ ounces bourbon
Sprig of mint

Dissolve sugar in the water to make a syrup. Crush mint leaves in syrup; remove leaves, filling cup with crushed ice. Add bourbon, but do not stir. Place sprig of mint in top of cup to serve.
Best if served in silver julep cup.

June Phillips

Eggnog I

Yield: 18 servings

1 dozen egg yolks
1 scant cup sugar
1 fifth whiskey
    or bourbon
½ cup rum

1 quart milk
1 quart half and half
1 pint heavy cream,
    whipped
Nutmeg

Beat egg yolks, adding sugar to taste. Stir in whiskey slowly; then add rum. Add milk and half and half. Fold in whipped cream. Sprinkle with nutmeg.

Gaye Mothershed

Eggnog II

Yield: 20 servings

¾ cup sugar
10 egg yolks
1 pint rye whiskey

1 quart heavy whipping cream
10 egg whites, stiffly
    beaten

Cream sugar and egg yolks. Slowly add whiskey, stirring constantly. Add heavy unwhipped cream; fold in beaten egg whites.

Sue Kirby
LaFayette, Georgia

Amaretto Coffee

Yield: 1 serving

1½ ounces Amaretto
Black coffee

Whipped cream

Pour Amaretto into stemmed glass or mug. Fill glass to within ½ inch with black coffee. Top with whipped cream.

Betty McDaniel

Irish Coffee

Yield: 1 serving

1½ ounces Irish whiskey
Black coffee

Sugar to taste
Whipped cream

Pour Irish whiskey into stemmed glass or mug. Fill to within ½ inch with black coffee. Add sugar to taste; stir well. Top with whipped cream.

Cookbook Committee

Hot Buttered Rum

Yield: 15 servings

1 cup butter
1½ cups sugar
⅛ teaspoon cloves
1 teaspoon ginger

1 teaspoon cinnamon
Boiling water
Rum
Cinnamon sticks (optional)

Blend first 5 ingredients ahead of time. Store in the refrigerator in a tightly covered container. At serving time, for each serving, place 1 tablespoon of reserved mixture in a small mug or cup. Add 2½ ounces boiling water and 1½ ounces rum. Garnish with cinnamon sticks, if desired.

Betty McDaniel

24-Hour Punch

Yield: 20 servings

4 cups water
1½ cups sugar
12 lemons

1 quart bourbon
1 (33.8-ounce) bottle
  ginger ale

Boil water and sugar until sugar dissolves. Remove from heat. Add the juice of the lemons, the bourbon and the lemon rinds. Let stand 30 minutes. Drain. Refrigerate overnight (may stand longer without hurting the punch). When serving, add at least 1 bottle of ginger ale. Two quarts of ginger ale may be preferable, according to individual taste.

Martha Nichols

Brandy Slush

Yield: 20 servings

9 cups water, divided
2 cups sugar
4 tea bags
1 (12-ounce) can frozen
orange juice concentrate

1 (12-ounce) can frozen
lemonade concentrate
2-4 cups brandy
Lemon-lime carbonated
drink

Boil 7 cups water and sugar; let cool. Boil the remaining 2 cups water and steep tea bags; let cool. Combine all ingredients. Stir thoroughly. Freeze. When ready to serve, fill glasses ¾ full with slush. Add lemon-lime drink to fill glasses.
Variation: a mint tea bag may be substituted.

Ann Johnson

Rum Punch

Yield: 2 gallons

1 quart light rum
1 (46-ounce) can tropical
fruit punch
1 (12-ounce) can frozen
limeade concentrate
1 (12-ounce) can frozen
orange juice concentrate

1 (33.8-ounce) bottle
lemon-lime carbonated
drink
1 lime, sliced
1 lemon, sliced
Strawberries

Combine rum, fruit punch, limeade, orange juice and lemon-lime drink. Chill. Garnish with fruit slices and strawberries. Serve in a punch bowl.

Susan Padgett

Champagne Punch

Yield: 3½ quarts

1 (25.4-ounce) bottle cold
duck, chilled
1 (25.4-ounce) bottle pink
champagne, chilled

4 cups cranberry juice
cocktail, chilled
1 (33.8-ounce) bottle ginger
ale, chilled

Combine all ingredients in a large punch bowl. Serve.

Wanda Roach

Coffee Knog

Yield: 1 gallon

4 cups strong hot coffee
2 quarts vanilla ice
cream

4 cups bourbon
1 cup light rum

Pour hot coffee over ice cream to melt it. Mix with bourbon and rum.

Cookbook Committee

Wassail Punch

Yield: 1½ gallons

1 gallon apple cider
1 quart orange juice
1 cup lemon juice
1 quart pineapple juice

24 whole cloves
4 sticks cinnamon
1 cup sugar

Mix all ingredients. Simmer for 10 minutes. Remove spices. Serve warm.
For a festive punch bowl, float small oranges that have been precooked about 10 minutes and studded with whole cloves.

Margaret Logan

Inexpensive Fruit Punch

Yield: 5-6 gallons

4 (0.41) packages cherry
   soft drink mix,
   unsweetened
4 cups sugar
8 quarts water
4 (46-ounce) cans tropical
   fruit punch

4 (46-ounce) cans pineapple
   juice
4 (33.8-ounce) bottles ginger
   ale, chilled

Blend soft drink mix, sugar and water. Add fruit punch and pineapple juice. Chill; add ginger ale just before serving.
Other flavors of the powdered drink mix may be substituted.

Emma Ridenhour

Wedding Punch

Yield: 100 servings

4 ounces citric acid
1 quart boiling water
2 (46-ounce) cans
   pineapple juice
6 lemons, squeeze and
   boil rinds

6 oranges, squeeze and
   boil rinds
5 pounds sugar

Dissolve acid in boiling water. Mix with sugar and fruit juices. Dilute to desired strength with water. Makes a tart, yellow punch which can be tinted with food coloring.
This is the recipe my mother used to make punch for almost every wedding or shower tea that took place for many years in Plains, Georgia.

Margaret Logan

Mock Champagne Punch

Yield: 30 servings

4 (24-ounce) bottles white
   grape juice, chilled
2 (33.8-ounce) bottles ginger
   ale, chilled

1 ice ring

Pour white grape juice into punch bowl. Gradually add ginger ale. Place ice ring into punch bowl. Serve immediately.

Judy Bishop

Strawberry Gelatin Punch

Yield: 2 quarts

1 cup boiling water
1 (3-ounce) box strawberry
   gelatin
1 (6-ounce) can frozen
   limeade concentrate

3 juice cans cold water
1 (33.8-ounce) bottle
   ginger ale, chilled
   Strawberries (optional)

Pour boiling water over gelatin; stir until dissolved. Add limeade and cold water. Pour into punch bowl; add ginger ale and ice just before serving. Punch will thicken slightly. Decorate with strawberries, if desired.

Margaret Logan

Mocha Punch

Yield: 50 servings

4 quarts boiling water
12 tablespoons instant
   coffee granules
3 cups sugar

1½ teaspoons vanilla extract
9 ounces chocolate syrup
6 quarts vanilla ice cream
3 quarts milk

Dissolve coffee granules in boiling water. Stir in sugar, syrup and vanilla. Cool. Add milk and ice cream to serve.
Very thick and rich.

Bonnie Massey

Pink Lady Punch

Yield: 20 servings

4 cups cranberry juice
   cocktail
1½ cups sugar

1 quart pineapple or
   grapefruit juice
2 (33.8-ounce) bottles
   ginger ale, chilled

Mix cranberry juice and sugar. Stir until sugar dissolves. Add fruit juice. Mix well. Chill. Add ginger ale when ready to serve.

Martha Nichols

Cranberry Punch

Yield: 30 cups

1 (32-ounce) bottle
   cranberry juice
1 (12-ounce) can frozen
   orange juice concentrate
1 (12-ounce) can frozen
   lemonade concentrate

3 cups water
Crushed ice
1 (33.8-ounce) bottle
   ginger ale

Mix juices and water. Pour over crushed ice. Add ginger ale just before serving.

Mary Winslow

Peppermint Punch

Yield: 24 servings

1½ pints vanilla ice
   cream, softened
6 cups dairy eggnog
5¼ cups carbonated water,
   chilled

1½ cups heavy cream,
   whipped
½ cup broken peppermint
   sticks

Spoon ice cream into punch bowl. Stir in eggnog and carbonated water. Top with puffs of whipped cream. Sprinkle with candy.
Children love this.

Gaye Mothershed

Golden Punch

Yield: 30 servings

1 (0.41-ounce) package
   pre-sweetened lemon
   soft drink mix
2 quarts water
2 (6-ounce) cans frozen
   orange juice concentrate

1 quart pineapple juice
1 (6-ounce) can frozen
   lemonade concentrate
1 (33.8-ounce) bottle
   ginger ale

Mix soft drink mix, water, orange juice, pineapple juice and lemonade in a large container. Refrigerate. To serve, pour this mixture into punch bowl. Add ginger ale to taste.

Betty Jo McDaniel

Country Club Punch

Yield: 4 gallons

4 (12-ounce) cans frozen
   orange juice concentrate
4 (12-ounce) cans frozen
   lemonade concentrate
2 (46-ounce) cans
   pineapple juice

1 cup sugar
2 (33.8-ounce) bottles
   ginger ale

Dilute frozen concentrates as directed. Add pineapple juice and sugar; blend well. Add ginger ale just before serving. Best if made a day ahead.
This recipe has been used for many years for social gatherings at the Americus Country Club.

Margaret Logan

Hot Percolator Punch

Yield: 7 cups

3 cups unsweetened pineapple
   juice
3 cups cranberry juice
1½ cups water
⅓ cup brown sugar,
   firmly packed

2 lemon slices
1 or 2 (4-inch) sticks
   cinnamon, broken
   (optional)
1½ teaspoons whole cloves
   Cinnamon sticks (optional)

Pour juices and water into a 12-cup percolator. Place remaining ingredients, except whole cinnamon sticks, in percolator basket. Perk through complete cycle. Serve with cinnamon stick, if desired.
This makes your house smell terrific.

Patty Mann

Banana Ale

Yield: 1 gallon

6 cups water
4 cups sugar
1 cup orange juice
5 bananas, sliced

2 tablespoons lemon juice
1 (46-ounce) can pineapple
   juice
Ginger ale

Boil water and sugar for 3 minutes; cool. Combine orange juice, bananas and lemon juice in a blender. Combine sugar syrup with other ingredients; add pineapple juice. Pour into a large container. Freeze. When ready to serve, fill blender container about half-full of frozen mixture. Process, adding ginger ale until slushy or desired consistency.
This keeps well, and children enjoy the slush, undiluted, as a snack.

Debbie Perry

Strawberry Slush

Yield: 18-20 servings

2 (0.41-ounce) packages
    unsweetened strawberry
    soft drink mix
2 quarts water
2 bananas, mashed

2 cups sugar
Juice of 2 lemons
1 (46-ounce) can pineapple
    juice

Mix all ingredients well. Freeze. Remove about 1 hour before serving. Stir occasionally. Serve as a slush.

Madelin Phelps

Hot Chocolate Mix

1 (8-quart) box powdered
    milk
1 (16-ounce) box chocolate-
    flavored drink mix

1 (16-ounce) box
    confectioners' sugar
1 (11-ounce) jar of coffee
    creamer

Mix all ingredients in a large bowl. Store in a tightly covered container. Use 3-4 heaping teaspoons per cup. Add hot water to serve.

Margaret Logan

Hot Spiced Tea

Yield: 8-10 servings

3 quarts water, divided
2 whole cinnamon sticks
1 teaspoon whole cloves
3 small tea bags

2 cups sugar
1 (46-ounce) can pineapple
    juice
Juice of 6 lemons
Juice of 6 oranges

Combine 1½ quarts water, cloves and cinnamon sticks; bring to a boil. Add tea bags; simmer for 8 minutes. Add remaining water, sugar, pineapple juice, orange juice and lemon juice. If using fresh oranges and lemons, float a couple of fruit halves in the tea. Heat thoroughly.

Judy Brandon

Hot Spiced Apple Juice

Yield: 16 servings

2 quarts apple juice
2 cups water
1 cup brown sugar,
  firmly packed
1 cup orange juice
6 tablespoons lemon
  juice

¼ teaspoon nutmeg
2 (3-inch) sticks cinnamon
  Orange slices (optional)
  Lemon slices (optional)

Combine all ingredients in a large saucepan. Stir until sugar is dissolved. Bring to a boil; reduce heat and simmer 15 minutes. Pour into heated serving cups. Garnish with thin orange or lemon slices, if desired.
The aroma of this on a cold day is unbeatable.

Margaret Logan

Easy Russian Tea Mix

2 cups Tang
½ cup instant tea mix
  with lemon and sweetener

1 teaspoon cinnamon
1 teaspoon allspice
½ teaspoon cloves

Mix all ingredients. Store in airtight container. Add about 2 heaping teaspoons to a cup of hot water to serve.

Cissy Cloud

Peach Punch

Yield: 32 servings

1 (48-ounce) can peach
  flavor juice drink
2 (6-ounce) cans frozen
  lemonade concentrate
2 (6-ounce) cans frozen
  orange juice concentrate
4⅓ juice cans water

12 ounces pineapple juice
1 (33.8-ounce) bottle
  ginger ale
  Cherries (optional)
  Mint sprigs (optional)

Mix juices and water. Chill. Add ginger ale just before serving. Garnish with cherries and sprigs of mint, if desired.

Mary Winslow

Soups

New England Clam Chowder

Yield: 15 servings

3 large potatoes, cubed
Salt
1 yellow onion, diced
1 stalk celery, diced
2 tablespoons butter
2 tablespoons all-purpose
  flour
1½ quarts clams
1½ bottles clam juice

2 teaspoons basil leaves
Lemon pepper to taste
Pinch of tarragon
½ gallon milk
1 pint light cream
1 cup butter
Chopped parsley
Salt to taste

Cook potatoes in salted water; set aside. Sauté onion and celery in 2 tablespoons butter until transparent; add 2 tablespoons flour to form a roux. Add clams and clam juice, then potatoes and seasonings. Stir. Add milk, cream and butter. Stir until desired consistency is reached. Garnish with parsley.

Gus White

Crab Bisque

Yield: 7 servings

1 (10½-ounce) can She-Crab
  soup
2 (10¾-ounce) cans cream
  of celery soup
1 (4-ounce) container whipped
  cream cheese with chives

1 (6-ounce) can white crab
  meat, undrained
3 soup cans milk or
  half and half
½ soup can dry sherry

Mix all ingredients together except sherry. Heat slowly, stirring often. Add sherry just before serving.

Martha Nichols

Southern Chowder

Yield: 4-6 servings

2 cups ground clams
  (more or less)
Clam liquor
2 or 3 slices salt pork
6 medium potatoes,
  peeled and diced

1 onion, diced
Water
Salt and pepper to taste

Grind or chop clams in liquor. Render fat from salt pork by frying. Put clams, liquor, potatoes and onion into a saucepan; add water to cover. Season with fat from salt pork, salt and pepper. Cook until potatoes are done.
Flavor is best when cooked over an open fire.

Skip Spears

New Orleans Oyster Stew

Yield: 6 servings

2 tablespoons margarine
3 tablespoons oil
4 tablespoons all-purpose
  flour
2 onions, finely chopped
1 clove garlic, minced
  Pepper to taste
2 stalks celery, finely
  chopped

1 beef bouillon cube
1 cup boiling water
¼ teaspoon ground mace
1 pint oysters with
  juice
1 quart milk
  Salt to taste

Heat margarine and oil over medium heat. Add flour, stirring constantly, until blended. Add onion, garlic, pepper and celery. Cook approximately 7 minutes. Dissolve bouillon in water; add to flour mixture. Add mace and oysters. Cook until oysters puff up and ruffle around the edges. Heat milk in another pan, but do not boil. Add milk to oyster mixture. Taste to see if stew is salty enough. Adjust seasonings. Serve immediately.
Can make oyster base ahead and refrigerate.

Donna Priestley

Old-Fashioned Oyster Chowder

Yield: 6-8 servings

8 slices bacon, diced
2 tablespoons butter
2 cups potatoes, cooked
  and coarsely chopped
½ cup green onion, sliced
½ cup celery, diced
1 medium carrot,
  coarsely shredded
½ cup water
2 cups milk

2 cups half and half
  or light cream
1 (12-ounce) can whole
  kernel corn, drained
1½ teaspoons salt
⅛ teaspoon pepper
2 dashes of Tabasco
1 pint oysters, undrained
  Chopped parsley

Fry bacon in large Dutch oven until crisp. Remove bacon; set aside. Remove all but 2 tablespoons bacon drippings from pan; add butter. Sauté potatoes until lightly browned. Add onion, celery, carrot and water. Cover; simmer 5 minutes or until vegetables are tender. Add milk, half and half, corn, salt, pepper and Tabasco. Simmer. Add oysters, oyster liquor and crumbled bacon. Heat just until edges of oysters curl. Garnish with parsley.

Ollie White

She-Crab Soup

Yield: 6-8 servings

3 quarts milk
½ cup butter
¼ medium onion,
    finely chopped
8 ounces crab meat
3 yolks of hard-cooked
    eggs, chopped

½ tablespoon paprika
¼ tablespoon Accent
¾ cup all-purpose flour
    Salt and pepper to taste
¼ cup sherry

Heat milk until hot, but do not boil. Melt butter in double boiler; add onion. Simmer a few minutes. Add crab meat and egg yolks. Stir. Add paprika and Accent. Stir. Fold in flour; simmer a few minutes. Pour milk in double boiler; stir until blended. Add salt, pepper and sherry. Keep on low heat for 25-30 minutes. Add a little sherry to each serving, if desired.

Linda Hasty

Cheese Chowder

Yield: 4 servings

½ cup carrots, coarsley
    shredded
½ cup onion, chopped
½ cup celery, chopped
3 tablespoons butter or
    margarine
¼ cup all-purpose flour

1 (10¾-ounce) can chicken
    broth
¼ teaspoon salt
2 cups milk or light cream
1½ cups American cheese,
    shredded

Cook carrots, onion and celery in butter over low heat until tender. Stir in flour. Add broth and salt. Cook and stir until thickened and bubbly. Stir in milk or cream and cheese, stirring until cheese melts and soup is heated through, but do not boil.
For a even better flavor, dissolve 1 chicken bouillon cube or 1 tablespoon chicken stock granules in the chicken broth before adding to the vegetables.

Anne Huey

Corn Chowder

Yield: 10 servings

1 pound bacon
3 onions, chopped
8 -10 potatoes, diced
Salt and pepper to taste

2 (17-ounce) cans cream-style corn
2 cups milk
1 tablespoon butter

Brown bacon until semi-crisp. Remove bacon; set aside. Sauté onion in bacon drippings. Remove with a slotted spoon; set aside. Combine potatoes, salt, pepper, onion and crumbled bacon in enough water to cover; cook until potatoes are tender. Add cream corn; boil 5 minutes. Add milk and butter; heat thoroughly. Serve.

Bonnie Massey

Cheddar Cheese Soup

Yield: 8-10 servings

1 cup margarine, divided
½ cup celery, chopped
½ cup onion, chopped
½ cup green pepper, chopped
½ cup carrots, chopped
½ cup cauliflower, chopped

2 cups water
2 chicken bouillon cubes
⅔ cup all-purpose flour
4 cups milk
½ pound sharp Cheddar cheese, shredded

Melt ½ cup margarine in a 4-quart saucepan. Add celery, onion, green pepper, carrots and cauliflower; cook until tender. Add water and bouillon. Heat to boiling. Cover; cook over low heat for 10 minutes. Melt remaining ½ cup margarine in a 2-quart saucepan. Stir in flour. Cook until bubbly. Remove from heat. Blend in milk with a wire whisk. Cook over medium heat, stirring often, but do not boil. Blend in cheese. Stir cheese mixture into vegetable mixture until well-blended. Serve immediately.

Madelin Phelps

Broccoli Chowder

Yield: 6-8 servings

2 pounds fresh broccoli
2 (13¾-ounce) cans chicken
   broth, divided
3 cups milk
1 cup cooked ham, chopped
2 teaspoons salt

¼ teaspoon pepper
1 cup half and half
2 cups (½-pound) Swiss
   cheese, shredded
¼ cup margarine

Combine broccoli and 1 can chicken broth in a Dutch oven; cover and cook 7 minutes or until broccoli is crisp-tender. Remove broccoli from broth; cool and chop coarsely. Add remaining can of chicken broth, milk, ham, salt and pepper to Dutch oven; bring to a boil over medium heat, stirring occasionally. Stir in broccoli and remaining ingredients. Cook over low heat until thoroughly heated, but do not boil.

Ann Fincher

Easy Cucumber Soup

Yield: 4 servings

½ cup onion, sliced
½ cup potatoes, diced
2 cups cucumbers, sliced
¼ teaspoon dry mustard

2 cups chicken broth
1 cup milk
   Salt and pepper to taste
   Chopped parsley to taste

Combine all ingredients except milk in saucepan. cook 10 minutes. Pour into blender; add milk. Blend until smooth. Chill.
Very easy and quick; can be made ahead.

Christi Kook

Celery Soup

Yield: 8 servings

3 cups celery with leaves,
   chopped
2 cups chicken stock
2 cups boiling water
½ cup onion, finely
   sliced

2 tablespoons butter
3 tablespoons all-purpose
   flour
2 cups milk
1 cup cream
   Salt and pepper to taste

Simmer the celery in the stock and water for 30 minutes. Cook the onion in butter until tender, about 5 minutes. Add the flour and milk; cook until thickened. Add the celery and liquid, cream, salt and pepper. Heat through, but do not boil.

Margaret Logan

Mushroom Bisque

Yield: 8 servings

¼ cup butter
1 small onion, chopped
1 celery stalk, chopped
¾ pound mushrooms, sliced
1 small potato, peeled
   and diced
1 cup water
1¼ teaspoon salt
¾ teaspoon fresh thyme,
   minced or ¼ teaspoon
   dried thyme, crumbled

Pinch of freshly ground
   white pepper
2 cups milk
¾ cup whipping cream
¼ cup dry sherry
2 teaspoons tamari soy sauce
Sour cream

Melt butter in large saucepan over medium-low heat. Add onion and celery. Cover; cook until transparent, about 10 minutes. Stir in mushrooms; cook until softened, about 6 minutes. Add potato, water, salt, thyme and pepper. Increase heat and simmer until potato is very soft, about 15 minutes. Purée mixture in food processor or blender until smooth. Return mixture to saucepan. Add milk, cream, sherry and soy sauce. Heat through, but do not boil. Garnish with sour cream.

Cookbook Committee

Swiss Onion Soup

Yield: 12 servings

½ cup butter
2 pounds onions, sliced
1½ teaspoons paprika
½ cup vegetable oil
¾ cup all-purpose flour
6 cups beef stock

¾ teaspoon celery salt
Salt and pepper to taste
1 (12-ounce) bottle dark or
   regular beer
Buttered toast
Parmesan cheese, grated

Melt butter. Add onions; sauté until soft. Add paprika, oil and flour. Brown evenly. Add stock; celery salt, salt and pepper. Simmer at least 2 hours. Add beer. Bring to serving temperature. Top with toast and Parmesan cheese.

Pat Contino

Potato Soup

Yield: 2 quarts

5 medium potatoes,
   peeled and diced
1 small onion, chopped
1 stalk celery, chopped
2 teaspoons celery salt
1 teaspoon seasoned salt
1 teaspoon whole dried basil
¼ teaspoon pepper
¼ cup green pepper, diced
2 tablespoons dried parsley
   flakes

2 chicken-flavored bouillon
   cubes
4 cups water
4 slices bacon
2 tablespoons all-purpose
   flour
1½ cups milk
½ cup fresh mushrooms,
   sliced

Combine first 11 ingredients in a large Dutch oven. Bring to a boil. Cover; reduce heat and simmer for 30-45 minutes. Cook bacon until crisp. Remove bacon, reserving 3 tablespoons drippings in skillet. Crumble bacon; set aside. Add flour and milk to drippings in skillet, stirring until smooth. Cook 1 minute, stirring constantly, until thick and bubbly. Gradually stir milk mixture and bacon into potato mixture. Add mushrooms. Simmer, uncovered, 15 minutes.

Frances Gober

"My" Potato Soup

Yield: 6-8 servings

6 cups potatoes,
   peeled and cubed
1 large onion, chopped
3 cups water
3 envelopes Herb Ox
   chicken-flavored
   instant broth

½ cup margarine
1½ cups milk, divided
   Salt and pepper to taste
1 tablespoon sugar

Cook potatoes and onion in water with chicken broth until tender; drain; reserve liquid. Add ½ cup milk. Put in food processor or blender with margarine; process until smooth. Pour back into pan. Add reserve liquid and enough remaining milk to make desired consistency. Adjust seasonings to taste. *Keeps in refrigerator one week; just heat in double boiler.*

Sarah Buffington

Vichyssoise

Yield: 6 servings

3 cups chicken broth
1 teaspoon salt
4 medium potatoes,
   peeled and diced
3 yellow onions, chopped
3 fresh leeks (white part
   and 2 inches green part)
   or an additional onion,
   chopped

1 teaspoon chervil
½ cup whipping cream
½ cup milk
2 tablespoons parsley,
   finely chopped

Heat chicken broth to boiling. Add salt, potatoes, onion and leeks. Cover; simmer 20 minutes. Add the chervil, whipping cream and milk. Simmer for 5 minutes. Purée the soup in a food processor or blender. Add the parsley. Chill for at least 4 hours.
Great on a hot summer day.

Elizabeth Haley

Creamy Turnip Soup

Yield: 6 cups

4 cups turnips, peeled
   and thinly sliced
2 medium onions, sliced
1 large carrot, sliced
1 stalk celery, chopped
1½ teaspoons salt

1 teaspoon sugar
⅛ teaspoon pepper
1 cup water
3 cups milk
1 cup half and half

Combine turnips, onions, carrot, celery, salt, sugar, pepper and water in a Dutch oven. Bring to a boil. Reduce heat and simmer 15-20 minutes or until vegetables are tender. Put vegetable mixture in a food processor or blender; process until smooth. Return to Dutch oven; add milk and half and half. Cook over low heat, stirring constantly, until thoroughly heated. Serve immediately.

Jerry Land

Brunswick Stew

Yield: 20 servings

2 pounds lean pork, cut
   in chunks
3½ pounds chicken pieces
3 pounds ground chuck
2 (28-ounce) cans tomatoes
3 (17-ounce) cans cream-style
   corn
Juice of 3 lemons
½ cup margarine

1 (32-ounce) bottle catsup
½ cup vinegar
½ cup sugar
¼ (10-ounce) bottle
   Worcestershire
2 large onions, chopped
Salt and pepper to taste
Tabasco

Cook pork and chicken in separate containers with enough water to cover. Reserve broth. Remove meat from chicken; set aside. Cook ground chuck in 2 cups of chicken broth. Drain, reserving liquid. Grind pork, chicken and ground chuck in food processor. Combine meat and reserved liquid with remaining ingredients in a large cooker. Cook slowly (add additional chicken broth, if necessary, to adjust thickness) for 2-3 hours. Stir frequently to avoid sticking.

Ann Ponder

Turtle Stew

Yield: 8 servings

½ cup butter
2 medium onions, finely
   chopped
¼ cup all-purpose flour
½ gallon milk, scalded

1 quart turtle meat
   with broth
1-3 teaspoons pepper to taste
Salt to taste
1 (5.33-ounce) can evaporated
   milk

Melt butter in skillet. Add onions; cook until transparent. Remove from heat. Add flour, stirring until smooth. Heat milk in a separate kettle. Add turtle and broth to flour mixture. Season to taste. Heat until bubbly. Add evaporated milk and scalded milk to turtle mixture. Simmer 10-15 minutes, but do not boil.

Jack Fincher

Delicious Chicken Gumbo

Yield: 8 servings

1 (2½-3-pound) whole fryer
  chicken
2 teaspoons Accent, divided
4 cups water
2 medium onions, chopped,
  divided
4 celery tops
2 teaspoons salt, divided
½ teaspoon pepper, divided
3 tablespoons butter
1 large green pepper,
  chopped

1 cup celery, chopped
2 tablespoons all-purpose
  flour
1 bay leaf
½ teaspoon thyme
2 (16-ounce) cans tomatoes
1 teaspoon Worcestershire
1 (10-ounce) package frozen
  okra, thawed

Combine chicken, 1 teaspoon Accent, water, 1 onion, celery tops, 1 teaspoon salt, ¼ teaspoon pepper; cook until tender. Strain broth. Refrigerate. Remove chicken from bones in large pieces. Heat butter, remaining onion, green pepper and celery together. Cook 5 minutes. Blend in flour gradually. Add refrigerated chicken stock and 1 teaspoon Accent, 1 teaspoon salt, ¼ teaspoon pepper, bay leaf, thyme, tomatoes and Worcestershire. Simmer 45 minutes. Add chicken pieces and okra. Simmer 15 minutes more. Remove bay leaf before serving.

Frances Gober

Sausage - Bean Chowder

Yield: 3 quarts

2 pounds bulk pork sausage
4 cups water
2 (16-ounce) cans kidney
  beans
2 (16-ounce) cans tomatoes
2 medium onions, chopped
2 medium potatoes, peeled
  and cubed

½ cup green pepper,
  chopped
1 bay leaf
½ teaspoon salt
½ teaspoon dried whole thyme
¼ teaspoon garlic powder
¼ teaspoon pepper

Brown sausage in Dutch oven, stirring to crumble. Drain off drippings. Stir in remaining ingredients. Bring to boil. Cover; reduce heat and simmer 1 hour. Remove bay leaf before serving.

Peggy Rutledge

Turkey, Vegetable & Noodle Soup

Yield: 6 servings

2 quarts Rich Turkey Broth
1 cup potatoes, peeled
  and cubed
1 cup carrots, sliced
1 cup celery, sliced
¼ cup onion, chopped

1 (10-ounce) package frozen
  baby lima beans
1 teaspoon salt
1 cup noodles, uncooked
2 cups cooked turkey,
  cut up

Combine turkey broth, potatoes, carrots, celery, onion, lima beans, salt and noodles. Simmer 15 minutes. Add turkey, Heat thoroughly. Serve.

Rich Turkey Broth

1 leftover cooked turkey
1 chicken bouillon cube
1 teaspoon salt
12 peppercorns

1 stalk celery, cut up
1 carrot, cut up
1 small onion, cut up

Strip as much meat as possible from the turkey. Put bones and skin into a large saucepan, barely covering with cold water. Add remaining ingredients. Cover. Simmer for 2-3 hours. Strain broth.

Brenda Satterfield

Ground Beef and Vegetable Soup

Yield: 4 servings

1 pound ground beef
1 (16-ounce) can tomatoes
2 cups water
4 medium potatoes, cut in
  large pieces

4 large carrots, cut in
  large pieces
2 teaspoons salt
  Dash of pepper

Brown beef in a large saucepan; drain. Add remaining ingredients. Simmer for at least 2 hours. Adjust seasonings.

Janice Ingram

Capitol Hill Bean Soup

Yield: 12-15 servings

1 pound dried navy beans
1 ham bone (about 1 pound)
½ cup mashed potatoes
3 cups celery, chopped
3 cups onion, chopped

¼ cup fresh parsley, chopped
1 clove garlic, minced
2 teaspoons salt
Black pepper to taste

Wash beans; place in a Dutch oven. Cover with water and soak overnight. Drain beans. Add ham bone; cover with water. Cover; bring to a boil. Reduce heat and simmer 1 hour. Add remaining ingredients. Simmer 1 more hour or until beans are tender. Remove ham from bone and dice; return ham to soup. Discard bone. Heat through. Serve.

Gus White

Original Kidney Bean Soup

Yield: 2-3 quarts

1 pound ground chuck
2 tablespoons oil
Salt and pepper to taste
2 medium onions, chopped
2 stalks celery, chopped
1 green pepper, chopped
2 quarts boiling water, divided

2 (16-ounce) cans stewed tomatoes
2 large potatoes, peeled and diced
2 (16-ounce) cans kidney beans, drained
½ teaspoon sugar

Brown meat in large Dutch oven in oil; drain. Season with salt and pepper. Add vegetables; cook until tender. Add 1 quart of boiling water and tomatoes. Simmer for 1 hour. Cook potatoes in 1 quart of water for 20 minutes. Add potatoes and water to meat and vegetable mixture. Add kidney beans and sugar. Simmer 45 minutes.
Serve with cornbread. This keeps well in the refrigerator and may be frozen.

Sara Jones

Breads

Heavenly Refrigerator Rolls

Oven: 450° - 7-10 minutes   **Yield:** 4 dozen

1 cup shortening
1 cup sugar
1½ teaspoons salt
1 cup boiling water
2 eggs, lightly beaten
2 packages active dry
    yeast

1 cup lukewarm water
6 cups all-purpose flour
Butter or margarine,
    melted

Place shortening, sugar and salt in a large mixing bowl. Add boiling water. Beat with an electric mixer until shortening is melted and mixture has cooled slightly. Add eggs; continue beating. Dissolve yeast in lukewarm water. Add to shortening mixture, beating well. Add flour gradually; continue to beat until soft dough forms. Mix by hand when it becomes too stiff for mixer. Cover; refrigerate overnight. Remove desired portion to floured surface. Roll to ¼-inch thickness. Cut with biscuit cutter. Brush surface with butter; fold over, pinching edges together slightly. Place on lightly greased baking sheet. Let rise 1½-2 hours. Bake at 450° for 7-10 minutes.
Dough keeps in refrigerator up to 10 days.

Susan Roach
Jackson, Georgia

Yeast Rolls

Oven: 425° - 10-13 minutes

1 package active dry
    yeast
¼ cup warm water
    (105° - 115°)
¼ cup butter
¼ cup sugar

1 egg, beaten
1 cup scalded milk
    (cooled to 105° - 115°)
1 teaspoon salt
4 cups all-purpose flour

Dissolve yeast in warm water; let stand 5-10 minutes. Cream butter, adding sugar slowly until mixture is light and fluffy. Sift flour and salt. Mix milk, egg and yeast. Slowly stir flour mixture into liquid mixture to form a soft dough. Place dough in well-greased bowl, turning several times to grease top of dough. Cover; place in refrigerator 24 hours. To cook, shape dough into ¾ to 1-inch balls and place three balls of dough in each muffin cup. Cover; let rise in a warm place until doubled in size. Bake at 425° for 10-13 minutes or until golden brown. Brush with melted butter when removed from oven.
Dough can be refrigerated for several days and cooked fresh as required.

Jim Hamrick

French Lemon Spirals

Oven: 375° - 12-15 minutes   **Yield:** 2 dozen

1	package active dry yeast	¾	cup sugar, divided
2½	cups all-purpose flour, divided	2	eggs, beaten
½	cup milk	4	teaspoons lemon rind, grated, divided
½	cup + 2 tablespoons butter or margarine, divided		

Combine yeast and 1 cup flour in a large mixing bowl. Combine milk, 6 tablespoons butter and ¼ cup sugar in a saucepan; cook over low heat until butter melts. Cook to lukewarm (105° - 115°). Stir into flour mixture, blending well. Add eggs and 2 teaspoons lemon rind. Beat at low speed of electric mixer until blended. Beat at high speed for 3 minutes. Stir in enough of remaining flour to make a stiff dough. Cover. Chill 2-3 hours. Divide dough in half; turn out onto a lightly floured surface. Roll each half into a 12x7-inch rectangle. Spread each with 2 tablespoons softened butter; sprinkle each with ¼ cup sugar and 1 teaspoon lemon rind. Roll up dough jellyroll fashion, starting at the long side. Pinch seams to seal. Cut each roll into 12 slices; place on greased baking sheets. Cover; let rise until doubled in bulk, about 1 hour. Bake at 375° for 12-15 minutes or until lightly browned.
Great for luncheons.

Wanda Roach

Bolillos Bread

Oven: 375° - 35-40 minutes   **Yield:** 2 dozen

1¼	tablespoons sugar	1	cup cold water
1	tablespoon salt	1	package active dry yeast
2	tablespoons shortening		
1	cup boiling water	6½	cups all-purpose flour

Mix sugar, salt and shortening with boiling water. Blend well. Add cold water, cooling mixture to lukewarm. Sprinkle yeast over mixture; let stand about 5 minutes. Stir well to dissolve. Blend in 4 cups flour; keep adding remaining flour until a stiff dough is formed. Knead on floured surface until smooth and elastic, about 4-5 minutes. Place dough in a greased bowl; brush top with additional shortening. Cover with a damp cloth. Let rise in a warm place for 1½ hours. Punch down and allow to rise again until double in size. Knead again. Divide into small bolillos about 2½-3 inches long, cylinders with pointed ends. Place on a greased baking sheet. Allow to rise, uncovered, in a warm place until double in size. Before baking, cut a ¼-inch deep slash down the length of the bolillos. Bake at 375° for 35-40 minutes or until golden brown. Cool on wire racks.
Bread is coarse with a hard crust.

Joan Anderson

English Muffins

Yield: 1½ dozen

2 cups milk
¼ cup margarine
2 tablespoons sugar
1 teaspoon salt
1 package active dry
   yeast

5 cups all-purpose flour,
   divided
1 egg
Cornmeal

Combine milk and margarine in a small saucepan. Heat until warm. Combine sugar, salt, yeast and 1½ cups flour in a large bowl. Blend liquid into dry ingredients. Beat 2 minutes. Gradually beat in egg and an additional 1 cup flour to make thick batter. Beat 2 minutes. Stir in 2½ cups flour to make a stiff dough. Knead 2 minutes on a floured surface. Place in greased bowl. Cover. Let rise until double (about 1½ hours). Punch down. Place on floured surface; cover with bowl; let rest for 15 minutes. Roll dough about ⅜ inch thick. Cut with 3-inch cookie cutter. Dip both sides in cornmeal. Place 1 inch apart on cookie sheet. Cover. Let rise until double (about 45 minutes). Brush a 12-inch skillet or griddle lightly with oil. On medium heat, cook muffins about 8 minutes on each side until lightly brown. Cool on wire racks.

Lillian Thomason

Parmesan Cheese and Dill Bread

Oven: 350° - 55 minutes   **Yield:** 1 large loaf or 2 regular loaves

1 (13-ounce) can evaporated
   milk
3 tablespoons sugar
3 tablespoons butter,
   cut into pieces
2 teaspoons salt
2 teaspoons dill seed
3 tablespoons instant minced
   onion

1 cup Parmesan cheese,
   grated
1½ packages active dry
   yeast
¼ cup warm water
   (about 110°)
3¾ cups all-purpose flour,
   sifted, divided
2 eggs

Combine milk, sugar, butter, salt, dill seed, onion and cheese in a saucepan. Heat, stirring to about 110° (butter and cheese may not melt completely). Dissolve yeast in the warm water. Add milk mixture. Beat in 1½ cups of the flour. Add eggs, 1 at a time, beating well after each addition. Gradually beat in 1½ cups more flour until batter is smooth. Beat in remaining ¾ cup flour with a spoon. Cover and let rise 45 minutes. Stir batter down and spoon into a generously greased 10-inch tube pan or 2 4½x8½-inch loaf pans. Cover and let rise in a warm place until almost doubled (about 45 minutes). Bake at 350° for about 55 minutes (45 minutes for loaf pans) or until bread sounds hollow when tapped.
A perfect bread for Italian food.

Helen Spears

Three Wheat Batter Bread

Oven: 350°
    45 minutes, small loaf
    60 minutes, large loaf

Yield: 2 small loaves or 1 large loaf

1 package active dry
   yeast
½ cup warm water (110°)
⅛ teaspoon ginger
3 tablespoons honey,
   divided
1 (13-ounce) can
   evaporated milk

1 teaspoon salt
2 tablespoons vegetable oil
2½ cups all-purpose flour
1¼ cups whole wheat flour
½ cup wheat germ
¼ cup cracked wheat

Combine yeast, water, ginger, and 1 tablespoon honey; let stand in a warm place until bubbly (about 20 minutes). Stir in remaining 2 tablespoons honey, milk, salt and oil. Mix together all flours and grains; add to liquid mixture one cup at a time, beating after each addition. Spoon batter evenly into a well-greased 2-pound coffee can or 2 greased 1-pound coffee cans. Cover with plastic lids. (Freeze at this point if you wish.) Let rise in a warm place until lids pop off, about 55 minutes for 1-pound cans; 1-1½ hours for 2-pound cans. Bake in can uncovered at 350° for about 45 minutes for 1-pound cans; about 60 minutes for 2-pound cans or until bread sounds hollow when tapped. Cool 10 minutes. Loosen crust around edge of can with thin knife; slide bread from can; let cool.
Hearty and nutritious.

Cookbook Committee

Dilly Bread

Oven: 375° - 35-40 minutes

Yield: 2 loaves

2 cups creamed cottage
   cheese
2 tablespoons butter
1 tablespoon dill seed
2 tablespoons scallions,
   minced
¼ cup sugar
¼ teaspoon baking soda

2 teaspoons salt
2 eggs
1 package active dry
   yeast
½ cup warm water
5 cups unbleached all-
   purpose flour

Slightly warm together the cottage cheese and butter. Add dill seed, onion, sugar, baking soda, salt and eggs. Beat until blended. Dissolve yeast in water; stir into cottage cheese mixture. Stir in as much flour as possible; then knead in the rest. Continue kneading until dough is smooth. Place in a greased bowl, turning batter to grease the top. Cover; let stand until doubled in bulk. Punch down. Shape into 2 loaves and place in greased 8x4-inch loaf pans. Cover; let rise until dough reaches tops of pans. Bake at 375° for 35-40 minutes or until browned and loaves sound hollow when tapped on top. Turn out and cool on racks.

Florence Cauble

Streamlined White Bread

Oven: 375° - 45-50 minutes   **Yield:** 1 loaf

1 package active dry
  yeast
1¼ cups warm water
2 tablespoons shortening
2 teaspoons salt

2 tablespoons sugar
3 cups all-purpose flour,
  sifted
Melted butter

Dissolve yeast in warm water. Add shortening, salt, sugar and 1½ cups sifted flour. Beat 2 minutes at medium speed. Add 1½ cups more flour; blend in with spoon. Cover; let rise in warm place about 30 minutes. Beat batter about 25 strokes and spread it evenly in a greased 9x5-inch loaf pan. Smooth top and pat into shape with floured hands. Let rise again until batter reaches 1 inch from top of loaf pan (about 40 minutes). Bake at 375° for 45-50 minutes until browned. Remove from pan. Place on cooling rack. Brush top with melted butter. Cool before cutting.
Tip: too much rising will cause bread to fall.

Carolyn Weaver

Whole Wheat Honey Bread

Oven: 375° - 40-45 minutes   **Yield:** 2 loaves

2½ cups warm water
  (105° to 115°)
⅓ cup instant nonfat dry
  milk powder
⅓ cup shortening
¼ cup honey

2 packages active dry
  yeast
1 tablespoon salt
3½ cups whole wheat flour
3½ cups all-purpose flour

Combine first 6 ingredients in a large mixing bowl; let stand 5 minutes. Add whole wheat flour; mix with electric mixer until blended. Increase speed to medium, beating 3 minutes. Gradually add remaining flour. Turn dough onto floured board (dough will be very sticky). Knead until smooth and elastic. Cover; let rest in a warm place (85°) free from drafts, 15 minutes. Dough will be soft. Divide dough in half; place each half in a greased 9x5-inch loaf pan. Cover; let rise in a warm place (85°) about 1½ hours or until doubled in bulk. Bake at 375° for 40-45 minutes or until loaves sound hollow when tapped. Transfer loaves to wire racks to cool.
Freezes well.

Helen Spears

Cinnamon Rolls or Sweet Dinner Rolls

Oven: 350° - 20 minutes

Yield: 24 cinnamon rolls
or 36 dinner rolls

Basic Recipe

1 cup shortening	2 eggs, beaten
1 cup boiling water	1 cup cold water
1 cup sugar	6 cups all-purpose flour,
1½ teaspoons salt	unsifted
3 packages active dry yeast	

Melt shortening in water. Stir in sugar and salt; dissolve. Add yeast, stirring to dissolve. Add eggs, water and flour to yeast mixture. Mix well. Cover; refrigerate overnight. Use dough to make cinnamon rolls or sweet dinner rolls.

Cinnamon Rolls

1 cup butter or margarine, softened	2 teaspoons cinnamon
½ cup brown sugar, firmly packed	3 tablespoons oil
½ cup sugar	6 tablespoons water
¼ teaspoon nutmeg	Raisins
	Nuts, chopped

Combine all ingredients except raisins and nuts. Set aside. Roll out 1 basic recipe of dough (½ at a time) into a rectangle 12x15x½ inches. Spread with ½ cinnamon-sugar mixture. Sprinkle with raisins. Roll up long side like a jelly roll. Cut into 12 rolls. Place in a greased 12x15-inch pan. Sprinkle with nuts. Let rise 1-2 hours. Bake at 350° for 20 minutes or until lightly browned. Make a glaze of powdered sugar and milk to drizzling consistency. Drizzle over rolls. Serve immediately. Repeat with remaining dough.

Sweet Dinner Rolls

Roll 1 basic recipe of dough to ½-inch thickness. Cut with 3-inch floured cookie cutter. Cut in half with knife. Brush with melted margarine. Fold over. Place 1 inch apart on greased cookie sheet. Let rise 1-1½ hours. Bake at 350° for 20 minutes.

Marcia Lutz

ALTA Almond Coffee Cake

Oven: 375° - 45 minutes   **Yield:** 12 servings

Crust

½ cup margarine,   2 tablespoons water
  softened
1 cup all-purpose flour

Mix margarine and flour with fork until crumbly. Add water and roll into 2 balls. Press balls together lining the bottom of a greased 9x13-inch pan.

Filling

1 cup water   3 eggs
½ cup margarine   2 teaspoons almond extract
1 cup all-purpose flour

Mix water and margarine and bring to a boil. Take off stove and add flour and eggs, beating well after each egg. Add almond extract and spread over crust. Bake at 375° for 45 minutes.

Frosting

1 cup confectioners'   Dash of vanilla extract
  sugar   Small amount of water
5 tablespoons margarine, Sliced almonds
  softened

Combine sugar, margarine, vanilla and water; mix until spreading consistency. Spread over warm cake. Sprinkle with sliced almonds.
It is best to make this coffee cake and serve it the same day, as it does not keep well.

Jo Ellen Wilson

Sour Cream Coffee Cake

Oven: 350° - 60-65 minutes   **Yield:** 12 servings

¾ cup pecans, finely   1½ cups sour cream
  chopped   3 eggs
1½ teaspoons cinnamon   1½ teaspoons baking powder
2 cups sugar, divided   1½ teaspoons baking soda
¾ cup margarine, softened   1½ teaspoons vanilla extract
3 cups all-purpose flour

Combine pecans, cinnamon and ¾ cup sugar. Set aside. In large bowl, beat margarine and 1¼ cups sugar until fluffy. Add flour and remaining ingredients. Beat 3 minutes. Grease and flour a 10-inch tube pan. Spread half of batter in pan. Sprinkle with half of nut mixture. Repeat with remaining batter and nut mixture. Bake at 350° for 60-65 minutes or until cake pulls away from sides of pan.

Elly Hobgood

Blueberry Coffee Cake

Oven: 350° · 50 minutes   **Yield:** 12 servings

1¼ cups fresh blueberries,
   or frozen blueberries,
   thawed
1⅓ cups sugar, divided
2 tablespoons cornstarch
½ cup margarine, softened
2 eggs
2 cups all-purpose flour
1 teaspoon baking powder
1 teaspoon baking soda
½ teaspoon salt
1 (8-ounce) carton sour
   cream
1 teaspoon almond extract
½ cup pecans, finely
   chopped
Glaze

Combine blueberries, ⅓ cup sugar and cornstarch in saucepan; cook over low heat 5-7 minutes until thickened. Set aside. Cream butter and gradually add 1 cup sugar, beating well until fluffy. Add eggs, one at a time, beating well after each. Combine flour, baking powder, soda and salt. Add to creamed mixture alternately with sour cream, beginning and ending with flour mixture. Stir in almond extract. Spoon half of batter into a greased and floured Bundt or 10-inch tube pan. Spoon half of blueberry sauce over batter. Repeat, then partially swirl through batter with a knife. Sprinkle with pecans. Bake at 350° for 50 minutes. Cool briefly in pan. Then invert on plate. Glaze when cool.
Even better the second day.

Glaze

¾ cup confectioners'
   sugar
1 tablespoon warm water
½ teaspoon almond extract

Combine sugar, water and almond extract; mix well.

Elly Hobgood

Applesauce Nut Bread

Oven: 350° · 50-55 minutes   **Yield:** 1 large loaf

1 cup raisins
   Hot water
1 cup shortening
1⅓ cups brown sugar,
   firmly packed
4 eggs, beaten
2 cups thick applesauce
4 cups all-purpose flour
2 teaspoons baking powder
2 teaspoons baking soda
1 teaspoon salt
½ teaspoon cinnamon
1 cup pecans, chopped
½ teaspoon cloves

Soak the raisins in a small amount of hot water; drain. Mix shortening, sugar and eggs; add applesauce. Blend in dry ingredients. Stir in nuts, raisins and cloves. Pour into a greased and floured 9x5-inch loaf pan. Bake at 350° for 50-55 minutes.

Shirley Pahl

Banana Bread

Oven: 350° - 45 minutes   **Yield**: 1 loaf

⅔ cup margarine, softened	¼ teaspoon salt
1½ cups sugar	4 tablespoons milk
2 eggs	1 cup bananas, mashed
1½ cups all-purpose flour	½ cup pecans, chopped
2 teaspoons baking powder	1 teaspoon vanilla extract

Cream margarine and sugar. Add eggs. Sift flour, baking powder and salt together. Add flour mixture and milk to creamed ingredients. Stir in mashed bananas, pecans and vanilla. Pour into a greased 9x5-inch loaf pan. Bake at 350° for 45 minutes.
Freezes well.

Wanda Roach

Date Nut Loaf

Oven: 350° - 1 hour - 1 hour 15 minutes   **Yield**: 1 loaf

8 ounces dates, chopped	1 egg, well beaten
1 teaspoon baking soda	2 cups all-purpose flour
1 cup boiling water	¼ teaspoon salt
½ cup shortening	1 cup nuts, chopped
¾ cup dark brown sugar, firmly packed	1-2 teaspoons vanilla extract

Mix dates, baking soda and boiling water. Let stand 10 minutes. Cream shortening and sugar. Gradually add egg, flour and salt. Add date mixture last. Fold in nuts and vanilla. Pour into a greased 9x5-inch loaf pan. Bake at 350° for 1 hour - 1 hour 15 minutes. Cool; then wrap tightly in foil and slice the next day.
This recipe is over 100 years old.

Era Hendrix

Poppy Seed Bread

Oven: 350° - 50 minutes   **Yield: 1 large or 2 small loaves**

2 eggs	1 teaspoon salt
1½ cups sugar	2 cups all-purpose flour
¾ cup vegetable oil	1 teaspoon baking powder
1 teaspoon vanilla extract	1 cup evaporated milk
¼ cup poppy seeds	

Beat eggs; add sugar, oil, vanilla and poppy seeds. Blend well. Sift together salt, flour and baking powder; add to mixture. Stir in milk. Pour into a greased 9x5-inch loaf pan or 2 small loaf pans. Bake at 350° for 50 minutes.
This freezes well.

Virginia Jones

Pumpkin Bread

Oven: 350° - 1 hour   **Yield:** 3 loaves

3⅓ cups all-purpose flour
2 teaspoons baking soda
1½ teaspoons salt
1 teaspoon cinnamon
1 teaspoon nutmeg
3 cups sugar
1 cup vegetable oil

4 eggs
⅔ cup water
2 cups canned pumpkin or
   2 cups fresh pumpkin,
   cooked
1 cup pecans, chopped

Sift flour, soda, salt, cinnamon, nutmeg and sugar. Make a well in dry mixture; add oil, eggs, water, pumpkin and nuts. Mix well. Divide into 3 greased 9x5-inch loaf pans. Bake at 350° for 1 hour.
This freezes well and makes great gifts.

Linda Hasty

Simple Sticky Buns

Oven: 350° - 30 minutes   **Yield:** 8 servings

1 package of 24 frozen
   yeast dinner rolls
1 (3-ounce) package
   butterscotch pudding
   (not instant)

½ cup nuts, chopped
½ cup brown sugar
½ cup butter

Grease large Bundt pan. Drop rolls, frozen, into bottom of pan. Sprinkle with pudding mix and nuts. Melt sugar with butter until dissolved. Pour over rolls. Cover. Let rise overnight. Bake at 350° for 30 minutes.
Wonderful to serve overnight guests for breakfast.

Marie Kook

Strawberry Nut Bread

Oven: 350° - 50-55 minutes   **Yield:** 2 loaves

1 cup butter
1½ cups sugar
1 teaspoon vanilla extract
¼ teaspoon lemon extract
4 eggs
3 cups all-purpose flour
1 teaspoon salt

1 teaspoon cream of
   tartar
½ teaspoon baking powder
1 cup strawberry jam
½ cup sour cream
1 cup pecans, chopped

Cream butter, sugar, vanilla and lemon until fluffy. Add eggs, one at a time, beating well after each. Sift flour, salt, cream of tartar and baking powder together. Combine jam and sour cream. Add jam mixture alternately with dry ingredients, beating well until combined. Stir in nuts. Pour into 2 greased and well-floured 9x5-inch loaf pans. Bake at 350° for 50-55 minutes. Cool in pans for 10 minutes; then remove from pans.

Doris Thacker

Zucchini Bread

Oven: 325° - 1 hour   **Yield:** 2 loaves

2 cups raw zucchini,
  shredded
1 cup vegetable oil
3 eggs, beaten
2 cups all-purpose flour
2 cups sugar

1 teapoon salt
1 teaspoon baking soda
1 teaspoon baking powder
3 teaspoons cinnamon
1 teaspoon vanilla extract
1 cup pecans, chopped

Mix all ingredients. Pour into 2 greased and floured 9x5-inch loaf pans. Bake at 325° for 1 hour.

Judi Whiddon

Sweet Potato Bread

Oven: 350° - 1 hour   **Yield:** 1 large loaf

2 cups self-rising flour
1 cup sugar
¼ cup vegetable oil
2 eggs
1 cup sweet potatoes,
  cooked

½ teaspoon allspice
½ cup milk
1 cup pecans, chopped

Combine all ingredients except pecans in a large mixing bowl; beat at low speed for 30 seconds and medium speed for 2 minutes. Stir in pecans. Pour into a greased and floured 7x5-inch loaf pan. Bake at 350° for 60 minutes. Cool for 10 minutes before removing from pan.

Shirley Pahl

Beer Bread

Oven: 425° - 30 minutes   **Yield:** 1 loaf

3 cups self-rising flour
3 tablespoons sugar

1 (12-ounce) can beer
  (not light)

Sift flour and sugar. Stir in beer. Pour into a well-greased 9x5-inch loaf pan. Bake at 425° for 30 minutes or until golden brown.

Nell Hamrick

Onion-Cheese Bread

Oven: 350° - 1 hour

Yield: 1 loaf

1 egg, beaten
½ cup milk
1 tablespoon vegetable oil
1½ cups Bisquick

½ cup onion, chopped
1 cup sharp Cheddar
   cheese, grated
1 tablespoon poppy seeds

Mix egg with milk and oil. Blend in Bisquick, onion and cheese. Pour into a greased 9x5-inch loaf pan. Sprinkle poppy seeds over top. Bake at 350° for 1 hour.

Sandra Bennett

Chocolate-Cinnamon Doughnuts

Yield: 2 dozen

4 cups all-purpose flour
⅓ cup unsweetened cocoa
4 teaspoons baking powder
1 teaspoon cinnamon
¾ teaspoon salt
¼ teaspoon baking soda
2 eggs, beaten

1¼ cups sugar
¼ cup vegetable oil
1 teaspoon vanilla extract
¾ cup buttermilk
Oil or shortening
Cinnamon Glaze

Stir together the flour, cocoa, baking powder, cinnamon, salt and baking soda. Beat eggs and sugar together until thick and lemon-colored. Stir in ¼ cup oil and vanilla. Add dry ingredients and buttermilk alternately to egg mixture, beginning and ending with dry ingredients. Beat just until blended after each addition. Cover; chill dough about 2 hours. Roll dough, ½ at a time, on lightly floured surface to ½-inch thickness. (Keep remaining dough chilled as other half is rolled.) Cut with floured 2½-inch doughnut cutter. Fry in deep hot fat (375°) about 1½ minutes per side; turning once. Drain. Dip warm doughnuts in Cinnamon Glaze.

Cinnamon Glaze

4 cups confectioners'
   sugar, sifted
1 teaspoon vanilla extract

½ teaspoon cinnamon
Milk

Combine confectioners' sugar, vanilla, cinnamon and enough milk to make a drizzling consistency.

Marcia Lutz

Apple Muffins

Oven: 450° - 15-20 minutes

Yield: 1 dozen (large) or
2 dozen (small)

1½ cups all-purpose flour
½ cup sugar
½ teaspoon cinnamon
2 teaspoons baking powder
½ teaspoon salt

1 egg, beaten
½ cup milk
¼ cup vegetable oil
1 cup raw apple, chopped

Sift together in mixing bowl the flour, sugar, cinnamon, baking powder and salt. Add egg, milk, oil and chopped apple to the dry ingredients. Stir together until ingredients are moistened. Fill greased muffin tins ⅔ full. Bake at 450° for 15-20 minutes until browned.

Jeanette Bagwell

Applesauce Raisin Bran Muffins

Oven: 350° - 20 minutes

Yield: 1½ dozen

1¼ cups 100% bran cereal
¾ cup milk
1¼ cups all-purpose flour
½ cup sugar
⅓ cup raisins
½ tablespoon baking powder
1 teaspoon cinnamon

½ teaspoon nutmeg
½ teaspoon baking soda
¼ teaspoon salt
½ cup applesauce
¼ cup vegetable oil
2 eggs, beaten

Soften cereal in milk 5 minutes. Mix flour, sugar, raisins, baking powder, spices, soda and salt. Make a well. Add applesauce and bran mixture, oil and eggs. Mix until moistened. Fill greased muffin tins. Bake at 350° for 20 minutes.

Carole Haley

Blueberry Yogurt Muffins

Oven: 400° - 20-25 minutes

Yield: 1 dozen

1 egg, beaten
¼ cup milk
1 (8-ounce) carton
blueberry yogurt

¼ cup vegetable oil
2 cups self-rising flour
¼ cup sugar

Combine egg, milk, yogurt and oil. Mix in flour and sugar, just until moistened. Fill greased muffin tins ⅔ full. Bake at 400° for 20-25 minutes or until browned.

Doris Thacker

Refrigerated Bran Muffins

Oven: 400° -10-15 minutes   **Yield:** 3 dozen

1 cup boiling water
3 cups All Bran cereal
2 cups buttermilk
1½ cups sugar, or 1¼
    cups sugar and ¼ cup
    molasses

2 eggs, beaten
½ cup vegetable oil
2½ cups all-purpose flour
2½ teaspoons baking soda
½ teaspoon salt

Pour hot water over cereal. Stir in buttermilk, sugar, eggs, oil, flour, baking soda and salt. Mix just until blended. Grease muffin tins; spoon in muffin mixture. Bake at 400° for 10-15 minutes.

Ruth Denney

Golden Muffin Mix

Oven: 400° - 10-15 minutes

2 cups All Bran cereal
2 cups bite-sized
    shredded wheat cereal
2 cups rolled oats
2 cups warm water
1 cup shortening
3 cups sugar

4 eggs, beaten
5 cups all-purpose flour
5 teaspoons baking soda
1 tablespoon salt
1 quart buttermilk
1 cup raisins,
    (optional)

Place cereals and water in a large bowl. Stir until smooth and cereals have softened. (Add a little more warm water if needed). In another bowl, cream shortening and sugar; beat in eggs, one at a time. Mix well. Combine dry ingredients. Add dry ingredients and buttermilk to cereal mixture. Stir in raisins, if desired. Mix until smooth; mixture will be thick. Store in a glass gallon jar. To cook, spoon into greased muffin tins. Bake at 400° for 10-15 minutes or until golden brown.

Mix will keep for months and will improve with age. It's great with butter or applesauce.

Audrey Turner

Graham Cracker Muffins

Oven 425° - 12-15 minutes   Yield: 1½ dozen

2⅔ cups graham cracker   3 tablespoons margarine,
    crumbs   melted
⅔ cup sugar   1 egg, beaten
1 tablespoon baking powder   1 tablespoon vanilla extract
  Pinch of salt   ½ cup pecans, chopped
¾ cup milk

Mix dry ingredients. Blend milk, margarine and egg together. Add to dry ingredients. Stir in vanilla and nuts. Fill greased muffin tins. Bake at 425° for 12-15 minutes. Watch carefully after 12 minutes to avoid getting the muffins too dark.
Can be made ahead and frozen.

Grace Hyatt

Molasses Refrigerator Muffins

Oven: 350° - 20 minutes   Yield: 3 dozen

4 cups all-purpose flour   ¼ teaspoon nutmeg
2 teaspoons baking soda   1 cup sugar
1 teaspoon salt   1½ cups shortening
1 teaspoon cinnamon   4 eggs, beaten
1 teaspoon ginger   1 cup molasses
¼ teaspoon cloves   1 cup buttermilk
¼ teaspoon allspice   1 cup raisins (optional)

Sift together flour, baking soda, salt, cinnamon, ginger, cloves, allspice and nutmeg. Cream sugar and shortening until light; add eggs, beating well. Blend in molasses and buttermilk. Add dry ingredients. Stir by hand just enough to moisten. Stir in raisins, if desired. Spoon into greased muffin tins, filling ½ full. Bake at 350° for 20 minutes or until golden brown.
Batter can be kept in refrigerator and used later.

Ruth Gramling

Streusel Orange Muffins

Oven: 400° - 18-20 minutes   Yield: 1 dozen

2 cups biscuit mix   ½ cup pecans, chopped
¼ cup sugar   3 tablespoons sugar
1 egg, beaten   1 tablespoon all-purpose
½ cup orange juice   flour
2 tablespoons vegetable oil   ½ teaspoon cinnamon
½ cup orange marmalade   ¼ teaspoon nutmeg

Combine biscuit mix and ¼ cup sugar; make a well in center of mixture. Combine egg, orange juice and oil; add to dry ingredients, stirring to moisten. Stir in marmalade and pecans. Spoon into greased muffin tins. Combine remaining 3 tablespoons sugar, flour and spices. Sprinkle 1 teaspoon of this mixture over batter in each muffin tin. Bake at 400° for 18-20 minutes.

Jeanette Black

Peach Muffins

Oven: 400° - 20 minutes

Yield: 1½ dozen

2 cups all-purpose flour
½ cup sugar
2 teaspoons baking powder
½ teaspoon baking soda
½ teaspoon salt
½ teaspoon cinnamon
½ teaspoon nutmeg
Dash of ground mace
1 egg, beaten
⅓ cup vegetable oil
⅓ cup milk

1 (8-ounce) carton
    peach yogurt
½ cup dried peaches,
    finely chopped
2 tablespoons all-purpose
    flour
2 tablespoons brown sugar
2 tablespoons pecans,
    chopped
½ teaspoon cinnamon
2 tablespoons margarine,
    softened

Combine first 8 ingredients in a large bowl; make a well in center of mixture. Combine egg, oil, milk, yogurt and dried peaches; add to dry ingredients. Stir until moist. Spoon batter into greased muffin tins, filled ⅔ full. Combine 2 tablespoons flour, brown sugar, pecans and ½ teaspoon cinnamon in a small bowl. Cut in margarine until mixture forms crumbs. Sprinkle 1 teaspoon crumb mixture over muffin batter. Bake at 400° for 20 minutes.
Good both warm or at room temperature.

Jeanette Black

Quick Biscuits

Oven: 425° - 10 minutes

Yield: 1 dozen

2 cups self-rising flour
1 (8-ounce) carton whipping
    cream

1 tablespoon sugar

Mix all ingredients. Roll out on floured board. Cut into rounds with a 2-inch biscuit cutter. Bake on a greased pan at 425° for 10 minutes or until golden brown.

Florence Cauble

Southern Drop Biscuits

Oven: 450° - 10 minutes   **Yield:** 1½ dozen

2 cups all-purpose flour
1 tablespoon baking powder
¾ teaspoon salt
½ teaspoon baking soda
½ teaspoon cream of
     tartar

4 tablespoons shortening
1 cup buttermilk
½ cup butter or
     margarine

Sift dry ingredients together twice. Cut shortening into flour mixture until well mixed. Add buttermilk; stir well. Drop level tablespoon of dough onto greased foil or cookie sheet. Place a pat of butter on each biscuit. Bake at 450° for 10 minutes.

Anne Huey

Mexican Cornbread

Oven: 450° - 25-30 minutes   **Yield:** 10 servings

1½ cups self-rising
       corn meal
1½ tablespoons sugar
1 medium onion, finely
     chopped
1 green pepper, finely
     chopped
1 Jalapeño pepper, finely
     chopped

½ cup sharp Cheddar
     cheese, grated
1 (8½-ounce) can cream-
     style corn
1 cup milk
3 eggs, slightly
     beaten
¼ cup vegetable oil

Combine all ingredients. Stir until well blended. Pour into a greased 9-inch square pan. Bake at 450° for 25-30 minutes.

Carolyn Weaver

Five-Item Cornbread

Oven: 400° - 20-25 minutes   **Yield:** 6 servings

½ cup vegetable oil
2 eggs, beaten
½ cup cream-style corn

1 cup self-rising corn meal
1 (8-ounce) carton sour
     cream

Put oil in iron skillet and heat in oven. Mix eggs, corn and corn meal. Add hot oil; mix well. Stir in sour cream. Pour mixture into the hot skillet. Bake at 400° for 20-25 minutes.
This is great to use in dressing.

Patsy Saxon

Spinach Cornbread

Oven: 350° - 30 minutes   **Yield:** 10 servings

1 (10-ounce) package frozen
   chopped spinach, thawed
   and drained
1 (8½-ounce) package
   Jiffy Corn Muffin Mix
4 eggs, beaten

6 ounces cottage cheese
½ cup margarine, melted
1 large onion, chopped
½ teaspoon salt

Mix all ingredients together. Pour into a greased 9-inch square pan. Bake at 350°
for 30 minutes.
Best when served hot!

Lila Stevens

Sourdough Cheese Toast

Oven: Broil 2-4 minutes   **Yield:** 6-8 servings

¼ cup mayonnaise
½ cup butter, softened
½ cup sharp Cheddar
   cheese, shredded

1 tablespoon garlic salt
   Sourdough bread,
   sandwich-sliced

Mix mayonnaise, butter, cheese and garlic salt together. Spread over 10 or
more slices of bread. Broil for 2-4 minutes.
Great with spaghetti.

Anne Harris

Chicken Dressing

Oven: 400° - 30-40 minutes

4 cups cornbread,
   broken up
3 cups biscuits,
   broken up
5 pieces white bread,
   broken up
4 cups chicken broth

¾ cup water
2 teaspoons sage
1½ cups celery, chopped
¾ cup onion, chopped
2 eggs, beaten
½ cup margarine, melted
   Salt and pepper to taste

Combine all ingredients; mix well. Pour into a 9x13-inch greased baking dish.
Bake at 400° for 30-40 minutes or until done.

Louise Roach

Cranberry Stuffing

1 cup celery, chopped
½ cup butter or
   margarine
1 (8-ounce) package stuffing
   mix

Poultry seasoning to taste
1 cup cranberries, chopped
1 cup chicken stock

Sauté celery in butter until light brown. Add stuffing mix, poultry seasoning, cranberries and chicken stock. Cool. Stuff bird. Roast as usual.

Elizabeth Jost

Dumplings That Work

1½ cups all-purpose flour
  2 teaspoons baking powder
  ½ teaspoon salt

1 egg yolk, beaten
Milk

Sift flour, baking powder and salt. Add egg yolk to small amount of milk. Mix into dry ingredients, adding just enough milk to make a drop batter. Drop by tablespoons into boiling broth or stew. Cover; cook without lifting the cover for 15-20 minutes.

Joan Satterfield

Hush Puppies

Yield: 6 servings

2 cups water ground
   corn meal
1 tablespoon all-purpose
   flour
½ teaspoon baking soda
1 teaspoon baking powder

1 teaspoon salt
1 egg, beaten
3 tablespoons onion,
   finely chopped
1 cup buttermilk

Mix dry ingredients together. Add onions, milk and egg. Blend well. Drop by teaspoonfuls into pan in which fish is being fried. Fry to a golden brown. Drain well. Serve hot.

Margaret McFather

Shrimp Paste

1 (7-ounce) can shrimp
   Juice of ½ lemon
3 tablespoons Durkee's
   Dressing

3 tablespoons mayonnaise
Onion juice to taste
Small shrimp for garnish

Mash shrimp until smooth. Add remaining ingredients; mix well. Refrigerate. Spread on bread rounds; garnish with small shrimp.

Marie Pressly

Frosted Ribbon Loaf

Ham Filling

2 cups ground ham
²/₃ cup celery, chopped
4 tablespoons pickle
   relish, drained

1 teaspoon prepared
   horseradish
½ cup mayonnaise

Combine ingredients for ham filling; blend well; set aside.

Egg Filling

8 hard-cooked eggs,
   chopped
²/₃ cup pimiento-stuffed
   olives, chopped

4 tablespoons green onion,
   chopped
4 teaspoons prepared mustard
½ cup mayonnaise

Combine ingredients for egg filling; blend well; set aside.

Frosting

3 (8-ounce) packages cream
   cheese, softened

²/₃ cup milk

Beat cream cheese with milk until fluffy. Set aside. Refrigerate.

To Assemble

1 Pullman loaf, unsliced
  Butter
  Ham filling

Egg filling
Frosting
Chopped parsley

Trim crust from bread. Slice lengthwise into 4 equal layers. Butter slices. Spread first slice with ham filling. Spread second and third slice with egg filling. Assemble and wrap in foil. Chill until firm. To complete, frost top and sides with prepared frosting. Sprinkle with parsley. Cover loosely and store in refrigerator. When ready to serve, slice.

Betty McDaniel

Dilled Cucumber and Cream Cheese Sandwiches

Yield: 16 finger sandwiches

1¹/₃ cups cucumber, peeled,
   seeded and chopped
¼ cup onion, minced
¼ cup snipped fresh dill
2 teaspoons fresh lemon juice

4 ounces cream cheese,
   softened
8 slices bread, crusts
   removed
Pepper to taste

Combine cucumber, onion, dill, lemon juice and cream cheese. Let mixture stand for 1 hour. Spread the filling on half the bread slices; sprinkle with pepper; top with remaining bread. Cut each sandwich into fourths.

Margaret Logan

Pimiento Cheese Spread - The Best

Yield: 3½ cups

1 (8-ounce) package cream
    cheese softened
2 teaspoons Worcestershire
    Salt and pepper,
    generously to taste
1 (4-ounce) jar pimientos,
    chopped, drained

1 teaspoon dry mustard
    (optional)
⅓ to ½ cup mayonnaise
12 ounces sharp Cheddar
    cheese, finely shredded

Beat cream cheese, Worcestershire, salt, pepper, pimientos, and mustard. Add mayonnaise and blend to spreadable consistency. Fold in Cheddar cheese and beat well. Adjust seasonings and consistency. Refrigerate in airtight container. Before spreading, remove from refrigerator and allow to soften slightly. *Keeps well for several days.*

Jeanette Black

Buttercups

Yield: 30 sandwiches

4 hard-cooked eggs,
    finely chopped
2 tablespoons radishes,
    chopped
1 tablespoon green onions,
    chopped
2 tablespoons mayonnaise

1 tablespoon Italian salad
    dressing
¼ teaspoon salt
¼ teaspoon Worcestershire
    Whole wheat bread,
    cut in rounds
    Radish slices

Combine first 7 ingredients. Chill. Spread on bread rounds. Arrange radish slices for garnish.

Brenda Satterfield

Chili Bean Franks

Yield: 10 servings

¼ pound ground beef
1 (11¼-ounce) can condensed
    chili beef soup
⅓ cup water

2 teaspoons prepared mustard
1 pound frankfurters, cooked
10 frankfurter buns,
    split and toasted

In saucepan, brown beef; stir to separate meat. Add soup, water and mustard. Heat; stir often. Place frankfurters in buns. Spoon soup over all.

Sue Wood

Orange Cream Cheese Crescents

Yield: 32 sandwiches

1 cup apple jelly
1 (11-ounce) can mandarin
   orange sections, drained
1 (8-ounce) package cream
   cheese, softened

1 tablespoon orange rind,
   grated
1 tablespoon milk
2 (8-ounce) cans orange-nut
   bread

Heat jelly just until melted in a small saucepan; remove from heat. Place orange sections, a few at the time, in jelly, turning to coat well. Lift out with a fork; place on wire rack set over waxed papper. Let stand until jelly sets. Blend cream cheese, orange rind and milk in a small bowl. Slice bread into 16 rounds; halve each. Spread with cheese mixture; top each with 1 orange section or 2 small sections.

Margaret Logan

Spiced Apricot Bread
Dainty Sandwiches

Oven: 350° - 1 hour

Yield: 3 dozen small sandwiches

1½ cups dried apricots, diced
  1 cup sugar
  ½ teaspoon cloves
  ¼ teaspoon nutmeg
  ½ teaspoon cinnamon
  ½ teaspoon salt
  6 tablespoons margarine,
    melted

1 cup water
1 egg, beaten
2 cups all-purpose flour
1 teaspoon baking soda
1 cup pecans or walnuts
  (may mix), chopped
Sandwich Fillings

Combine apricots, sugar, spices, salt, margarine and water in a saucepan. Cook for 5 minutes and cool thoroughly. Add egg, then flour mixed with soda. Stir in nuts; mix well. Pour into a greased 9x5x3-inch loaf pan. Bake at 350° for 1 hour. For a party, chill bread; slice thinly and make small dainty sandwiches. Use one of the following Sandwich Fillings.

Sandwich Fillings

1. Softened cream cheese flavored with honey and lemon juice.

2. One cup chopped dates mixed with ¼ cup orange juice and ¼ cup finely chopped walnuts.

3. Four ounces cream cheese mixed with 1 tablespoon grated orange rind, ¼ cup chopped seedless raisins, 2 tablespoons chopped pecans and 2 tablespoons orange juice.

Margaret Logan

Salads

Blueberry Congealed Salad

Yield: 12 servings

2 (3-ounce) packages
    blackberry gelatin
2 cups boiling water
1 (16-ounce) can blueberries
1 (8-ounce) can crushed
    pineapple
1 (8-ounce) package cream
    cheese, softened

½ cup sugar
1 (8-ounce) carton sour
    cream
½ teaspoon vanilla extract
½ cup nuts, chopped

Disslove gelatin in water. Drain blueberries and pineapple; reserve juices. Measure juice to make a cup (about ½ blueberries and ½ pineapple). Add to gelatin. Stir in blueberries and pineapple. Pour into a 2-quart pan. Chill until firm. Combine cream cheese, sugar, sour cream and vanilla; spread over congealed gelatin. Sprinkle nuts on top. Cut into squares.

Christie Geiger

Apricot Delight

Yield: 10-12 servings

½ cup pineapple juice
½ cup sugar
1 egg yolk
1 tablespoon all-purpose
    flour
1 tablespoon butter
1 (8-ounce) package cream
    cheese
2 bananas, sliced
1 (20-ounce) can crushed
    pineapple, drained

1 (6-ounce) package apricot,
    orange, or pineapple
    gelatin
1 cup hot water
    Miniature marshmallows
1 (8-ounce) carton frozen
    whipped topping

Combine pineapple juice, sugar, egg yolk, flour and butter. Cook over low heat until thick. Stir in cream cheese. Place bananas in an 8x10-inch pan. Pour crushed pineapple over bananas. Dissolve gelatin in water. Pour over crushed pineapple. Put 1 layer of marshmallows. Mix whipped topping with cooled cooked mixture; spread over marshmallows. Chill. Cut into squares.

Jeanette Bagwell

Bing Cherry Salad

Yield: 10-12 servings

2 envelopes unflavored gelatin
1 cup cold water
1 (16-ounce) can pitted black
   cherries
1 (20-ounce) can pineapple
   chunks

¾ cup sugar
½ cup lemon juice
   Dressing

Dissolve gelatin in cold water. Drain cherries and pineapple; reserve juice. Add enough water to the cherry and pineapple juice to make 2 cups. Bring this to a boil. Pour over dissolved gelatin. Add sugar and lemon juice, then fruit. Mix thoroughly. Pour into a 2-quart shallow dish. Congeal. Serve with the Dressing.

Dressing

1 (3-ounce) package cream
   cheese, softened
½ cup mayonnaise
½ cup heavy cream, whipped

12 large marshmallows,
   cut up
½ cup pecans, chopped

Beat cream cheese and mayonnaise until smooth. Fold in whipped cream, then marshmallows and nuts.

Peggy Jones

Rich's Magnolia Room Fruit Salad

Yield: 20-24 servings

1 (8-ounce) package cream
   cheese, softened
½ cup confectioners' sugar
⅓ cup mayonnaise
2 teaspoons vanilla extract
1 (6½-ounce) can sliced
   peaches, well drained
½ cup maraschino cherries,
   well drained
1 (26-ounce) can fruit
   cocktail, drained

1 (13-ounce) can crushed
   pineapple, drained
2 cups miniature
   marshmallows
½ cup whipping cream,
   whipped
   Few drops food coloring,
   if desired

Place cream cheese in mixer bowl. Add confectioners' sugar; blend in the mayonnaise. Add vanilla extract. Fold in the fruit and marshmallows gently. Fold in whipped cream. Pour into large paper-lined muffin tins; freeze. Before serving, take out of freezer about 10-15 minutes, but do not allow to become soft. Remove paper liners before serving.

Jerry Land

Cranberry Salad Souffle'

Yield: 8 servings

1 (3-ounce) package lemon
 gelatin
1 cup boiling water
1 (16-ounce) can whole
 cranberry sauce
½ cup mayonnaise
1½ ounces (half of 3-ounce
 package) cream cheese,
 softened

1 tablespoon lemon juice
¼ teaspoon salt
2 oranges, sectioned
 and diced
½ cup pecans, chopped
½ cup celery, chopped

Dissolve gelatin in water. Heat cranberry sauce until melted; strain ½ cup juice, adding to dissolved gelatin. Blend together mayonnaise and cream cheese. Add to gelatin mixture with lemon juice and salt. Blend thoroughly. Put in a freezing tray; chill until firm, about 20-25 minutes. Put in a bowl and whip until fluffy. Fold in remaining cranberry, diced oranges, nuts and celery. Pour into a mold. Chill until firm.

Julia Ellis

Cranberry Salad

Yield: 12-14 servings

1 (6-ounce) package raspberry
 gelatin
1 envelope unflavored gelatin
1 (16-ounce) can whole
 cranberries, drained

1 (8-ounce) can crushed
 pineapple, drained
1 pound red seedless grapes,
 halved
1 cup pecans, chopped

Combine gelatins. Mix according to package directions, decreasing the amount of water by ½ cup. Add remaining ingredients. Pour in a 9x13-inch pan. Chill until firm. Cut into squares.

Julia Ellis

Pineapple Aspic

Yield: 8-10 servings

1 (20-ounce) can crushed
 pineapple
1 (6-ounce) bottle maraschino
 cherries
 Juice of 2 lemons
 Scant cup of sugar

2 tablespoons unflavored
 gelatin
1 tablespoon water
 Sections of 2 grapefruits
1 cup nuts, chopped

Drain pineapple and cherries, reserving juices. Mix pineapple, cherry and lemon juice with sugar. Boil 5 minutes. Soften gelatin in water. Add gelatin to boiled mixture; cool. Add fruits and nuts. Pour into oiled individual molds. Chill until firm.

Virginia Jones

Pineapple Cheddar Salad

Yield: 9 servings

1 (3-ounce) package lemon
    gelatin
1 cup boiling water
1 (8-ounce) can crushed
    pineapple, undrained
¾ cup sugar

½ pint whipping cream,
    whipped
1 cup mild Cheddar cheese,
    shredded
½ cup pecans, chopped
    (optional)

Dissolve gelatin in boiling water. Stir in pineapple and sugar; cool. Fold in remaining ingredients; add pecans, if desired. Spoon into a 9-inch square pan; chill until firm. Cut into squares to serve.

Lillian Thomason

Molded Orange Salad

Yield: 14-16 servings

2 (3-ounce) packages orange
    gelatin
1 cup boiling water
1 (6-ounce) can frozen orange
    juice concentrate, thawed
2 juice cans water
2 (11-ounce) cans mandarin
    oranges, drained

1 (20-ounce) can crushed
    pineapple, drained
1 (8-ounce) can water
    chestnuts, drained and
    thinly sliced

Dissolve gelatin in boiling water; cool until partially congealed. Mix orange juice concentrate with water. Combine gelatin, orange juice, mandarin oranges and pineapple. Mix well; add water chestnuts. Pour into a lightly oiled 8-cup mold. Chill until firm.

Joan Anderson

Pretzel Salad

Oven: 400° - 8 minutes

Yield: 10-12 servings

2 cups pretzels, finely
    crushed
¾ cup margarine, melted
1 cup + 3 tablespoons
    sugar, divided
1 (8-ounce) package cream
    cheese, softened

1 (8-ounce) carton frozen
    whipped topping
1 (6-ounce) package
    strawberry gelatin
1½ cups boiling water
2 (10-ounce) packages frozen
    strawberries

Mix together pretzels, margarine and 3 tablespoons sugar; pat into a 9x13-inch pan. Bake at 400° for 8 minutes. Cool. Combine cream cheese, 1 cup sugar and frozen whipped topping; spread over pretzel crust. Dissolve gelatin in the boiling water; stir in strawberries. Cool until mixture begins to congeal. Spoon over cream cheese mixture. Refrigerate overnight. Cut into squares.

Lillian Thomason

Strawberry Jello Salad

Yield: 8 servings

2 (3-ounce) packages
  strawberry gelatin
2 cups boiling water
2 (10-ounce) packages frozen
  strawberries, thawed

1 (20-ounce) can crushed
  pineapple, undrained
2 large ripe bananas,
  finely diced
1 cup sour cream

Dissolve gelatin in boiling water. Add strawberries, pineapple and bananas. Pour half of mixture in an 8x8x2-inch pan. Chill until firm. Spread evenly with sour cream. Pour remaining gelatin mixture over sour cream. Chill until firm. Cut into squares; top with additional sour cream, if desired.

Barbara Helton

Deluxe Waldorf Salad

Yield: 6-8 servings

2 large tart red apples,
  unpeeled and diced
1 large green apple,
  unpeeled and diced
Lemon juice
½ pound seedless green
  grapes, halved
½ cup pecans, coarsely
  chopped

½ cup celery, finely diced
⅓ cup raisins
2 tablespoons maraschino
  cherries, sliced
¼ cup + 2 tablespoons
  mayonnaise
Lettuce

Toss apples with lemon juice. Add remaining ingredients; mix well. Spoon into a lettuce-lined bowl.
A beautiful salad.

Sylvia Peterson

Frosty Fruit Cup

Yield: 8 servings

½ watermelon, chilled
1 honeydew melon, chilled
2 cantaloupes, chilled
½ cup light corn syrup
¼ cup fresh lime juice
2 tablespoons snipped mint
  leaves

½ pint blueberries
½ pint strawberries
1 medium bunch seedless
  grapes
Mint leaves for garnish

Cut out small balls using a scoop from watermelon, honeydew melon and cantaloupes; place in bowl. Combine corn syrup, lime juice and mint leaves; pour over melon balls. Cover. Refrigerate. About 1 hour before serving, add blueberries, strawberries and grapes; mix with melon balls. Remove fruit with slotted spoon and fill chilled sherbet dishes. Serve with a small amount of marinade poured over fruit. Garnish with mint leaves.

Elizabeth Garrett

Fruit Salad

Yield: 6-8 servings

2 (16-ounce) cans fruits
for salad, drained
1 Winesap apple, unpeeled
and chopped
¼-½ pound purple
grapes, seeded and
halved

2 bananas, chopped
1 cup pecans, coarsely
chopped
1 cup sour cream
Lettuce
1 carton fresh
blueberries

Cut fruit into desired sized pieces. Toss fruits, nuts and sour cream together. Refrigerate. Spoon salad on lettuce-lined individual plates. Top with a mound of fresh blueberries.

Vern Wheeler

Avocado-Citrus Salad

Yield: 8-10 servings

2 (32-ounce) jars grapefruit-
orange sections
Lettuce leaves
1 ripe avocado,
peeled and sliced

1 green pepper,
sliced into rings
⅓ cup walnuts, chopped
Orange French Dressing

Drain fruit, reserving juice. Arrange grapefruit and orange sections on individual plates lined with lettuce. Dip avocado slices in reserved juice; then add to salad. Top each with a green pepper ring and sprinkling of walnuts. Top with Orange French Dressing.

Orange French Dressing

1 (6-ounce) can frozen orange
juice concentrate, thawed
½ cup vegetable oil
¼ cup vinegar

2-3 tablespoons sugar
½ teaspoon dry mustard
¼ teaspoon salt

Combine all ingredients; mix well. Chill before serving.

Joan McFather

Minted Citrus Salad

Yield: 6 servings

2 cups fresh grapefruit
   sections
2 or 3 oranges, peeled
   and thinly sliced
Salad greens
Mint leaves for garnish

3 tablespoons mint jelly
1 tablespoon honey
Grated peel of 1 lime
Juice of 1 lime
Juice of 1 lemon

Arrange grapefruit sections and orange slices on a bed of salad greens on individual serving plates. Garnish with mint leaves. Blend together mint jelly, honey, grated lime peel, lime juice and lemon juice. Spoon some of the dressing on each serving.

Ann Weeks

Mandarin Orange Salad

Yield: 4 servings

½ cup vegetable oil
¼ cup tarragon-flavored
   vinegar
1½ teaspoons sugar
½ teaspoon tarragon
¼ teaspoon salt
⅛ teaspoon pepper

Dash of hot sauce
1 head romaine lettuce,
   torn into pieces
1 (11-ounce) can mandarin
   oranges, drained
1 (2-ounce) package slivered
   almonds, toasted

Mix first 7 ingredients in a jar; shake well. Combine lettuce, mandarin oranges and almonds. Pour dressing over salad. Serve.

Susan Roach
Jackson, Georgia

Asheville Salad

Yield: 8-10 servings

2 envelopes unflavored gelatin
½ cup cold water
1 (10¾-ounce) can tomato
   soup
2 (3-ounce) packages cream
   cheese
1 cup mayonnaise
   Any 2 of the following:

1 cup celery, chopped
2 green peppers, chopped
½ cup pecans, chopped
½ cup pimiento-stuffed
   olives, sliced
1 cup cooked shrimp,
   chopped

Soak gelatin in water. Heat soup slowly; stir in cream cheese. Add gelatin, stirring until dissolved. Cool. Add mayonnaise and remaining ingredients. Pour into a 9-inch square dish or a 6-cup mold. Chill until firm.

Lane Towers

Harriette's Salad

Yield: 8 servings

½ cup water
1 (17-ounce) can early peas, drained, reserve juice
1 (3-ounce) package lemon gelatin
1 cup celery, chopped
1 tablespoon onion, grated

1 tablespoon pimiento, chopped
1 tablespoon vinegar
1 tablespoon sugar
1 cup mayonnaise
1 teaspoon salt

Boil water and ½ cup reserved juice from peas. Add gelatin and dissolve. Cool. Add the remaining ingredients. Pour in a greased 4-cup mold. Chill until firm.

Linda Schwamlein

Molded Bean Salad

Yield: 8-10 servings

1 (6-ounce) package lemon gelatin
1⅓ cups boiling water
1 (15½-ounce) jar spaghetti sauce with mushrooms
2 tablespoons vinegar

1 (15-ounce) can garbanzo beans, drained
1 (8-ounce) can red kidney beans, drained
½ cup celery, sliced
½ cup green pepper, chopped

Dissolve gelatin in water. Add spaghetti sauce and vinegar. Congeal until consistency of egg whites. Add garbanzo beans, kidney beans, celery and green pepper. Pour into an oiled 6-cup mold. Chill until set.

Virginia Spears

Artichoke-Rice Salad

Yield: 8 servings

1 (6-ounce) package chicken-flavored rice
4 green onions, sliced
½ green pepper, chopped
12 pimiento-stuffed olives, sliced

2 (6-ounce) jars marinated artichoke hearts, sliced
¾ teaspoon curry
⅓ cup mayonnaise

Cook rice according to package directions omitting butter. Add green onions, green pepper and olives. Drain artichoke hearts; reserve liquid. Add artichoke hearts to rice mixture. Cool. Combine half of reserved artichoke marinade, curry and mayonnaise. Combine with rice mixture; toss. Refrigerate.
Best if made a day ahead.

Ann Cullens

Broccoli Cauliflower Salad

Yield: 6-8 servings

1 bunch fresh broccoli,
   cut into flowerets
½ head cauliflower,
   cut into flowerets
½ cup pimiento-stuffed
   olives, sliced
2 onions, sliced
2 hard-cooked eggs,
   chopped

½ cup fresh bacon bits
½ cup mayonnaise
¼ cup sour cream
2 tablespoons cheese and
   garlic salad dressing mix
   (like the Good Seasons
   packages)

Steam broccoli and cauliflower until crisp tender. Add olives, onions, eggs and bacon. Mix mayonnaise, sour cream and dressing mix. Toss with vegetable mixture. Chill at least 2 hours before serving.
Easy and good with any meat.

Anne Harris

Broccoli Pasta Salad

Yield: 12 servings

1 (6-ounce) jar marinated
   artichoke hearts, chopped
1 large bunch fresh broccoli,
   cut into flowerets
⅔ cup pimiento-stuffed
   olives, chopped
1 small bunch green onion,
   chopped
4 hard-cooked eggs,
   chopped
3 cups cooked fancy pasta,
   (bow ties, small egg
   noodles, etc.)
½ pound fresh mushrooms,
   sliced (optional)

1 (8-ounce) can water
   chestnuts, sliced
1 egg
2 tablespoons Parmesan
   cheese, grated
1 whole clove garlic,
   crushed
½ teaspoon Dijon mustard
   Salt to taste
   Fresh ground pepper to taste
½ cup vegetable oil
⅓ cup lemon juice

Toss artichoke hearts, broccoli, olives, onions, hard-cooked eggs, pasta, mushrooms and water chestnuts. Set aside. In a food processor or blender, mix the remaining ingredients. Pour over pasta mixture; toss. Chill 2-3 hours before serving.

Deborah Fincher

Three-Week Slaw

3 pounds cabbage, chopped
1 green pepper, chopped
2 onions, chopped
2 cups sugar

1 cup vinegar
1 cup vegetable oil
1 tablespoon celery seed
1 tablespoon salt

Combine cabbage, green pepper, onions and sugar; set aside. In a saucepan, combine vinegar, oil, celery seed and salt. Bring to a boil. Pour over cabbage mixture; stir well. Refrigerate.
Keeps well in refrigerator for 3 weeks.

Lois Cloud

Creamy Pea Salad

Yield: 4 servings

1 (10-ounce) package frozen
   green peas, thawed
¼ cup onion, chopped
¼ cup celery, chopped
¼ teaspoon salt
⅛ teaspoon pepper
⅛ teaspoon whole basil leaves

½ cup sour cream
9 slices bacon, cooked
   and crumbled
½ cup cashews, coarsley
   chopped
Lettuce

Combine first 7 ingredients, stirring gently. Chill 3-4 hours. Stir in bacon and cashews when ready to serve. Serve on lettuce leaves.

Wanda Roach

Hot German Potato Salad

Yield: 10-12 servings

6 medium potatoes (boiled
   in their jackets) or 1
   (24-ounce) can boiled
   potatoes
6-8 slices bacon
¾ cup onion, chopped
2 tablespoons all-purpose
   flour

1-2 tablespoons sugar
1½ teaspoons salt
½ teaspoon celery seed
Dash of pepper
¾ cup water
⅓ cup garlic vinegar
Parsley (optional)
Chives (optional)

Slice potatoes thin. Fry bacon slowly in large skillet and remove when crisp. Sauté onion in bacon fat until golden brown. Blend in flour, sugar, salt, celery seed and pepper. Cook over low heat until smooth and bubbly. Remove from heat. Stir in water and vinegar. Heat to a boil, stirring constantly. Carefully stir in potatoes and crumbled bacon bits. Mix well. Remove from heat and allow to stand. One hour before serving, reheat and serve hot. May sprinkle parsley and chives on top.
Tangy, hot potato salad. Good accompaniment for winter meals.

Deborah Fincher

Pinto Bean Salad

Yield: 6 servings

1 hard-cooked egg,
   chopped
1 medium green pepper,
   chopped
1 stalk celery, chopped
1 tablespoon mustard

1 (16-ounce) can pinto beans,
   drained
Salt to taste
Garlic to taste
Mayonnaise to mix

Mix all ingredients together. Chill.
This may be prepared one day ahead.

Tammie Curtis

Bean Salad

Yield: 6 servings

1 (16-ounce) can French-style
   green beans, drained
1 (16-ounce) can yellow
   wax beans, drained
1 (16-ounce) can red kidney
   beans, drained
1 (15-ounce) can garbanzo
   beans, drained
1 small onion, minced

½ cup green pepper,
   chopped
¾ cup cider vinegar
1 cup sugar
1 teaspoon celery seeds
½ cup vegetable oil
1 teaspoon salt
1 teaspoon pepper

Combine beans, onion and green pepper in large bowl. Combine remaining
ingredients; heat to a boil. Pour over vegetables, mixing well. Cover; refrigerate
for several hours.
Easy to prepare. Keeps very well in refrigerator for several days.

Marie Moore

Sauerkraut Salad

Yield: 8 servings

1 cup sugar
¼ cup vinegar
2 tablespoons vegetable oil
1 (14½-ounce) can sauerkraut,
   drained and chopped
½ cup pimiento, chopped

½ cup green pepper,
   chopped
½ cup onion, chopped
½ cup celery, chopped
½ cup carrots, shredded

Heat together sugar, vinegar and oil. Pour over combined vegetables. Refrigerate several hours or overnight.
Very good and colorful.

Myrtie Whidby

Day Ahead Spinach Salad

Yield: 6 servings

¾ pound fresh spinach,
  stems removed, washed,
  well dried and torn
  into pieces
½ medium cucumber, thinly
  sliced
½ cup radishes, thinly
  sliced
¼ cup green onions,
  thinly sliced

2 hard-cooked eggs,
  sliced
Garlic salt to taste
¾-1 cup thick commercial
  Bleu cheese dressing
5 slices bacon, crisply
  fried and crumbled
½ cup salted Spanish peanuts

Arrange spinach evenly in shallow salad bowl. Layer with all of cucumber slices, radishes, onions and eggs. Sprinkle with garlic salt to taste. Spread dressing evenly over top. Cover. Chill overnight. Just before serving, sprinkle with bacon and nuts. To serve, lift out portions carefully. Be sure to get all layers.

Helen Spears

Spinach Salad

Yield: 6 servings

1 pound spinach, stems
  removed, washed, well
  dried and torn
  into pieces
6 strips bacon, fried
  and crumbled
1 (14-ounce) can bean
  sprouts, drained
1 (8-ounce) can water
  chestnuts, sliced

3-4 hard-cooked eggs,
  chopped
¾ cup sugar
½ cup catsup
1 cup vegetable oil
1 small onion, chopped
1 teaspoon Worcestershire
1 teaspoon salt
¼ cup vinegar

Combine the spinach, bacon, bean sprouts, water chestnuts and eggs; toss. Combine the next 7 ingredients in a jar. Shake well. Pour over spinach mixture just before serving.

Lynn Payne

Greek Appetizer Salad

Yield: 4-6 servings

1 (8-ounce) can green
    beans, drained
3 small zucchini, cut into
    ½-inch slices
1 small cauliflower, cut
    into flowerets
½ cup olive oil
¼ cup lemon juice
1 teaspoon salt

½ teaspoon sugar
½ teaspoon oregano leaves
1 clove garlic, finely
    chopped
Lettuce leaves
1 small onion, separated
    into rings
Cherry tomatoes for garnish
Ripe olives for garnish

Bring 1-inch salted water to boiling in a 3-quart saucepan; add beans. Simmer, covered, for 5 minutes. Add zucchini and cauliflower. Heat to boiling. Reduce heat and cook, covered, about 5 minutes or just until tender; drain. Place vegetables in a shallow dish. Mix oil, lemon juice, salt, sugar, oregano and garlic; pour over vegetables. Cover. Refrigerate for a least 2 hours, spooning marinade over vegetables occasionally. Remove vegetables with slotted spoon to lettuce-lined plates. Top with onion rings. Garnish with cherry tomatoes and olives.

Cathy Lacy

Marinated Summer Salad

Yield: 10-12 servings

1 cup cauliflower flowerets
1 cup carrots, thinly
    sliced
1 cup fresh mushrooms,
    sliced
1 cup brussels sprouts,
    sliced
1 cup yellow squash,
    thinly sliced
1 cup broccoli flowerets
1½ cups zucchini, thinly
    sliced

¾ cup lemon juice
¾ cup vegetable oil
3 tablespoons sugar
1-1½ teaspoons dried whole
    oregano
1 tablespoon salt
½ teaspoon pepper
½ cup radishes, thinly
    sliced

Combine first 7 ingredients in shallow container. Combine remaining ingredients, except radishes, mixing well. Pour marinade over vegetables; toss. Cover. Chill overnight. Stir in radishes before serving.
Easy and quick, if you use a food processor.

Linda Hasty

Layered Vegetable Salad

Yield: 12 servings

1 small head lettuce,
  chopped
1 (16-ounce) can tiny English
  peas, drained
4 stalks celery, finely
  chopped
6 green onions, chopped

1 tablespoon sugar
1 pint mayonnaise
1 (9-ounce) can grated
  Parmesan cheese
9 slices bacon, crisply
  fried and crumbled

Layer first 4 ingredients in order given in a 9x11-inch pyrex dish. Sprinkle sugar over this. Spread mayonnaise evenly. Sprinkle Parmesan cheese over mayonnaise. Refrigerate. Crumble bacon over dish just before serving.

Barbara Manous

Macaroni Salad

Yield: 4-6 servings

8 ounces macaroni
1 cup sour cream
½ cup Italian salad
  dressing
½ pound bacon, fried
  and crumbled

2 hard-cooked eggs,
  chopped
1 tomato, chopped
  Salt and pepper to taste

Cook macaroni according to package directions until tender; drain. Toss with remaining ingredients. Refrigerate.
Variations: May add sliced avocados or chopped chicken instead of bacon.

Terri Edwards
Alpharetta, Georgia

Cracker Salad

Yield: 6 servings

5 hard-cooked eggs,
  chopped
1 cup sweet pickle
  cubes
1 (2-ounce) jar pimientos,
  diced

1 small onion, chopped
1 cup mayonnaise
1 stack of soda crackers,
  coarsely crumbled

Combine all ingredients; mix well. Chill slightly.
Great with cold plate in summer.

Ovalene Pettit

Caesar Salad with Avocado

Yield: 6-8 servings

½ cup vegetable oil
¼ cup lemon juice
½ teaspoon garlic salt
½ teaspoon Worcestershire
⅛ teaspoon dry mustard
¼ teaspoon pepper
½ cup Parmesan cheese, grated
1 large or 2 small heads lettuce, torn into pieces

1 (¾-ounce) can anchovies, drained and chopped
1 egg
1 avocado, peeled and diced
1 cup garlic-flavored salad croutons

Combine oil, lemon juice, garlic salt, Worcestershire, mustard, pepper and cheese in salad bowl. Add lettuce and anchovies; toss. Break egg onto salad; toss until flecks of yolk disappear. Add avocado and croutons; toss gently.

Barry Bishop

Oriental Salad

Yield: 6 servings

1 (20-ounce) package frozen tiny peas, thawed and drained
½ pound fresh cooked shrimp, shelled and deveined
1 cup celery, finely chopped
¾ cup mayonnaise (homemade, if possible)

1 tablespoon fresh lemon juice
½ teaspoon curry powder
Garlic salt to taste
½ cup unsalted cashews
1 (5½-ounce) can chow mein noodles
Lettuce

Combine first 7 ingredients in a large bowl; toss well. Cover. Refrigerate for at least 30 minutes. Add nuts and noodles; toss again. Serve on lettuce.
Lobster or crab meat can be substituted.

Helen Spears

Shrimp and Feta Salad

Yield: 6 servings

1½ pounds cooked large
shrimp, shelled and
deveined
1 bunch scallions or
green onions, minced
½ pound Feta cheese,
cut into ½-inch
pieces
2 tomatoes, cut into
½-inch pieces
2 hard-cooked egg
yolks
¼ cup olive oil

¼ cup vegetable or
safflower oil
¼ teaspoon salt
Pepper to taste
1½ teaspoons white wine
vinegar
Juice of ½ lemon
1 tablespoon fresh dill
weed, minced or 1
teaspoon dried dill
weed
½ head romaine or
other lettuce

Toss shrimp with scallions, Feta, and tomatoes; set aside. Mash egg yolks. Put in jar with the next 7 ingredients. Shake well. Pour over shrimp mixture; toss. Serve on lettuce.

Joan McFather

Shrimp Salad on Avocado Ring

Yield: 8 servings

1 pound cooked shrimp,
shelled and deveined
1 cup celery, chopped
2 fresh tomatoes,
peeled and diced
¼ cup green pepper,
chopped
2 tablespoons pimiento,
chopped
1 tablespoon green onion,
chopped
½ teaspoon salt

Dash of pepper
1 cup sour cream
½ cup catsup
1 tablespoon soy sauce
1 tablespoon onion,
grated
1 tablespoon lemon juice
2 teaspoons horseradish
1 teaspoon salt
½ teaspoon dry mustard
8 avocado rings,
½-inch thick
Lettuce leaves

Combine first 8 ingredients in a bowl. Blend together sour cream, catsup, soy sauce, onion, lemon juice, horseradish, salt and dry mustard; pour over shrimp salad; mix lightly. Arrange avocado rings on crisp lettuce. Fill center of each ring with shrimp salad.

Peggy Jones

Super Chicken Salad

Yield: 4-6 servings

3 pounds chicken breasts
1 (8-ounce) package cream
   cheese, softened
2 tablespoons mayonnaise
¾ cup pecans, chopped
1 tablespoon onion,
   grated

2 tablespoons sweet pickle
   juice
1 cup celery, finely
   chopped
¼ teaspoon curry powder
   Salt and pepper to taste
   Lettuce

Cook chicken in salted water. Remove chicken from bones and coarsely chop. Combine cream cheese and mayonnaise until smooth. Add pecans, onion, pickle juice, celery, curry powder, salt and pepper. Stir until well blended. Combine chicken and cream cheese mixture. Mix until well blended. Serve on lettuce leaves.

Frances Gober

Chinese Chicken Salad

Yield: 6 servings

½ cup soy sauce
¼ cup vegetable oil
¼ cup dry sherry
2 tablespoons honey
2 teaspoons brown sugar
3 cups cooked chicken,
   diced
8 ounces linguine
1 (6-ounce) package frozen
   snow peas

½ head cabbage, chopped
1 red pepper, thinly
   sliced
½ (8-ounce) can water
   chestnuts, drained and
   sliced (more or less
   according to taste)
½ cup cashews
2 scallions

Combine soy sauce, oil, sherry, honey and brown sugar in medium bowl. Stir until well blended. Place chicken in medium bowl. Pour half of soy sauce mixture over chicken; mix well. Cover and refrigerate 2 hours. Meanwhile, break linquine in half; cook according to package directions. Rinse and drain. Place in large bowl. Cook snow peas according to package directions. Run under cold water until cool. Add to linguine. Gently stir in remaining ingredients and soy sauce mixture. Toss to coat; then stir in chicken.

Ann Ruppel

Beef Salad with Asparagus and Broccoli

Yield: 4 servings

1 small flank steak	1 bunch broccoli,
Salt to taste	cut into flowerets
4 cups fresh asparagus,	Ginger Dressing
cut diagonally into	Lettuce leaves
bite-sized pieces	

Broil flank steak to desired doneness. Cool and slice. Bring large pot of salted water to boil. Add asparagus; blanch 30 seconds. Remove with slotted spoon. Add broccoli; blanch 30 seconds; drain well. Cool. Toss meat slices in Ginger Dressing. Add vegetables; toss. Serve at room temperature on a bed of lettuce.

Ginger Dressing

⅓ cup light soy sauce	1 teaspoon sugar
¼ cup white vinegar	Freshly ground white
3 tablespoons sesame oil	pepper
1 (1½-inch) piece fresh ginger, peeled and grated	

Combine all ingredients; mix well.

Helen Spears

Smooth But Spicy Dressing

Yield: 4-6 servings

½ cup sour cream	1-2 tablespoons oil and
½ cup mayonnaise	vinegar dressing
1-2 teaspoons Durkees Sauce	

Combine all ingredients. Refrigerate. Use on tossed salad or tomato and lettuce sandwiches.
Easy. Do ahead.

Sarah Buffington

Hot Bacon Dressing

Yield: 4-6 servings

4 slices bacon	1 tablespoon sugar
¼ cup water	1 tablespoon onion, minced
½ cup vinegar	Dash of cayenne pepper
½ teaspoon salt	

Fry bacon in pan until crisp. Drain on paper towels, then crumble. Combine bacon and remaining ingredients. Add to pan drippings. Heat to boiling. Pour over salad.

Cookbook Committee

Celery Seed Dressing

Yield: 1½ cups

⅓ cup sugar
1 teaspoon dry mustard
1 teaspoon salt
1 teaspoon paprika

1 heaping teaspoon celery
   seeds
3 tablespoons + 1
   teaspoon vinegar, divided
1 cup vegetable oil

Combine sugar, dry mustard, salt, paprika and celery seeds. Mix in 1 teaspoon vinegar. Add alternately oil and 3 tablespoons vinegar, beating briskly with a wire whisk or fork until dressing looks creamy. Serve over fresh fruit or grapefruit and avocado salad.
Keeps well in refrigerator.

Selene Hendrix

Mustard Dressing

Yield: ¾ cup

1 teaspoon Dijon mustard
½ cup vegetable oil
¼ cup fresh lemon juice

3 tablespoons parsley,
   chopped
Salt and pepper to taste

Blend mustard and oil. Gradually add lemon juice; mix until smooth. Stir in parsley and seasonings.

Frances Owen

Honey-Mustard Dressing

Yield: 2½ cups

¾ cup vegetable oil
½ teaspoon paprika
¼ cup honey
¼ cup lemon juice

½ teaspoon salt
¼ teaspoon dry mustard
Dash of cayenne pepper

Combine all ingredients in a covered jar. Shake well. Chill. Pour over salad just before serving.
A good accompaniment for fried chicken fingers.

Christi Kook

Basil Dressing

Yield: 2 cups

1½ cups mayonnaise
¼ cup light corn syrup
¼ cup onion, finely
   chopped
3 tablespoons lemon
   juice

1 teaspoon dried basil
   leaves
½ teaspoon salt
¼ teaspoon pepper

Combine all ingredients. Pour over fresh, crisp vegetables.

Mandy Mills

Roquefort-Bleu Cheese Dressing

1 quart mayonnaise
1 medium white onion,
    finely chopped
Juice of 2 lemons
Dash of salt
1 (8-ounce) package Bleu
    cheese or 1 (4-ounce)
    Roquefort and 1 (4-ounce)
    Bleu cheese, crumbled

2 tablespoons
    Worcestershire
Milk (optional)

Combine all ingredients except milk. Mix with electric mixer until lumps are gone and dressing is creamy. Add milk, if necessary, to thickness desired.

Betty McDaniel

Buttermilk Dressing

1 quart mayonnaise
3 cups buttermilk
1 teaspoon salt
1 teaspoon ground black
    pepper

1 teaspoon Accent
1 teaspoon garlic powder

Mix ingredients well. Chill.
Use as a dip, salad dressing or topping for baked potatoes. Will keep in refrigerator for weeks.

Frances Gober

Italian Salad Dressing

Yield: 1 cup

½ cup olive oil
2 tablespoons onion, minced
1 tablespoon Parmesan
    cheese, grated
2 teaspoons salt
¾ teaspoon Worcestershire
¾ teaspoon dried basil leaves

¾ teaspoon dry mustard
¾ teaspoon oregano leaves
¾ teaspoon sugar
¾ teaspoon pepper
¼ cup red wine vinegar
1 tablespoon lemon juice

Combine first 10 ingredients in container of blender or processor; process for 30 seconds. Add vinegar and lemon juice; process 30 seconds. Refrigerate.

Cookbook Committee

Eggs and Cheese

Breakfast Casserole

Oven: 350° - 45 minutes   **Yield:** 8 servings

> 6 slices white bread
> Butter or margarine
> 1 pound pork sausage
> 1½ cups Cheddar cheese,
>   grated

> 6 eggs, beaten
> 2 cups half and half
> 1 teaspoon salt
> 1 teaspoon dry mustard
>   (optional)

Remove crusts from bread; spread with butter. Place in a greased 13x9-inch baking dish. Set aside. Cook sausage until browned, stirring to crumble; drain well. Spoon over bread slices. Sprinkle with cheese. Combine eggs, half and half, salt, dry mustard, if desired; mix well. Pour over cheese. Cover, chill overnight. Bake, uncovered, at 350° for 45 minutes or until set.

Charlotte Boyd

Woodchuck

Yield: 8 servings

> ½ cup butter
> ½ cup all-purpose flour
> 3 cups milk
> 10 ounces sharp Cheddar
>   cheese, grated
> 1 green pepper, chopped
>   and sautéed until
>   tender
> 1 (2-ounce) jar pimiento,
>   chopped

> 1 (4-ounce) can mushroom
>   stems and pieces, drained
> Salt and pepper to taste
> 8 hard-cooked eggs,
>   sliced
> 2 (5-ounce) cans Chinese
>   noodles
> Tomato wedges for garnish

Melt butter in top of double boiler, over boiling water; stir in flour until smooth. Add milk slowly, stirring constantly until thickened. Add cheese; stir until melted. Add green pepper, pimiento and mushrooms. Season with salt and pepper. At serving time, add hard-cooked eggs. Serve over warm Chinese noodles. Garnish with tomato wedges.
Variation: Can use 4 hard-cooked eggs plus 1½ cups cubed cooked chicken, turkey or shrimp.

Wanda Roach

Glorified Eggs

Yield: 2-4 servings

2 tablespoons butter
2 tablespoons all-purpose
  flour
½ teaspoon salt
⅛ teaspoon pepper
1 cup milk
2 teaspoons onion, minced
1 tablespoon pimiento,
  chopped

⅓ cup celery, thinly
  sliced
⅓ cup English peas,
  cooked
3 hard-cooked eggs,
  quartered

Melt butter; blend in flour, salt and pepper. Slowly add milk. Bring to a slow boil. Add onion, pimiento, celery and peas just before serving. Fold in eggs. Serve over biscuit halves or toast.
Recipes doubles and triples easily.

Elly Hobgood

Garlic Cheese Grits

Oven: 350° - 15-20 minutes

Yield: 6 servings

4 cups water
½ teaspoon salt
1 cup regular uncooked
  grits
½ cup butter or
  margarine
1 (6-ounce) roll process
  garlic cheese

2 cups Cheddar cheese,
  shredded
2 tablespoons Worcestershire
½ teaspoon garlic salt
  Paprika (optional)

Combine water and salt in a saucepan; bring to a boil. Add grits. Reduce heat to low and cook, covered, for 10 minutes or until thickened, stirring occasionally. Remove from heat. Add butter, cheese roll, Worcestershire and garlic salt. Stir until cheese melts. Pour mixture into a greased 1½-quart baking dish. Sprinkle with paprika, if desired. Bake at 350° for 15-20 minutes.

Cookbook Committee

Cheese Soufflé

Oven: 350° - 1 hour

Yield: 6 servings

3 eggs, beaten
2 cups milk
½ teaspoon Worcestershire
½ teaspoon dry mustard
¼ teaspoon salt

⅛ teaspoon cayenne pepper
7 slices white bread
½ cup butter, melted
8 ounces sharp Cheddar
   cheese, grated

Blend eggs, milk and seasonings; set aside. Trim crusts from bread; cut into cubes. Pour butter over bread cubes, stirring gently; let stand until butter is absorbed. Layer half of bread cubes in a lightly greased soufflé dish; top with half of cheese. Repeat layers. Pour egg mixture over all. Refrigerate several hours or overnight. Remove from refrigerator 1 hour before baking. Bake at 350° for 1 hour or until firm.
This is a never-fail soufflé.

Jeannie Adams

Blintz Soufflé

Oven: 350° - 1 hour

Yield: 6-8 servings

½ cup butter, melted
12 frozen blintzes
4 eggs, beaten
1 (16-ounce) carton sour
   cream

½ cup sugar
¼ cup orange juice
1-2 teaspoons vanilla
   extract

Line a 10x13-inch pan with melted butter. Put blintzes in pan. Beat together remaining ingredients. Pour mixture over blintz. Bake at 350° for 1 hour.
Blintzes can be purchased from freezer section of larger grocery store.

Dorothy Rosenblum

Macaroni Casserole

Oven: 300° - 25 minutes

Yield: 10-12 servings

1 (16-ounce) box elbow
   macaroni, cooked and
   drained
¼ (2-ounce) jar pimiento
   (optional)
1 small onion, chopped
1 pound Cheddar cheese,
   grated

1 (4-ounce) can mushrooms,
   chopped
1 (10¾-ounce) can cream
   of mushroom soup
1 cup mayonnaise
3 tablespoons butter,
   melted

Combine all ingredients. Pour in a greased 13x9-inch baking dish. Bake at 300° for 25 minutes or until bubbly.
Freezes well; bake first.

Doris Thacker

Family-Style Swiss Cheese Fondue

Yield: 4 cups

3 tablespoons butter or margarine
3 tablespoons all-purpose flour
½ teaspoon garlic salt
½ teaspoon salt
Dash of white pepper
Dash of nutmeg

2½ cups milk
1 pound processed Swiss cheese, shredded
1 teaspoon Worcestershire
Dash of hot sauce
French bread, cut into 1-inch cubes

Melt butter in fondue pot over moderate heat. Stir in flour, garlic salt, salt, pepper and nutmeg. Stir in milk; cook, stirring constantly, until smooth and slightly thickened. Add cheese, small amount at a time; cook over low heat, stirring until cheese is melted. Stir in Worcestershire and hot sauce. Spear cubes of bread with fondue fork and twirl bread in cheese until coated. Cool slightly.

This can be prepared in the microwave and poured into fondue pot right before serving.

Ollie White

Cheese Sausage Quiche

Oven: 375° - 35-40 minutes

Yield: 4-6 servings

¾ pound link pork sausage
½ cup onion, chopped
⅓ cup green pepper, chopped
1½ cups sharp Cheddar cheese, grated
1 tablespoon all-purpose flour

2 eggs, beaten
1 cup evaporated milk
1 tablespoon parsley flakes
¾ teaspoon seasoned salt
¼ teaspoon garlic salt
¼ teaspoon pepper
1 (9-inch) deep dish pastry shell, unbaked

Fry sausage until cooked, drain on paper towels. Slice sausage. Reserve 2 tablespoons fat, using this to sauté onion and green pepper 2-3 minutes. Combine cheese and flour. Stir in sausage slices, green pepper and onion. Spread in pie crust shell. Mix remaining ingredients; pour into shell. Bake at 375° on cookie sheet for 35-40 minutes or until browned and filling is set.

Cindy Holcomb

Mexican Quiche

Oven: 350° - 45 minutes   **Yield:** 6-8 servings

½ pound cooked ham, chopped
4 slices bacon, cooked and crumbled
1 cup Swiss cheese, shredded
1 cup sharp Cheddar cheese, shredded
¼ cup onion, chopped
1 medium tomato, peeled and chopped

2 Jalapeño peppers, seeded and chopped
2 tablespoons fresh mushrooms, chopped
1 tablespoon parsley flakes
1 teaspoon dry mustard
½ cup sour cream
4 eggs, beaten
1 (10-inch) pastry shell, unbaked

Combine all ingredients; blend well. Pour into pastry shell. Bake at 350° for 45 minutes or until filling is set and browned.

Julia Dennis

Olive-Swiss Quiche

Oven: 375° - 25-30 minutes   **Yield:** 6 servings

½ pound mushrooms, coarsley chopped
1¼ cups pitted ripe olives, coarsley chopped, divided
3 tablespoons butter
¼ cup dry bread crumbs
½ cup green onion, chopped

1½ cups Swiss cheese, grated
1 cup cottage cheese
3 eggs
½ teaspoon thyme
¾ cup parsley, finely chopped

Sauté mushrrooms and ¾ cup olives in butter in skillet until moist and coated, about 20 seconds. Stir in bread crumbs. Spoon into a 9-inch quiche pan or pie plate; press evenly against bottom and sides. Combine green onions, Swiss cheese and ½ cup olives. Sprinkle into shell. Process cottage cheese, eggs and thyme in a blender or food processor until smooth. Pour into shell. Bake at 375° for 25-30 minutes or until knife inserted in center comes out clean. Cover loosely with foil if it starts to get too brown. Let stand 10 minutes. Sprinkle with parsley just before serving.

Debbie Perry

Tomato Quiche

Oven: 375° - 25-30 minutes　　　　　**Yield:** 4-6 servings

¼ cup onion, minced
6 tablespoons olive oil,
　divided
1 (14½-ounce) can tomatoes
　with basil, drained and
　coarsely chopped
1 large clove garlic,
　mashed
½ teaspoon oregano,
　basil or thyme
½ teaspoon salt
⅛ teaspoon pepper

1 egg + 3 egg yolks
3 tablespoons tomato
　paste
3 tablespoons parsley,
　chopped
1 teaspoon paprika
　Pinch of cayenne pepper
1 (8-inch) pastry shell,
　partially cooked
¼ cup Parmesan cheese,
　grated

Cook onions in 2 tablespoons olive oil in medium skillet 5 minutes or until tender, stir in tomatoes. Add garlic, oregano, salt and pepper. Cover; cook 5 minutes, shaking pan occasionally, to evaporate juice almost entirely. Allow to cool slightly. Beat together egg and egg yolks, 3 tablespoons olive oil, tomato paste, parsley, paprika and cayenne pepper. Fold gradually into the cooked tomatoes. Spread mixture into pastry shell. Sprinkle Parmesan cheese over top and dribble 1 tablespoon olive oil over it. Bake at 375° for 25-30 minutes or until puffed and browned on top.

Good also served at room temperature as a luncheon dish.

Kathleen Harbin

Side Dishes

Baked Apricots

Oven: 300° - 1 hour   **Yield:** 10-12 servings

2 (15-ounce) cans apricot
   halves, drained
Light brown sugar

Ritz crackers, roughly
   crushed
Butter

Layer 1 can of apricots in a buttered baking dish. Sprinkle liberally with brown sugar. Cover with layer of Ritz crackers. Dot with butter. Repeat, using second can of apricots and ending with butter. Bake, covered, at 300° for 1 hour.

Joan McFather

Curried Fruit

Oven: 350° - 40 minutes   **Yield:** 8-10 servings

1 (29-ounce) can salad
   fruits, drained
1 cup dark pitted
   cherries
½ cup maraschino
   cherries
2 bananas

½ cup butter, melted
½ cup brown sugar
2 tablespoons cornstarch
1 tablespoon curry
   powder

Combine salad fruits and cherries. Cut bananas into salad-sized pieces; add to other fruits. Add butter. Combine sugar, cornstarch and curry powder. Sprinkle over fruit mixture. Mix fruit very lightly. Pour into a buttered 2-quart baking dish. Bake at 350° for 40 minutes.

Joan Anderson

Hot Fruit Compote

Oven: 350° - 1 hour   **Yield:** 16-20 servings

½ cup butter
Dash of salt
¾ cup light brown sugar
2 tablespoons cornstarch
1 cup cream sherry wine
1 (16-ounce) can peach
   halves, drained
1 (16-ounce) can pear
   halves, drained

1 (16-ounce) can apricot
   halves, drained
1 (20-ounce) can pineapple
   chunks, drained
1 (16-ounce) can dark
   pitted cherries,
   drained

Melt butter; add salt, brown sugar and cornstarch. Cook until slightly thickened. Add sherry. Arrange fruit in large shallow baking dish. Pour butter mixture over fruit. Bake, covered, at 350° for 1 hour. Reheat at 350° for 20 minutes. Can be reheated several times.
Fruits can be added or deleted accordingly. Reheating improves taste.

Nell Hamrick

Pineapple Casserole

Oven: 350° - 45 minutes   **Yield:** 8 servings

¾ cup margarine,
   softened
1½ cups sugar
   Dash of salt
2 quarts soft bread
   cubes (8-10 slices)

3 eggs, beaten
2 tablespoons milk
1 (20-ounce) can unsweetened
   crushed pineapple,
   undrained

Cream margarine, sugar and salt. Add bread cubes, eggs, milk and pineapple. Pour into a greased 2-quart casserole. Bake at 350° for 45 minutes.

Deborah Fincher

Sweet Fried Apples

Yield: 4-6 servings

6-8 slices bacon
4 tablespoons bacon
   drippings
6 cups apples slices,
   unpeeled

½-1 cup brown sugar,
   firmly packed

Cook bacon until crisp; drain and keep hot. Leave about 4 tablespoons drippings in skillet. Add apples; brown lightly. Sprinkle brown sugar over apples. Cover. Cook slowly until tender. Remove cover and let apples brown, cooking off excess juice. Add crumbled bacon. Serve immediately.
Good for side dish in winter with pork.

Helen Spears

"Extra Special" Rice Casserole

Oven: 350° - 25 minutes   **Yield:** 10-12 servings

1 cup long grain rice,
   uncooked
1 (15½-ounce) can chicken
   broth
   Water
1 pound Monterey Jack
   cheese, grated
1 (16-ounce) carton sour
   cream

⅓ cup creamy Italian
   dressing
1 (4-ounce) can green
   chili peppers, chopped
1 (8-ounce) can water
   chestnuts, sliced
   and drained

Combine rice, chicken broth, plus enough water to make 2 cups liquid. Cook rice until tender. Add cheese, sour cream, dressing, chili peppers and water chestnuts; stir until well blended. Pour into a 9x13-inch baking dish or 2 8-inch square baking dishes. Bake, uncovered, at 350° for 25 minutes.
Can be made the day before. Freezes well.

Patsy Saxon

Fried Rice

Oven: 350° - 1 hour   **Yield:** 6 servings

1 (10¾-ounce) can onion soup
1 (10½-ounce) can beef
  bouillon

1 cup rice, uncooked
½ cup butter

Combine all ingredients. Put in a greased 1½-quart baking dish. Bake at 350° for 1 hour or until rice is tender.

John Dunn

Rice Casserole

Oven: 350° - 1 hour   **Yield:** 4-6 servings

¼ cup margarine
1 cup regular rice,
  uncooked
1 (10¾-ounce) onion soup
1 (8-ounce) can water
  chestnuts, sliced and
  drained

¾ cup water
1 (4-ounce) can sliced
  mushrooms, drained
1 tablespoon dried onion

Melt margarine in a skillet; add rice and brown. Add remaining ingredients. Pour into a greased 2-quart baking dish. Bake, covered, at 350° for 1 hour.

Pat Champion

Mexican Rice

Yield: 6 servings

⅔ cup onion, chopped
1 cup green peppers,
  chopped
3 tablespoons butter
1 cup rice, uncooked
1 teaspoon chili powder

1 (14½-ounce) can whole
  tomatoes, diced or 1
  (10-ounce) can Rotel
  tomatoes and chiles
2 teaspoons salt
2 cups water

Sauté onion and green pepper in butter. Stir in rice, chili powder, tomatoes and salt. Add water. Do not stir. Boil. Reduce heat. Simmer, covered, for 20 minutes.

Janis Farr

Asparagus Casserole Superb

Oven: 375° - 30 minutes　　　　**Yield:** 8-10 servings

3　hard-cooked eggs,
　　sliced
2　(14½-ounce) cans green
　　asparagus spears
1　(8-ounce) can water
　　chestnuts, sliced
½　cup milk
6　tablespoons all-purpose
　　flour

¼　cup butter
½　teaspoon salt
¼　teaspoon pepper
1　cup extra sharp
　　Cheddar cheese, grated
2　tablespoons pimiento
¾　cup fresh bread
　　or cracker crumbs

Slice eggs. Drain asparagus and water chestnuts, reserving 1½ cups of liquid. Blend together milk and flour until smooth; combine with vegetable juice, butter, seasonings and cheese. Cook over low heat until thickened, stirring constantly; add pimiento. Place asparagus in a buttered 9x13-inch baking dish. Top with water chestnuts and sliced eggs. Pour cheese sauce over asparagus. Sprinkle with crumbs. Bake at 375° for 30 minutes.
Makes a very colorful dish.

Myrna Pruett

Baked Beans

Oven: 350° - 3 hours.　　　　**Yield:** 8-10 servings

2　cups small dried white
　　navy beans
5　cups cold water
2　medium onions, sliced
2　bay leaves
1　teaspoon salt
¼　teaspoon pepper

1　ham bone and
　　leftover ham
2　cups catsup
2　cups light brown sugar
⅓　cup cider vinegar
2　tablespoons Worcestershire
1　tablespoon dry mustard

Soak beans overnight in water. Drain and rinse beans. Put in a 6-quart Dutch oven; cover with 5 cups cold water. Add onions, bay leaves, salt, pepper and ham bone. Bring to a boil; simmer until beans are tender, about 1 hour. Remove ham bone and bay leaves. Drain beans (reserving liquid for later use). Add leftover ham, catsup, brown sugar, vinegar, Worcestershire and dry mustard; mix well. Pour into a Dutch oven. Add enough reserved liquid to cover beans. Bake, covered, at 350° for 3 hours.
Worth the trouble; turns a leftover holiday ham into a delicacy.

Elly Hobgood

Green Beans with Cheese

Yield: 6 servings

1½ pounds fresh green
    beans, ends and
    strings removed
Boiling water
1 clove garlic
1 teaspoon salt
¼ cup + 1 tablespoon
    butter, melted, divided

¼ teaspoon basil, crushed
3 tablespoons Cheddar
    cheese, grated
2 tablespoons fine dry
    bread crumbs

Cover beans with boiling water. Add garlic and salt. Cook uncovered on high heat for about 7 minutes or until tender but still crisp and green. Drain well; discard garlic. Add ¼ cup butter, basil and cheese. Combine bread crumbs and 1 tablespoon butter; sprinkle over beans. Serve immediately.

Ann Weeks

Mary Elizabeth's Green Beans

Yield: 12 servings

3 (28-ounce) cans green
    beans, cooked
6 tablespoons vinegar
6 tablespoons sugar

1 medium onion, sliced
8 slices bacon, cooked
    and crumbled

Combine beans and remaining ingredients. Simmer for about 1 hour.

Pat Stewart

Swiss-Style Green Beans

Oven: 400° - 20 minutes

Yield: 4-6 servings

2 tablespoons butter or
    margarine
2 tablespoons all-purpose
    flour
1 teaspoon salt
1 teaspoon sugar
¼ teaspoon pepper
½ teaspoon onion, grated

1 cup sour cream
2 (16-ounce) cans French-
    style green beans,
    drained
¼ cup Swiss cheese,
    grated
1 cup corn flakes,
    crushed
Parmesan cheese

Melt 2 tablespoons butter; stir in flour and seasonings until smooth. Add onion. Add sour cream, stirring constantly. Simmer until heated through. Add beans; mix well. Pour into a greased 2-quart baking dish. Top with Swiss cheese and corn flakes. Sprinkle with Parmesan. Bake at 400° for 20 minutes.

Susan Roach
Jackson, Georgia

Curried Lima Beans

Oven: 325° - 25 minutes   **Yield:** 6-8 servings

2 (10-ounce) packages frozen
    baby lima beans
2 slices bacon, diced
1 medium onion, finely
    chopped
1 clove garlic, crushed
½ teaspoon curry powder
1 (10¾-ounce) can cream
    of mushroom soup

½ cup sour cream
2 tablespoons dry white
    wine, sherry or milk
1 (3½-ounce) can French
    fried onions, slightly
    crushed

Cook beans according to package directions until tender; drain. Fry bacon until crisp in skillet; sauté onion, garlic and curry powder for about 5 minutes. Blend soup, sour cream and wine in a bowl until smooth. Add to skillet; heat to just under boiling point; stir in beans and bacon bits. Turn into a 1½-quart shallow casserole; top with French fried onions. Bake at 325° for about 25 minutes. *May be prepared ahead of time to bake later.*

Linda Hasty

Cranberry Beets

Yield: 4 servings

1 (16-ounce) can small
    whole beets, undrained
1 (8-ounce) can whole-berry
    cranberry sauce
1 tablespoon orange peel,
    grated

1 tablespoon cornstarch
1 tablespoon cold water

Put beets and cranberry sauce into saucepan; heat until blended. Stir in orange peel, then cornstarch which has been dissolved in cold water. Cook over low heat, stirring constantly, until thickened.
Leftovers reheat well.

Martha Nichols

Orange Beets

Yield: 4-6 servings

1 tablespoon cornstarch
1 tablespoon sugar
¾ teaspoon salt
1 cup orange juice

1 teaspoon orange rind,
    grated
1 tablespoon butter
1 (20-ounce) can beets,
    drained

Combine cornstarch, sugar and salt in saucepan. Blend in orange juice gradually. Cook over low heat, stirring constantly, until mixture thickens and comes to a boil. Stir in orange rind, butter and beets; heat thoroughly.

Sue Cannon

Broccoli Casserole

Oven: 350° - 45 minutes   **Yield:** 6-8 servings

2 (10-ounce) packages frozen
 chopped broccoli
1 (10¾-ounce) can cream
 of mushroom soup
1 cup sharp Cheddar
 cheese, grated

1 medium onion, chopped
¼ cup mayonnaise
3 eggs, beaten

Cook broccoli in salted water until tender; drain. Mix well with remaining ingredients. Pour into a greased 2-quart casserole dish. Bake at 350° for 45 minutes.

Hortensia McNeill

Broccoli with Olive Sauce

Yield: 8-10 servings

2 pounds fresh broccoli
 or 2 (10-ounce) packages
 frozen broccoli

Olive Sauce

Steam broccoli over small amount of water for 10-15 minutes, until tender. Arrange in serving dish. Pour Olive Sauce over broccoli.

Olive Sauce

¾ cup butter, melted
2 cloves garlic, minced
 or 1 teaspoon garlic
 salt or ½ teaspoon
 garlic powder

¼ cup lemon juice
12 pimiento-stuffed olives,
 chopped

Combine all ingredients. Heat thoroughly, but do not boil.

Louise Forrester

Mother's Broccoli and Rice Casserole

Oven: 350° - 20 minutes   **Yield:** 8 servings

1 (10-ounce) package
 frozen chopped broccoli
½ cup butter or
 margarine
½ cup celery, chopped
½ cup onion, chopped

1½ cups cooked rice
 (not instant)
1 (8-ounce) jar Cheese
 Whiz
1 (10¾-ounce) can cream
 of mushroom soup

Cook broccoli according to package directions; drain. Melt butter; sauté celery and onion until clear. Combine broccoli, vegetables, rice, cheese and mushroom soup; blend well. Pour into a 2-quart baking dish. Bake at 350° for 20 minutes.

May be prepared ahead, frozen and cooked when ready to serve.

Jo Ellen Wilson

Marinated Broccoli

Yield: 10-12 servings

3 bunches fresh broccoli
1 cup cider vinegar
1 tablespoon sugar
1 tablespoon dried dill
   weed
1 teaspoon salt

1 teaspoon garlic salt
1 teaspoon pepper
1½ cups vegetable oil
   Lemon slices (optional)

Separate broccoli into flowerets. Wash thoroughly, drain well. Place in a large, shallow container; set aside. Combine remaining ingredients; mix well. Pour over broccoli. Toss gently to coat. Chill at least 24 hours, stirring several times. Garnish with lemon slices if desired.
Fresh dill makes it even better. May also be used as an appetizer.

Ann Fincher

Broccoli-Onion Deluxe

Oven: 350° - 25 minutes

Yield: 6 servings

1 - 1½ pounds fresh broccoli,
      cut into 1½-inch pieces
3 small onions, coarsely
   chopped
4 tablespoons butter or
   margarine, melted,
   divided
2 tablespoons all-purpose
   flour

1 cup milk
1 (3-ounce) package cream
   cheese, cubed
¼ teaspoon salt
⅛ teaspoon pepper
½ cup sharp Cheddar
   cheese, shredded
1 cup soft bread
   crumbs

Cook broccoli and onion in a small amount of boiling water 3-4 minutes or until tender; drain well. Melt 2 tablespoons butter in a heavy saucepan over low heat; add flour, stirring until smooth. Cook 1 minute, stirring constantly. Gradually add milk; cook over medium heat, stirring constantly, until thickened and bubbly. Remove from heat. Add cream cheese; stir until melted. Stir in salt and pepper. Pour over vegetables; stir gently. Spoon into a lightly greased 1½-quart casserole; top with cheese. Cover. Bake at 350° for 25 minutes. Combine remaining 2 tablespoons butter and bread crumbs; toss gently. Uncover casserole, and sprinkle with buttered bread crumbs. Bake 5 additional minutes or until golden brown.
Delicious!

Cissy Cloud

Stir-Fry Broccoli

Yield: 6 servings

¼ cup boiling water
2 tablespoons soy sauce
1 tablespoon dry sherry
1 teaspoon sugar

¼ teaspoon salt
1 bunch fresh broccoli
¼ cup peanut oil
1 small onion, chopped

Combine first 5 ingredients, stirring well; set aside. Trim off large outer leaves of broccoli and remove tough ends of stalks. Wash thoroughly in cold water. Cut stalks diagonally into 1-inch slices. Cut flowerets into 1-inch pieces. Pour oil around top of preheated wok, allowing to heat for 2 minutes. Add broccoli. Stir-fry for 2 minutes. Add onion, stir-fry for 3 minutes. Add soy sauce mixture. Cover; reduce heat to low. Cook 5 minutes or until broccoli is crisp tender.

Ollie White

Brussel Sprouts with Caraway Cheese Sauce

Yield: 6 servings

1½ pounds fresh brussel
    sprouts, or 2 (10-ounce)
    packages frozen
1 cup evaporated milk
1½ cups sharp Cheddar
    cheese, shredded

1 teaspoon caraway seeds
¼ teaspoon dry mustard
½ teaspoon Worcestershire
4-6 drops hot sauce

Remove discolored outer leaves from brussel sprouts; trim ends and wash thoroughly. Cook, covered, in about 1 inch boiling, salted water for 8-10 minutes or until fork tender. Drain well. Combine remaining ingredients in a small saucepan; cook over medium heat until the cheese is melted, stirring constantly. Serve brussel sprouts with sauce over them, or serve sauce in another dish.
Easy and colorful.

Jerry Land

Hungarian Casserole

Yield: 4-6 servings

1 medium head cabbage,
    chopped
2 medium onions, chopped
    Vegetable oil

1 (12-ounce) package medium
    egg noodles
Salt and pepper to taste

Fry cabbage and onions in oil until well done. Cook noodles according to package directions; drain. Mix together. Salt and pepper to taste. Put in a casserole to keep warm.
Cabbage lovers will really enjoy this side dish.

Mary Winslow

Stir-Fried Chinese Cabbage

Yield: 4 servings

2 tablespoons vegetable
   oil
1 fresh ginger root,
   sliced
1 pound Chinese cabbage
   Several stalks bok choy,
   cut diagonally into
   ¼-inch slices

3 stalks celery, cut
   diagonally into ¼-inch
   slices
½ teaspoon salt
½ teaspoon sugar
3 tablespoons chicken
   broth
1 teaspoon sesame oil
   (optional)

Heat oil in the wok. Brown and discard the ginger slice. Stir-fry the Chinese cabbage, bok choy and celery for 2-3 minutes. Add salt, sugar and chicken broth. Cover; heat for 1 minute. Sprinkle with sesame oil, if desired. Serve at once.

Ollie White

Carrot Ring

Oven: 350° - 30 minutes

Yield: 8 servings

1½ cups fresh bread
   crumbs, divided
3 cups carrots,
   cooked and mashed
¼ cup butter or
   margarine
½ teaspoon salt

½ cup sugar
2 eggs, beaten
¾ cup milk
½ teaspoon nutmeg
   Baby lima beans or
   parsley

Prepare a 1-quart ring mold, well greased and breaded with ½ cup bread crumbs. Cook carrots in boiling water until tender; mash. Mix with remaining ingredients. Pack into prepared mold. Bake at 350° for 30 minutes. Unmold onto serving plate. Fill center ring with baby lima beans or parsley.

Anne Huey

Heavenly Carrots

Yield: 16 servings

2 pounds carrots,
   sliced
1 small green pepper,
   sliced
1 medium onion, sliced
1 (10¾-ounce) can tomato
   soup

½ cup vegetable oil
1 cup sugar
¾ cup vinegar
1 teaspoon prepared
   mustard
1 teaspoon Worcestershire
   Salt to taste

Boil carrots until tender crisp in salted water. Place cooked carrots, pepper and onions in layers. Combine remaining ingredients, blending well. Pour over carrots. Refrigerate overnight.
Keeps up to 3 weeks in the refrigerator.

Doris Thacker

Carrots, Israeli Style

Yield: 6 servings

1½ pounds young carrots,
    cut into ¼-inch slices
4 tablespoons butter or
    margarine
⅓ cup dry white wine

½ teaspoon nutmeg
⅔ cup white raisins
3 tablespoons light brown
    sugar

Place carrots, butter, wine and nutmeg in a saucepan. Cover. Cook over low heat until carrots are tender. Stir in raisins and sugar, cooking a few minutes longer until raisins are plump and carrots are glazed.

Martha Nichols

Carrot and Rice Ring

Oven: 350° - 30 minutes

Yield: 12 servings

3 cups cooked regular
    rice
2 cups carrots, grated
¼ cup onion, grated
2 tablespoons all-purpose
    flour
1 (11-ounce) can Cheddar
    cheese soup, undiluted

1 egg, slightly beaten
1 teaspoon salt
¼ teaspoon pepper
1 teaspoon Worcestershire
1 (10-ounce) package frozen
    English peas
Carrots curls or radish
    roses (optional)

Combine rice, carrots, onion and flour in a large bowl. Add next 5 ingredients. Pack mixture into a greased 8-inch ring mold. Bake at 350° for 30 minutes. Allow to cool 10 minutes. Cook peas according to package directions; drain. Invert rice ring on platter; fill center with peas. Garnish with carrot curls and radish roses, if desired.

Variation: Can substitute 1 can cream of mushroom soup for cheddar cheese soup and add 1 cup grated Cheddar cheese for an even better rice ring for mushroom lovers.

Colorful and perfect for a party.

Carole Haley

Cauliflower Casserole

Oven: 400° - 20 minutes   **Yield:** 6-8 servings

1 cauliflower, broken into flowerets	Dash of salt
1 (10-ounce) box frozen English peas or 1 (16-ounce) can peas	Dash of paprika
	2 cups White Sauce
	½ cup sharp Cheddar cheese, grated
Butter	1 cup bread crumbs

Cook cauliflower and peas separately; drain. Place in casserole, a layer of each. Dot with butter, a dash of salt and paprika, and over each layer a sprinkling of bread crumbs and white sauce to which the grated cheese has been added. Top with bread crumbs. Bake at 400° for 20 minutes.

White Sauce

4 tablespoons butter	½ teaspoon salt
3-4 tablespoons all-purpose flour	2 cups milk

Melt butter over low heat. Add flour and salt, stirring for 3-4 minutes. Stir in milk. (Can add seasonings of celery salt, lemon juice, Worcestershire or onion juice to taste, if desired.) Simmer, stirring constantly, until thick. **Yield:** 2 cups.

Florence Cauble

Frosted Cauliflower

Oven: 350° - 15 minutes   **Yield:** 6-7 servings

1 head cauliflower	¼ teaspoon dry mustard
½ cup mayonnaise	1½ teaspoons dried parsley flakes or 1 tablespoon fresh parsley, finely minced
⅓ cup Parmesan cheese, grated	
1 tablespoon lemon juice	
Salt to taste	2 egg whites

Steam or simmer cauliflower head for about 20 minutes or until crisp tender. Combine mayonnaise, Parmesan cheese, lemon juice, salt, dry mustard and parsley. Beat egg whites until stiff; fold into the mayonnaise mixture. Cover cauliflower with sauce. Bake at 350° for 15 minutes or until frosting begins to brown. Remove whole to serving dish. Serve immediately.

May be prepared early in the day except for final baking.

Anne Huey

Spanish Corn

Oven: 350° - 45 minutes-1 hour **Yield:** 6-8 servings

2 eggs
1 teaspoon sugar
1 teaspoon salt
½ teaspoon dry mustard
1 (20-ounce) can yellow
   whole kernel corn,
   drained
½ cup green pepper,
   finely chopped

¼ cup pimiento, diced
1 tablespoon onion,
   finely chopped
½ cup sharp Cheddar
   cheese, finely grated
2 tablespoons butter,
   melted
Buttered bread crumbs

Combine first 4 ingredients; beat with electric mixer until well blended. Add corn, green peppers, pimiento, onion, cheese and butter. Pour into a 2-quart baking dish. Cover with bread crumbs. Bake at 350° for 45 minutes-1 hour.

Julia Ellis

Eggplant Casserole

Oven: 350° - 45 minutes **Yield:** 6 servings

3 cups eggplant, parboiled
1 cup bread crumbs
2 cups milk
2 eggs, beaten

1 teaspoon salt
Pepper to taste
½ pound sharp Cheddar
   cheese, grated

Cook eggplant until tender. Layer eggplant with bread crumbs in a 9x13-inch baking dish. Mix milk, eggs, salt and pepper; pour over layers. Cover with cheese. Bake at 350° for 45 minutes.

Sylvia Peterson

Oven Fried Okra

Oven: 425° - 1 hour **Yield:** 4-6 servings

4-6 cups fresh okra,
   sliced
1 egg, beaten
¼ - ½ cup corn meal

¼ - ½ cup vegetable oil
1 teaspoon salt
¼ teaspoon pepper

Toss okra with egg; roll in corn meal. Preheat oven to 425°. Place metal baking dish in oven with oil and preheat. Add battered okra. Cook 1 hour, turning occasionally.
Much easier than frying; also allows okra to cook more evenly and crisper.

Linda Hasty

Creamed Onions

Oven: 350° - 30 minutes   **Yield:** 12 servings

3 pounds onions,
    peeled and quartered
1 (10¾-ounce) can cream
    of mushroom soup
1 cup Cheddar cheese,
    grated

Dash of Worcestershire
1 (2-ounce) jar pimientos,
    chopped

Cook onions in boiling water until tender. Drain onions in a colander for 2 hours. Layer onions, soup and cheese in a 3-quart casserole. Add Worcestershire and pimientos. Bake at 350° for 30 minutes or until hot and bubbly.

Barbara Manous

Onion Casserole

Oven: 350° - 30 minutes   **Yield:** 6 servings

½ cup margarine
4 medium onions,
    sliced
12 saltine crackers,
    crushed
1 (10¾-ounce) can cream
    of mushroom soup

2 eggs, beaten
½-1 cup milk
    Salt and pepper to taste
    Sharp Cheddar cheese,
    grated

Melt margarine; cook onions until tender. Butter a casserole dish; line with cracker crumbs. Add onions and soup in layers until dish is full. Combine eggs, milk, salt and pepper. Pour over top of casserole. Sprinkle grated cheese and a few more cracker crumbs over the top. Bake at 350° for 30 minutes until brown and bubbly.
Especially good with Vidalia onions in season. Can be assembled as much as a day ahead of time and cooked just before your meal.

Nancy Payne

Potato and Onion Casserole

Oven: 325° - 2 hours   **Yield:** 4 servings

4 medium potatoes,
    peeled and sliced
1 medium onion,
    thinly sliced
1 teaspoon salt

2 tablespoons butter
1 (10¾-ounce) can cream of
    mushroom, celery or
    onion soup
½ cup water

Place potatoes and onions in several layers in deep baking dish. Add salt. Dot with butter. Cover with soup and water. Bake at 325° for 2 hours.
Easy to fix.

Barbara Whidby

Stuffed Potatoes

Oven: 375° - 20 minutes   **Yield:** 6 servings

4 baking potatoes
1 (3-ounce) package cream
  cheese (with chives
  if desired)
3 tablespoons margarine
½ cup Parmesan cheese,
  grated

2 tablespoons sour cream
1 egg
½ teaspoon salt
  Dash of pepper
  Paprika

Bake potatoes at 400° until tender. Split in half lengthwise; carefully scoop out. Put into processor bowl or large bowl of mixer. Add remaining ingredients except egg; beat until smooth. Add egg; beat until creamy. Fill 6 shells, discarding the remaining 2. Sprinkle top of each potato with additional Parmesan cheese and paprika. Bake at 375° for 20 minutes or until puffed and lightly browned.

Potatoes may be prepared ahead of time and frozen before baking; thaw and add topping of Parmesan and paprika just before baking.

Linda Hasty

Potato-Zucchini Au Gratin

Oven: 350° - 1 hour 30 minutes   **Yield:** 8 servings

4 medium Idaho potatoes,
  peeled and cut into
  ⅛-inch slices
2 cups Cheddar cheese,
  shredded, divided
6 tablespoons butter,
  divided
2 tablespoons all-purpose
  flour

1 teaspoon salt
⅛ teaspoon pepper
1 cup milk
4 medium zucchini,
  thinly sliced
1 cup dry bread crumbs
¼ cup parsley, chopped

Layer potato slices with 1 cup cheese in buttered 13x9-inch baking dish. Melt 2 tablespoons butter in saucepan; remove from heat. Stir in flour, salt and pepper; stir in milk. Cook, stirring constantly, over medium heat until sauce boils and thickens. Pour sauce over potato slices. Bake, covered, at 350° for 50 minutes. Remove cover. Layer zucchini slices and remaining cheese over potatoes. Mix bread crumbs, parsley and 4 tablespoons melted butter. Sprinkle over zucchini. Bake, uncovered, at 350° for 40 minutes.

Deanie Fincher

Sloppy Potato Skins

Oven: 350° - 4-6 minutes   **Yield:** 4 servings

1 (16-ounce) package frozen
   potato wedges
Salt to taste
1 small onion, sliced
   (optional)
1 (0.4-ounce) package
   Hidden Valley Ranch
   Dressing mix

1 cup mayonnaise
1 cup buttermilk
1 (8-ounce) package
   Velveeta cheese, grated

Deep fry wedges until done; drain on paper towels; add salt. Stir-fry onions, if desired; set aside. Place potatoes in an 8x10-inch baking dish. Combine dressing mix, mayonnaise and buttermilk; pour over potatoes. Bake at 350° for 4-6 minutes. Remove from oven; top with cheese then onions, if desired. Return to oven to melt cheese. Serve immediately.
Delicious!

Dora Bobo

Spinach with Artichokes

Oven: 350° - 30 minutes   **Yield:** 8-10 servings

4 (10-ounce) packages
   frozen chopped spinach
11 ounces cream cheese,
   softened
5 tablespoons margarine,
   melted

Juice of 1 lemon
Salt and pepper to taste
Seasoned salt to taste
Several dashes of nutmeg
2 (14-ounce) cans artichoke
   hearts, drained

Cook spinach according to package directions; drain well. Set aside. Blend cream cheese and margarine until smooth; add lemon juice; combine with spinach. Stir in seasonings, blending well. Place artichoke hearts in a 16x8-inch baking dish. Spoon spinach mixture over artichokes. Cover with foil; punch a few holes in the foil. Bake at 350° for 30 minutes.
May be put together in the morning before baking later in the day.

Linda Hasty

Spinach Casserole

Oven: 350° - 10-15 minutes   **Yield:** 6-8 servings

1 (8-ounce) package cream cheese
1 (10¾-ounce) can cream of mushroom soup
2 (10-ounce) packages frozen chopped spinach

1 (3½-ounce) can French fried onions
½ cup butter, melted
Cheese Ritz cracker crumbs

Melt cream cheese in soup over low heat. Cook spinach according to package directions; drain well. Add to soup mixture. Add onions. Melt butter; add crumbled crackers until butter is absorbed. Pour spinach mixture in shallow layer in square baking dish. Cover with cracker crumb mixture. Bake at 350° for 10-15 minutes.
Tastes even better when reheated.

Florence Cauble

Squash Fritters

Yield: 10 servings

1 cup self-rising corn meal
1 egg, beaten
⅔ cup milk

1 cup squash, cooked and mashed
Salt to taste
Vegetable oil for frying

Combine all ingredients; blend well. Spoon 1 tablespoon batter into hot oil. Fry until browned on both sides. Drain on paper towels. Serve immediately.

Judi Whiddon

Butternut Squash Casserole

Oven: 350° - 45 minutes   **Yield:** 8 servings

2 cups butternut squash, cooked, drained and mashed
3 eggs, beaten
6 tablespoons margarine
1 cup milk or ½ cup milk and ½ cup orange juice

1 cup sugar
½ teaspoon ginger
2 tablespoons flaked coconut
Butter bread crumbs or crushed corn flakes

Combine all ingredients, mixing well. Pour into a lightly greased 2-quart baking dish. Set in a pan of water. Bake at 350° for 45 minutes or until knife inserted into center comes out clean. Just before removing from oven, sprinkle lightly with buttered bread crumbs or crushed corn flakes.
An excellent choice as a change from potato soufflé. Can be prepared ahead, frozen and baked when needed.

Grace Hyatt

Tip: To prepare the extremely hard butternut squash more easily, drop into a pot of boiling water for 6-10 minutes before trying to peel. Remove from water and cool. Peel, remove seed pulp, dice and cook in small amount of water until tender.

Baked Stuffed Squash

Oven: 350° - 30 minutes

Yield: 12 servings

6 medium to large
  yellow squash
1 egg
Salt and pepper to taste

1 medium onion, chopped
Oven-toasted rice
  cereal
Margarine

Boil squash in salted water in covered saucepan about 10 minutes; drain. Do not overcook. Squash should be firm. Slice squash in half lengthwise. Place in a greased baking dish. Remove pulp. Mix pulp, egg, salt, pepper and onion. Fill squash with mixture. Cover with rice cereal. Dot with margarine. Bake at 350° for 30 minutes or until lightly browned.

Ruth Denney

Baked Squash

Oven: 375° - 1 hour

Yield: 6 servings

3 pounds yellow squash,
  cooked and mashed
½ cup onion, chopped
2 eggs, beaten
1 tablespoon sugar

1 teaspoon salt
½ teaspoon pepper
½ cup margarine, melted
½ cup cracker meal
  or bread crumbs

Combine squash, onion, egg, sugar, salt and pepper. Mix until well blended. Pour mixture into a 1½-quart baking dish. Spread margarine over top; sprinkle with cracker meal or bread crumbs. Bake at 375° for 1 hour or until brown on top.

Denise Swords

Squash Soufflé Casserole

Oven: 350° - 30 minutes

Yield: 6-8 servings

2 cups squash
1 small onion, chopped
2 eggs, beaten
½ cup mayonnaise
1½ cups sharp Cheddar
  cheese, grated

Salt and pepper to taste
½ cup margarine
1½ cups saltine crackers,
  crushed

Cook squash with chopped onion; drain. Add remaining ingredients except crackers and margarine. Beat squash mixture with electric mixer until only slightly lumpy. Pour into buttered 2-quart baking dish. Brown cracker crumbs in butter in skillet until just lightly brown. Place crumbs on top of squash. Bake at 350° for 30 minutes. Center should be firm.

Can be done ahead and refrigerated, then baked before serving.

Julia Dennis

Mexican Squash

Yield: 4 servings

10 small zucchini
2 medium onions, chopped
1 tablespoon vegetable
   oil
4 large tomatoes,
   peeled and diced
2 cloves garlic, minced

3 green chilies, cleaned
   and diced
1 teaspoon salt
½ teaspoon oregano
½ pound Longhorn cheese,
   grated

Cut zucchini into pieces. Fry onions in oil until tender. Add squash and remaining ingredients except cheese. Simmer 10-15 minutes. Sprinkle with cheese. Serve immediately.

Ann Hopkins

Zucchini Casserole

Oven: 350° - 30-35 minutes   **Yield:** 8 servings

2 eggs, separated
1 (8-ounce) carton sour
   cream
2 tablespoons all-purpose
   flour
   Salt to taste
7 zucchini squash,
   scrubbed and sliced

1¾ cups Cheddar cheese,
    shredded
8 slices bacon, cooked
   and crumbled
⅓ cup dry bread crumbs
1 tablespoon butter,
   melted

Beat egg yolks. Stir in sour cream and flour. Beat egg whites and salt; fold into sour cream mixture. Layer half of squash in a 12x8-inch pan. Pour on half of egg mixture. Sprinkle with half of cheese; add bacon. Layer remaining squash, egg mixture and cheese. Combine bread crumbs and butter; sprinkle on top. Bake at 350° for 30-35 minutes.

Anne Huey

Sweet Potato Beignets

Yield: 4-6 servings

1 (15½-ounce) can sweet
   potatoes, drained and
   mashed
1 egg + 1 yolk
2 ounces sherry or
   Madeira wine

¼ teaspoon nutmeg
  Salt to taste
  All-purpose flour
  Almonds or pecans,
  finely chopped
  Vegetable oil

Mix sweet potatoes with 2 egg yolks, sherry, nutmeg and salt. Beat until light and smooth. Cool in refrigerator. Form into croquettes; roll in flour. Beat 1 egg white until frothy. Dip croquettes into egg white. Roll in almonds or pecans. Fry in deep fat until golden brown. Serve immediately.
Dry bread crumbs can be substituted for nuts.

June Phillips

Sweet Potato Soufflé I

Oven: 350° - 35 minutes   **Yield:** 8 servings

3 cups sweet potatoes,
   cooked and mashed
1 cup sugar
½ cup milk
⅓ cup butter

1 teaspoon orange,
   lemon or vanilla extract
2 eggs, beaten
½ teaspoon salt
Topping

Combine all ingredients; beat until smooth. Pour into a buttered 2-quart baking dish. Add Topping. Bake at 350° for 35 minutes.

Topping

1 cup brown sugar,
   firmly packed
⅓ cup all-purpose flour

⅓ cup butter, melted
1 cup pecans, chopped

Combine all ingredients.

Judy McClure

Sweet Potato Soufflé II

Oven: 350° - 40 minutes   **Yield:** 8 servings

4 medium to large sweet
   potatoes, cooked
   and mashed
1 cup margarine,
   melted
2 eggs, beaten
1½ cups sugar
1 (5.33-ounce) can evaporated
   milk

½ teaspoon cinnamon
½ teaspoon cloves
½ teaspoon allspice
¼ teaspoon nutmeg
⅛ teaspoon ginger
1 tablespoon vanilla extract

Combine all ingredients. Beat until smooth. Pour into a buttered 2-quart baking dish. Bake at 350° for 40 minutes.

Juanita Jones

Sweet Potato Casserole

Oven: 350° - 30 minutes   **Yield:** 6 servings

2½ pounds sweet potatoes,
   cooked and mashed
3 tablespoons bourbon
   or dry sherry
½ cup brown sugar,
   firmly packed

½ teaspoon salt
3 tablespoons butter,
   melted
Grated rind of 1 orange
Juice of 1 orange

Combine all ingredients; beat until smooth. Pour into a buttered 1½-quart baking dish. Cook, covered, at 350° for 30 minutes.

Elizabeth Haley

Yams and Apples

Oven: 350° - 40 minutes   **Yield:** 6 servings

3½ **pounds sweet potatoes**	1¾ **cups sugar**
5 **apples**	1 **teaspoon cinnamon**
½ **cup water**	½ **teaspoon nutmeg or**
¾ **cup butter**	**cloves**

Peel potatoes; cut into 1-inch slices. Peel and core apples; cut into eighths. Place apples and potatoes into a greased 13x9-inch baking dish. Add water. Cut up butter, dotting on top of potatoes and apples. Sprinkle sugar and spices over top. Cover. Bake at 350° for 45 minutes, stirring once or twice to mix spices.

Susan Roach
Jackson, Georgia

Summer Tomato Pie

Oven: 400° - 15 minutes   **Yield:** 1 (9-inch) pie
      350° - 20 minutes

1 **recipe for pie pastry**	2 **tablespoons freshly cut**
4-6 **ripe tomatoes,**	**basil or 1 teaspoon**
peeled and thickly	**dried basil**
sliced	1 **cup sharp Cheddar**
1 **teaspoon salt**	**cheese, shredded**
1 **teaspoon freshly ground**	1 **cup mayonnaise**
pepper	

Line a 9-inch pie plate with pastry. Cover with layers of sliced tomatoes. Sprinkle with salt, pepper and basil. Blend cheese and mayonnaise; spread over tomatoes. Cover with pastry for crust. Bake at 400° for 15 minutes; then reduce heat to 350° and bake about 20 minutes or until crust is slightly browned.
A summer must!

Helen Spears

Tomato Provencale

Oven: 450° - 10-15 minutes   **Yield:** 8 servings

4 **medium tomatoes,**	2 **tablespoons parsley,**
halved	**finely chopped**
Prepared mustard	1 **tablespoon onion,**
Seasoned salt to taste	**grated (optional)**
Pepper to taste	1 **tablespoon olive oil,**
1 **cup soft bread crumbs**	**vegetable oil or butter**

Arrange tomatoes, cut side up, in a greased shallow pan. Spread tomatoes lightly with mustard. Sprinkle with salt and pepper. Combine bread crumbs, parsley, onion if desired, and olive oil; sprinkle over tomatoes. Bake at 450° for 10-15 minutes or until bread crumb mixture is golden.
Olive oil and onion give this dish a great flavor!

Judy Bishop

Greek Tomato Pilaf

Yield: 4-6 servings

2 tablespoons margarine
2 medium tomatoes, chopped
2 tablespoons onion, chopped
2 cups water

1 cup regular rice, uncooked
1 teaspoon instant beef bouillon
¾ teaspoon salt
⅛ teaspoon pepper

Melt margarine in a saucepan. Add tomatoes and onion. Cook over medium heat. Add remaining ingredients. Heat to boiling, stirring once or twice. Reduce heat. Simmer, covered, for 14 minutes.

Cathy Lacy

Glazed Turnips

Oven: 350° - 1 hour   **Yield:** 4 servings

6 medium turnips
2 tablespoons butter
¼ cup honey

¼ cup water
¼ teaspoon nutmeg
¼ teaspoon salt

Peel and dice turnips. Steam just until tender. Place drained turnips in a buttered baking dish. Combine butter, honey, water, nutmeg and salt in a small saucepan. Heat until butter melts. Pour over turnips. Bake at 350° for 1 hour or until turnips are lightly browned and glazed.

Florence Cauble

Vegetable Supreme

Yield: 6 servings

1 cup mayonnaise
1 (8-ounce) can water chestnuts, sliced and drained
1 medium onion, chopped
2 hard-cooked eggs, chopped
2 tablespoons vegetable oil
1 tablespoon Worcestershire

1 teaspoon prepared mustard
1 (16-ounce) can French-style green beans, cooked and drained
1 (16-ounce) can small lima beans, cooked and drained
1 (16-ounce) can English peas, cooked and drained

Combine first 7 ingredients. Blend well. Add cooked vegetables. Serve dish either hot or cold.
Sauce can be made ahead of time and refrigerated until needed.

Patsy Neese

Vegetable Casserole

Oven: 350° - 30 minutes   **Yield:** 4-5 servings

1 (16-ounce) can mixed
    vegetables, drained
1 (17-ounce) can whole
    kernel corn, drained
1 (10¾-ounce) can cream
    of chicken soup
1 cup Cheddar cheese,
    grated

½ cup mayonnaise
¼ cup onion, chopped
    (optional)
¼ cup celery, chopped
    (optional)
Salt and pepper to taste
Cracker crumbs
Margarine, melted

Mix together all ingredients except cracker crumbs and margarine. Pour into a greased 1½-quart baking dish. Top with cracker crumbs mixed with margarine. Bake at 325° for 30 minutes.

Nan Cox

Spicy Paella-Style Vegetables

Oven: 350° - 25-28 minutes   **Yield:** 6 servings

¾ pound broccoli, sliced
    or 1 (10-ounce) package
    frozen chopped broccoli
2 cups small zucchini,
    sliced ¼-inch thick
1½ cups medium green or
    red sweet peppers,
    chopped
½ cup onion, chopped
2 cloves garlic, minced
¼ cup olive oil or
    vegetable oil
1 (16-ounce) can tomatoes,
    cut up

1 teaspoon salt
½ teaspoon ground red
    pepper
⅛ teaspoon pepper
2¾ cups chicken broth
1½ cups long grain rice,
    uncooked
1 tablespoons lemon juice
1 cup fresh or frozen
    peas, thawed
⅔ cup Parmesan cheese,
    grated
6 eggs

Cook fresh broccoli in a small amount of boiling, lightly salted water for 5 minutes or until crisp-tender; drain. (If using frozen, cook according to package directions.) In a paella pan or 12-inch ovengoing skillet, cook zucchini, sweet pepper, onion and garlic in olive oil until onion is tender. Stir in undrained tomatoes, salt, red pepper and pepper. Stir in chicken broth, rice and lemon juice; mix well. Bring to boiling. Bake, covered, at 350° for 10 minutes. Stir in broccoli, peas and Parmesan cheese. Make 6 depressions in rice mixture with the back of spoon. Carefully break the eggs into he depressions. Sprinkle eggs lightly with salt. Bake, covered, 15-18 minutes more or until eggs are set and rice is tender.
This is a meal in a dish. All you need is a beverage and fruit for dessert.

Margaret Logan

Barbecue Sauce

Yield: 4¼ cups

1 cup catsup
¾ cup vinegar
2 tablespoons lemon juice
¾ cup water
½ cup vegetable oil
½ cup brown sugar,
   firmly packed
½ cup Worcestershire

1 tablespoon salt
4 teaspoons dry mustard
4 teaspoons chili powder
4 teaspoons paprika
2 teaspoons red pepper
2 teaspoons liquid hot
   sauce (optional)

Place all ingredients in blender. Blend until completely mixed.
Sauce can be used to baste grilled meats or can be heated and served as an accompaniment for meat dishes such as roast pork.

Linda Merrell

Hunters' Deer Sauce

½ cup butter
1 (15-ounce) bottle
   A-1 Sauce
1 tablespoon dried
   minced onion
1 (8-ounce) jar grape
   or apple jelly

1 tablespoon black pepper
1 beef bouillon cube
4 tablespoons brown sugar
4 tablespoons vinegar
4 tablespoons Worcestershire
4 tablespoons sherry
   Juice of 4 lemons

Combine all ingredients in a saucepan. Cook over low heat until butter and jelly have melted. Do not boil.
Great to use over a venison roast.

C. J. Gober

Meat Marinade

Yield: 1½ cups

½ cup soy sauce
¼ cup water
½ cup vegetable oil
2 tablespoons instant
   minced onions
2 tablespoons sesame
   seeds

1 tablespoon sugar
1 teaspoon ginger
¾ teaspoon salt
½ teaspoon ground red
   pepper

Combine all ingredients, blending well.
Good marinade for chicken, shrimp and fish.

David Cannon

Raisin Sauce

Yield: 8-10 servings

1 cup raisins
1¾ cups water
⅓ cup brown sugar,
    firmly packed
¼ teaspoon cinnamon
¼ teaspoon cloves

¼ teaspoon dry mustard
¼ teaspoon salt
1½ tablespoons cornstarch
1½ tablespoons water
1 tablespoon vinegar

Boil raisins in 1¾ cups water 5 minutes. Add sugar, spices, mustard and salt. Mix cornstarch with 1½ tablespoons water; add to mixture. Cook, stirring until thickened. Blend in vinegar. Serve over ham slices.
Can also be used as a glaze for ham.

Donna Priestley

Sauce for Ham

Yield: 6-8 servings

1 (8-ounce) can crushed
    pineapple, undrained
1 tablespoon cornstarch
1 cup brown sugar,
    firmly packed

2 tablespoons lemon juice
2 tablespoons prepared
    mustard

Mix all ingredients together in a saucepan. Cook until thickened. Serve over ham.

Julia Dennis

Cranberry Walnut Sauce

Yield: 4 cups

1 pound fresh cranberries
1 cup sugar
1 cup red currant jelly
1 cup water
1 cup walnuts, chopped

3 teaspoons lemon rind,
    grated
3 teaspoons orange rind,
    grated

Combine in large saucepan cranberries, sugar, jelly and water. Bring to a boil. Reduce heat; simmer, uncovered, for 25 minutes. Remove all green unpopped berries. Stir in walnuts and grated rinds. Refrigerate overnight. Sauce will thicken as it cools.

Judi Whiddon

Mustard Cream

Yield: 1 cup

2 tablespoons margarine
2 tablespoons all-purpose
flour
2 tablespoons dry mustard
1 tablespoon sugar
1 teaspoon salt

Dash of cayenne pepper
1 cup milk
1 egg, beaten
2 tablespoons cider
vinegar

Melt margarine in a medium saucepan; stir in flour, mustard, sugar, salt and cayenne. Cook, stirring constantly, until bubbly. Stir in milk; continue cooking and stirring until sauce thickens and boils 1 minute. Stir ½ cup of the hot mixture into beaten egg in a small bowl; stir back into remaining sauce in pan; cook, stirring constantly, 1 minute longer. Remove from heat; stir in vinegar. Cool. Chill in tightly covered container. Beat until smooth just before serving. *Goes well with meats and is especially good on ham biscuits. Keeps well.*

Margaret Logan

Cocktail Sauce for Shrimp

Yield: 1¼ cups

1 cup catsup
2 tablespoons lemon juice
½ teaspoon salt
¼ teaspoon Tabasco

1 tablespoon horseradish
2 tablespoons celery,
minced
1 teaspoon onion, grated

Combine all ingredients. Chill.

Janice Ingram

Marinara Sauce

Yield: 6 servings

2 tablespoons olive or
vegetable oil
1 small onion, chopped
2 garlic cloves, minced
1 tablespoon sugar
2 teaspoons basil

1½ teaspoons salt
1 (16-ounce) can tomatoes,
undrained
1 (6-ounce) can tomato
paste

Cook onion and garlic in hot olive oil until tender, about 5 minutes. Stir in sugar, basil, salt, tomatoes with liquid and tomato paste. Break tomatoes into small pieces. Reduce heat to low. Cook, covered, 20 minutes or until mixture is thickened, stirring occasionally. Serve over spaghetti.

Wanda Roach

Chili Sauce

1 gallon tomatoes	3 tablespoons salt
2 cups onions, chopped	1 tablespoon celery seed
2 cups sweet red pepper	3 tablespoons mixed spices
1 pod hot red pepper	2½ cups vinegar
1 cup sugar	

Skin tomatoes before chopping. Chop all vegetables before measuring. Tie mixed spices in a bag. Mix all ingredients except spices and vinegar. Add spice bag after mixture has boiled 30 minutes. Cook until very thick; add vinegar and boil until there seems to be no more free liquid. Taste and add more seasonings if necessary. Pour while boiling hot into jars and seal.
This is an old family recipe. Total cooking time is 3-4 hours.

Margaret Logan

Aristocratic Pickles

Yield: 6 pints

24 medium cucumbers, thinly sliced	6 cups sugar
	1 quart vinegar
Salt (sufficient quantity to make "brine water")	1 teaspoon cloves
	1 teaspoon allspice
2 tablespoons alum	1 teaspoon cinnamon
2 tablespoons ginger	

Soak cucumbers in brine water for 7 days; stir daily. On 8th day, drain off brine water. Wash cucumbers in fresh water; drain. Boil 10 minutes in "alum water" to cover; drain. Boil 10 minutes in "ginger water" to cover; drain. Boil for 30 minutes in sugar, vinegar, cloves, allspice and cinnamon mixture. Pack in jars; cover with remaining syrup and seal. (Note: "Brine water" - use about 1 gallon of water and add enough salt to float an egg.)
Makes a lovely holiday gift or accompaniment for a nice dinner.

Ruth Gramling

Paula's Pickles

16 cups cucumbers, sliced	5 cups sugar
2 large onions, chopped or sliced	2 tablespoons mustard seed
	1½ teaspoons tumeric
2 large green peppers, chopped or sliced	1½ teaspoons celery seed
	½ teaspoon cloves
1 cup salt	
5 cups dark vinegar	

Place cucumbers, onion and peppers in a large bowl. Sprinkle salt over vegetables. Cover with ice or cold water. Refrigerate for 3 hours; drain. Rinse with fresh water 3 or 4 times. Combine vinegar, sugar, mustard seed, tumeric, celery seed and cloves in large pan. Bring to a boil. Add vegetables. Heat throughout or scald. Do not boil. Pack in hot jars. Seal.

Mary Wuestefeld

Squash Pickles

Yield: 5-6 pints

8 cups squash, sliced
3 green peppers, sliced
2 cups onion, sliced
Salt
2½ cups sugar

2 teaspoons mustard seed
2 cups vinegar
2 teaspoons celery seed
½ teaspoon dry mustard

Layer squash, peppers and onions in a large Dutch oven. Sprinkle with salt. Let stand 1 hour. Drain. Heat other ingredients. Pour over vegetables. Bring to full, rolling boil. Spoon into sterilized jars. Seal.

Linda Hasty

Cucumber Lime Pickles

Yield: 7-8 pints

7 pounds cucumbers,
    sliced crosswise
2 gallons water
2 cups pickling lime
8 cups distilled apple
    cider vinegar

8 cups sugar
2 teaspoons mixed pickling
    spices

Soak clean cucumbers in 2 gallons water and lime mixture in crockery or enamel ware for 24 hours. Wash three times in clean water; soak in fresh ice water for 3 hours. Combine remaining ingredients; bring to a low boil. Stir until sugar is dissolved. Add cucumbers; soak 5-6 hours or overnight. Boil pickles in soaking liquid for 35 minutes. Fill sterilized quart jars with cucumbers slices; pour syrup over cucumbers, leaving ⅛-inch head space. Cap each jar when filled.

Sylvia Peterson

Pear Preserves

1 pound fresh pear
    slices
¾ pound sugar

1 lemon or lime,
    thinly sliced
Cinnamon stick (optional)

Put pears in clear water to cover. Boil gently until tender and can be pierced with a fork; drain. Layer pears and sugar in bowl. Cover with a cloth. Allow to stand overnight. Pour off syrup from pears; reserve. Add lemon or lime slices to syrup; bring to a boil. Add pears. Continue to cook until clear and syrup is thick as preserve syrup. Cook slowly, stirring often, but gently so as not to break the fruit. Can add a cinnamon stick for a spicy marmalade flavor. Remove any scum while cooking. Pour in jelly jars. Seal.

Deborah Fincher

Hot Pepper Jelly

Yield: 12-14 (8-ounce) jars

6 green peppers, seeded
20 hot peppers, seeded
3 cups white cider
vinegar

5 pounds sugar
2-2½ bottles Certo
Red or green food
coloring

Chop peppers by hand (use rubber gloves) or in blender; set aside. Combine vinegar and sugar in a large boiler. Bring almost to a boil. Add peppers. Return to a boil; continue boiling for 8-10 minutes. Remove from heat; strain (if desired). Add Certo and food color. Reheat to boiling. Remove from heat. Ladle into jars. Seal.

Jelly is delicious with crackers and cream cheese.

Emma Ridenhour

Cranberry-Orange Relish

Yield: 2½ cups

1 (16-ounce) package
cranberries
2 cups sugar

1 teaspoon orange peel,
grated
1¼ cups orange juice

Combine cranberries, sugar, grated orange peel and orange juice in a saucepan. Bring to a boil; reduce heat. Boil gently, uncovered, until cranberry skins pop, 8-10 minutes. Stir once or twice. Cool. Store in covered container in refrigerator until ready to serve.

Keeps well and goes beautifully with Thanksgiving and Christmas turkeys.

Margaret Logan

Zucchini Relish

Yield: 7½ pints

10 cups ground zucchini
4 cups ground onion
5 teaspoons plain or
pickling salt
2¼ cups white vinegar
1 teaspoon dry mustard
¼ teaspoon pepper

1 teaspoon nutmeg
3 cups sugar
2 teaspoons celery salt
1 teaspoon tumeric
1 teaspoon cornstarch
1 red bell pepper,
chopped (optional)

Combine zucchini and onions in large glass or plastic bowl. Sprinkle with pickling salt. Let stand overnight. Drain and rinse several times with cold water. Add remaining ingredients. Cook for 30 minutes. Seal in pint jars.

Makes excellent hamburger - hotdog relish. Equally good with cold meats. Even people who don't like squash, like this.

Elly Hobgood

Maple Syrup

Yield: 2½ cups

4 cups sugar
½ cup brown sugar,
     firmly packed

2 cups water
1 teaspoon vanilla extract
1 teaspoon maple extract

Boil sugars and water for 1 minute. Cool slightly; add extracts. Refrigerate overnight before using.
Keeps well in refrigerator.

Shirley Bursmith

Lemon-Pepper Butter

Yield: 2 cups

2 cups butter or
     margarine, softened
¼ cup snipped chives,
     fresh or freeze-dried
1½ teaspoons lemon peel,
     grated

2 tablespoons lemon juice
½ teaspoon black pepper

Cream butter until light and fluffy. Add remaining ingredients. Mix thoroughly to blend ingredients well. Store in refrigerator in a tightly covered container. *Use this seasoned butter to add flavor to vegetables and to brush over broiled fish, beef steaks and pork cutlets. Spread it on toast for the beginning of a tasty hot sandwich, on English muffins for brunch or dinner rolls.*

Cookbook Committee

Main Dishes

Spicy Pot Roast

Yield: 8-10 servings

2 cups apple juice
1 teaspoon salt
1 teaspoon cinnamon
¼ teaspoon ginger
¼ teaspoon cloves
¼ teaspoon pepper

1 (5-pound) boneless
   chuck roast
¼ cup + 3 tablespoons
   all-purpose flour,
   divided
2 tablespoons vegetable oil

Combine apple juice, salt, cinnamon, ginger, cloves and pepper in large shallow container; add roast turning to coat. Cover. Marinate overnight in refrigerator. Remove roast. Reserve liquid. Dredge roast in ¼ cup flour; brown on all sides in hot oil in a Dutch oven. Add reserved liquid; bring to boil. Reduce heat and simmer, covered, 2½ hours or until roast is tender. Remove roast, reserving pan drippings. Combine 3 tablespoons flour and ½ cup pan drippings; stir until smooth. Pour flour mixture into remaining pan drippings; cook, stirring constantly, until thickened and bubbly. Serve gravy with roast.

Jim Hamrick

Stuffed Tenderloin

Oven: 325° · 1 hour 15 minutes

Yield: 6-8 servings

1 (3-pound) beef
   tenderloin
6 tablespoons butter
½ cup onion, chopped
½ cup celery, chopped

3 cups soft bread crumbs
1 (6-ounce) can sliced
   mushrooms, drained
Salt and pepper to taste
3 slices bacon

Split and flatten tenderloin. Melt butter; sauté onion and celery. Stir in bread crumbs and mushrooms. Spread mixture over half of meat. Bring second side over; fasten edges with skewers. Season with salt and pepper. Top with bacon slices. Roast, uncovered, in a shallow pan at 325° for 1 hour 15 minutes or until rare or medium rare.

Cissy Cloud

Eye of Round Roast

Oven: 350° · 20 minutes per pound

Yield: 6 servings

1 teaspoon oregano
1 teaspoon salt
½ teaspoon garlic powder
½ teaspoon paprika

½ teaspoon pepper
1 (3-3½ pound) eye of round
   roast
1 tablespoon vegetable oil

Mix seasonings together. Rub roast with oil, then with seasoning mixture. Roast, uncovered, at 350° for 20 minutes per pound.
Very easy - always comes out tender.

Pat Gold

Juicy Roast Beef

Oven: 500°

1-3 boxes ice cream
    salt, depending upon
    size of roast

1 standing rib or
    sirloin tip roast of
    desired size

Place bed of ice cream salt at least ½-inch thick in bottom of deep pan. Sprinkle with water. Place roast on salt. Cover sides and top of roast with salt. Salt must be thick enough to form a solid ½ - 1-inch jacket around roast. Sprinkle liberally with water. Insert meat thermometer. Cook at 500° until desired doneness is reached. Remove from oven. Let cool slightly. Break salt jacket, using mallot if necessary. Remove all remaining salt. Serve immediately.
Salt holds in all juices. Meat is tender, juicy and not salty.

Jim Hamrick

Beef Wellington

Oven: 425° - 25 minutes
       425° - 10 minutes
       375° - 20 minutes

Yield: 12 servings

1 (5-pound) fillet of beef
  Butter
⅓ cup brandy

1 box frozen puffed pastry
  Duxelles
1 egg white, slightly beaten

Trim fillet and rub with butter. Roast on rack at 425° for 25 minutes or until meat thermometer reads 120° (very rare). Remove from oven. Flambé with brandy. Let meat cool to room temperature. Roll out part of puffed pastry into a rectangle 1½ inches larger in width and length than fillet. Spread with Duxelles leaving 1 inch uncovered on all edges. Center fillet on rolled out dough. Roll out remaining dough; shape it over the entire fillet. Brush edges with egg white. Secure top and bottom pastry together, finger pinching all around. Use excess dough for decorations. Brush remaining egg white over entire surface; place decorations on top. Place covered fillet on a greased baking sheet. Bake at 425° for 10 minutes. Reduce heat to 375°. Bake for 20 minutes or until crust is golden brown. Allow to stand 15 minutes before slicing. Serve immediately.

Duxelles

¼ cup onions, chopped
2 tablespoons butter
3 tablespoons olive oil
¾ pound fresh mushrooms,
    finely chopped

¼ teaspoon grated nutmeg
  Salt and pepper to taste

Sauté onions in butter and olive oil. Add mushrooms, nutmeg, salt and pepper. Sauté on high heat. Cool.

Helen Spears

Burgundy Beef Tips

Oven: 300° - 1-3 hours   Yield: 6-8 servings

3 pounds sirloin roast
   (or other boneless roast),
   cut into 1-inch cubes
3 tablespoons vegetable oil
¾ cup beef bouillon
1 tablespoon tomato
   paste
2 cloves garlic, minced
½ medium onion, grated
2 tablespoons soy sauce
½ teaspoon thyme

¾ cup Burgundy
2 tablespoons cornstarch
⅓ cup beef bouillon
½ pound fresh mushrooms,
   sliced
2 tablespoons butter
Salt and pepper to taste
Pearl onions (optional)
Cooked rice

Sauté meat in oil until browned on all sides. Do not crowd meat. Transfer meat to a baking dish. Deglaze skillet with a little wine. Pour over meat. Add ¾ cup bouillon, tomato paste, garlic, onion, soy sauce, thyme and wine. Bake, covered, at 300° for 1-3 hours, depending on meat used, until fork tender. Extra wine or bouillon may be added during cooking time if needed. Remove from oven. Skim off any fat accumulated on surface. Drain off gravy into a saucepan. Combine cornstarch and ⅓ cup bouillon to form a paste; add to saucepan. Stir until gravy is thickened. Sauté mushrooms in butter. Add mushrooms and gravy to meat. Season to taste. Add pearl onions, if desired. Serve over rice.

Frances Owen

Chuck Roast with Mushroom Soup

Oven: 350° - 2 hours 30 minutes   Yield: 6 servings

1 (3-pound) beef chuck
   roast
1 large onion, sliced
4 large carrots, sliced
6 large potatoes, sliced
1 large green pepper,
   sliced
1 stalk celery, sliced
1 teaspoon salt

1 teaspoon pepper
2 teaspoons Nature's
   Seasons, seasoning
   blend
1 (4-ounce) can sliced
   mushrooms, drained
1 (10¾-ounce) can cream
   of mushroom soup
2½ soup cans water

Place roast in large roasting pan. Arrange vegetables around roast. Sprinkle with salt, pepper and Nature's Seasons seasoning. Add mushrooms. Pour cream of mushroom soup and water into pan. Cover with aluminum foil. Bake at 350° for 2 hours 30 minutes.
Easy!

Shirley Pahl

Rib Roast

Oven: 375° - 2 hours

1 rib roast   **Salt and pepper**

Rub roast with salt and pepper. Place on a rack, uncovered, in a cold oven. Turn oven to 375°. Bake for 2 hours. Allow to stand for 20 minutes before cutting. *This cooks any size rib roast just right - crispy brown on the outside and rare on the inside.*

Florence Cauble

Braised Short Ribs

Oven: 350° - 1 hour 15 minutes   **Yield:** 2 servings

1½ **pounds beef short ribs**
1 **tablespoon all-purpose flour**
2 **tablespoons vegetable oil**
¼ **cup onion, chopped**
¼ **cup celery, chopped**
1 **(6-ounce) can V-8 juice**
¼ **teaspoon salt**
Dash of pepper
Dash of cloves

Coat ribs with flour; set aside. In heavy skillet, over medium heat, cook onion and celery lightly in oil. Remove with slotted spoon. Increase heat and brown ribs on all sides. Place browned ribs in deep 1-quart baking dish. Drain off any remaining fat from skillet. Return to heat. Add onion, celery, V-8, salt, pepper and cloves. Bring to boil, loosening brown bits from skillet. Pour over ribs. Bake, covered, at 350° for 1 hour. Uncover. Bake 15 minutes more.

Elly Hobgood

Sirloin Shish-Kabobs

Yield: 6 servings

1 **teaspoon ginger**
1 **teaspoon dry mustard**
½ **cup soy sauce**
½ **cup vegetable oil**
3 **cloves garlic, pressed**
3 **pounds sirloin beef, cut into cubes**
Tomatoes, quartered
Small whole onions
Green pepper, cut into large strips
Small whole mushrooms

Combine ginger, dry mustard, soy sauce, vegetable oil and garlic. Let stand 24 hours. Place beef cubes in a shallow dish. Pour marinade over cubes. Marinate for 12 hours. Put beef on skewers with tomatoes, onions, green peppers and mushrooms. Grill over medium coals until desired doneness is reached or broil in oven about 7 minutes per side.

Barry Bishop

Beef Stew

Yield: 4-6 servings

6 tablespoons shortening
3 pounds beef, cut in
    1½-inch cubes
2 medium onions, chopped
1½ cups red wine
    (Chianti)
4 cups water
2 beef bouillon cubes
1 clove garlic,
    finely chopped
2 tablespoons parsley,
    chopped or parsley
    flakes
1 bay leaf

⅛ teaspoon dried thyme
    leaves
1½ tablespoons salt
1 teaspoon pepper
6 medium potatoes,
    quartered
6 medium carrots, sliced
3 stalks celery, sliced
2 medium green peppers,
    sliced
2 medium tomatoes, chopped
    or 1 (8-ounce) can
    tomatoes

Melt shortening. Brown meat cubes on all sides. Place meat in a Dutch oven. Combine onions, wine, water, bouillon cubes and seasonings; add to meat. Simmer, covered, for 2 hours. Add vegetables; cook until tender. Add more water, if necessary. Serve.

Linda Merrell

Mary Ellen's Easy Beef Stew

Oven: 300° - 2 hours 30 minutes   **Yield:** 8 servings

2 pounds lean stew beef,
    cut into 1-inch cubes
½ cup all-purpose flour,
    divided
4 potatoes, quartered
6 carrots, cut into
    2-inch lengths
1 cup celery, sliced

4 large onions, quartered
1 cup water
¼ cup sherry
2 teaspoons sugar
1 teaspoon salt (optional)
½ teaspoon pepper
3 tablespoons soy sauce

Place half of meat in large greased baking dish. Sprinkle lightly with flour. Add layer of vegetables; sprinkle with more flour. Repeat process ending with flour. Mix water, sherry, sugar, salt, if desired, pepper and soy sauce. Pour over mixture. Bake, covered, at 300° for 2 hours 30 minutes.
Tastes even better warmed over the second day.

Martha Nichols

Stir-Fry Beef and Snow Peas

Yield: 6 servings

1 pound boneless sirloin
  steak
3 tablespoons soy sauce,
  divided
3 teaspoons cornstarch,
  divided
2½ teaspoons sugar,
  divided
2 tablespoons wine
2 carrots, scraped
½ pound Chinese pea pods

4 tablespoons peanut oil
  or vegetable oil, divided
2 slices ginger root
1 (8-ounce) can water
  chestnuts, drained and
  sliced
1 (15-ounce) can straw
  mushrooms, drained
2 tablespoons rice wine

Partially freeze steak; slice diagonally across grain into 2x¼-inch strips. Combine 1 tablespoon soy sauce, 2 teaspoons cornstarch, ½ teaspoon sugar and wine; pour over steak. Marinate 1 hour at room temperature or overnight in refrigerator. Cut 4 or 5 lengthwise triangular grooves ⅛-inch deep at even intervals down length of carrots. Slice carrots ⅛-inch thick. Set aside. Pour 1 tablespoon oil around top of preheated wok coating sides; heat to 325°. Add pea pods to wok; stir-fry 1-2 minutes. Remove. Arrange around border of serving platter. Pour 2 tablespoons oil around top of wok, coating sides. Add ginger root and steak; stir-fry 4-5 minutes. Remove. Pour 1 tablespoon oil around top of wok, coating sides. Add carrots, water chestnuts and mushrooms; stir-fry 2-3 minutes. Combine 2 tablespoons soy sauce, rice wine, 2 teaspoons sugar and 1 teaspoon cornstarch, mixing well; add to carrot mixture. Cook until thickened, stirring constantly. Stir in steak. Pour steak mixture into center of platter.

Ollie White

Beef Stroganoff

Yield: 6 servings

¼ cup butter
2 medium onions,
  finely chopped
3 pounds sirloin, cut into
  finger-sized pieces
  Salt and pepper to taste
  Garlic powder to taste
2 cups beef bouillon

¼ cup red wine
1 pound fresh mushrooms,
  sliced
1 package powdered beef
  gravy mix
1 pint sour cream
  Cooked rice or egg
  noodles

Melt butter; add onions. Sauté until the onions are soft. Add the meat; brown quickly for several minutes. Sprinkle with salt, pepper and garlic powder. Pour beef bouillon and red wine over mixture. Cook for about 10 minutes. Add mushrooms; cook for 5 more minutes. Combine beef gravy mix with enough cold water to make it soupy. Stir this mixture into the meat. Add sour cream, stirring thoroughly. Cook until hot. Serve the dish with either white rice or broad egg noodles.

Bob Stubbs

Speedy Stroganoff

Yield: 6 servings

1 pound beef sirloin,
   cut into strips
1 tablespoon shortening
1 medium onion, chopped
1 clove garlic, minced
1 (10¾-ounce) can cream
   of mushroom soup

1 cup sour cream
1 (4-ounce) can sliced
   mushrooms, drained
2 tablespoons catsup
2 teaspoons Worcestershire
   Cooked noodles

Brown sirloin strips in shortening. Add onion and garlic. Cook until onion is crisp and tender. Combine soup, sour cream, mushrooms, catsup and Worcestershire. Pour over meat. Cook, stirring occasionally, over low heat until hot. Serve over cooked noodles.

Wanda Austin

Stuffed Meat Rolls

Oven: 400° - 60 minutes

Yield: 6 servings

2 pounds beef round
   steak
1 teaspoon basil, crushed
⅛ teaspoon pepper
4 ounces cooked ham, thinly
   sliced and cut into
   strips
2 hard-cooked eggs,
   chopped
¼ cup Parmesan cheese,
   grated
½ cup onion, chopped
¼ cup green pepper,
   chopped

1 tablespoon butter
   or margarine
1 tablespoon vegetable oil
1 cup beef broth
¼ cup Marsala wine or
   dry sherry
2 tablespoons brandy
¼ cup cold water
2 tablespoons cornstarch
   Salt and pepper to taste
   Cooked spaghetti, noodles,
   or rice

Cut round steak into 6 rectangular pieces; pound each piece flat with a meat mallet to about ¼-inch thickness. Combine basil and pepper; sprinkle over meat. Layer a sixth of the ham over each piece of meat. Sprinkle with chopped egg and grated Parmesan. Roll up jelly-roll style from short side and tie with a piece of string. In a large skillet, cook onion and green pepper in butter or margarine and cooking oil until tender. Add meat, beef broth and wine or dry sherry. Cover; simmer, covered, for 30 minutes. Transfer to a 13x9-inch baking dish. (Cover with moisture-vapor-proof wrap. Seal, label and freeze for serving later or continue with sauce for serving now.) Before serving: Bake, covered, at 400° for 50 minutes, or until heated through. Add brandy; bake 10 minutes more. Remove meat rolls to platter and remove strings; keep warm. Pour broth from baking dish into saucepan. Boil until reduced to 1⅓ cups. Combine cold water and cornstarch; stir into hot broth. Cook and stir until thickened and bubbly. Cook and stir 1-2 minutes more. Season to taste with salt and pepper. Serve sauce with meat rolls over the hot cooked spaghetti, noodles or rice.

Gaye Mothershed

California Casserole

Oven: 350° - 45 minutes
　　　　425° - 25 minutes

Yield: 6 servings

2　**pounds round steak**
⅓　**cup all-purpose flour**
1　**teaspoon paprika**
¼　**cup vegetable oil**
1¾ **cups small cooked or**
　　　canned onions

2　**(10¾-ounce) cans cream**
　　　of mushroom soup,
　　　divided
1　**soup can water**
　　　Dumplings
1　**cup sour cream**

Coat round steak with a mixture of flour and paprika. Pound mixture into steak. Cut into 2-inch cubes. Brown thoroughly in oil. Place in a large deep baking pan; add onions. In the skillet used for browning the meat, combine 1 can mushroom soup and 1 soup can of water. Bring to a boil; pour over meat and onions. Bake at 350° for 45 minutes. Top with Dumplings. Increase oven to 425°. Bake about 25 minutes until dumplings are done. Combine remaining can of mushroom soup with sour cream. Heat thoroughly. Serve with casserole.

Dumplings

2　**cups all-purpose flour**
4　**teaspoons baking powder**
½　**teaspoon salt**
1　**teaspoon poultry**
　　　seasoning
1　**teaspoon celery seed**
1　**teaspoon dry onion**
　　　flakes

1　**tablespoon poppy seed**
¼　**cup vegetable oil**
1　**cup milk**
¼　**cup butter, melted**
1　**cup Ritz crackers,**
　　　crushed

Sift together flour, baking powder, salt and poultry seasoning. Add celery seed, dry onion flakes and poppy seed. Add oil and milk. Stir until just moistened. Drop rounded tablespoons dough into the mixture of melted butter and crushed Ritz crackers, rolling to coat dumplings with crumbs.

Irene Brown

Pepper Steak

Yield: 6 servings

1½ pounds sirloin steak,
  1-inch thick
  Boiling water
4 cups green pepper
  rings, thinly sliced
3 tablespoons vegetable oil
3 cups onions, thinly
  sliced
¾ teaspoon salt
2 cloves garlic, minced
5 green onions, sliced

2 teaspoons monosodium
  glutamate
1½ teaspoons sugar
  Dash of pepper
⅓ cup sherry
1½ teaspoons ginger
¾ cup beef broth
3 tablespoons cornstarch
2 tablespoons soy sauce
¾ cup water
  Cooked rice

Put beef in freezer for a few minutes. Slice into slivers. Pour just enough boiling water over green pepper rings to cover. Let stand about 3 minutes; rinse in cold water. Heat oil in large skillet. Add green pepper rings, onions, salt, garlic and green onions. Cook 3 minutes over high heat. Add beef slivers; cook 2 minutes. Add monosodium glutamate, sugar, pepper, sherry and ginger; cook 1 minute. Add broth. Bring mixture to a boil. Combine cornstarch, soy sauce and ¾ cup water. Stir into skillet. Cook until sauce in thickened. Serve hot over rice.

Frances Gober

Smothered Swiss Steak

Yield: 6 servings

¼ cup all-purpose flour
1-1½ teaspoons seasoned
  salt
¼ teaspoon pepper
2 pounds round steak
2 tablespoons shortening
  or vegetable oil
1 (16-ounce) can whole
  tomatoes, undrained
2 medium onions, sliced

1 (8-ounce) can tomato
  sauce
1 large green pepper,
  cut into rings
2 cloves garlic,
  crushed
6 carrots, peeled and
  sliced lengthwise
  Cooked rice (optional)

Combine flour, salt and pepper. Sprinkle half of flour mixture on steak; pound into steak. Turn steak and repeat process. Cut steak into 6 serving pieces. Heat shortening in a 10-inch skillet; brown meat on both sides. Pour tomatoes over meat. Combine onion, tomato sauce, green pepper and garlic; pour over steak. Simmer, covered, for 30 minutes. Add carrots; cover and continue cooking 1 hour. Serve with hot rice, if desired.

Sylvia Peterson

Beef and Potato Boats

Oven: 400° - 1 hour 20 minutes

Yield: 4 servings

4 large baking potatoes
4 slices bacon
¾ pound ground beef
1 onion, chopped or
   1 tablespoon onion
   salt

1½ teaspoons salt
½ cup sour cream
2 tablespoons butter
¼ cup milk
¼ cup processed American
   cheese, grated

Bake potatoes at 400° for 1 hour. Set aside. Cook bacon; drain and crumble. Mix beef and onions; shape into patties. Brown in a skillet for 5 minutes on each side. Break up into small chunks. Add salt, sour cream and bacon; set aside. Split potatoes; scoop out. Combine with milk and butter; mash until smooth. Put beef in potato shell. Put mashed potatoes on top. Sprinkle with cheese. Bake at 400° for 20 minutes.

Judy McClure

Lasagna I

Oven: 375° - 50 minutes

Yield: 8 servings

1 pound sweet or hot
   Italian sausage
½ pound ground beef
½ cup onion, finely
   chopped
2 cloves garlic,
   crushed
2 tablespoons sugar
2 tablespoons salt,
   divided
1½ teaspoons dried basil
   leaves
½ teaspoon fennel seed
¼ teaspoon pepper
4 tablespoons parsley,
   chopped, divided

4 cups canned tomatoes,
   undrained or 1 (35-ounce)
   can Italian-style
   tomatoes
1 (12-ounce) can tomato
   paste
½ cup water
12 lasagna noodles
1 (15-ounce) carton Ricotta
   or cottage cheese
1 egg
½ teaspoon salt
¾ pound Mozzarella cheese,
   thinly sliced
¾ cup Parmesan cheese,
   grated

Sauté sausage, beef, onion and garlic; drain. Add sugar, 1 tablespoon salt, basil, fennel, pepper and 2 tablespoons parsley. Mix well. Add tomatoes, tomato paste, ½ cup water. Mash tomatoes with a fork. Bring to a boil; simmer, covered, stirring occasionally for 1 hour 30 minutes. Boil noodles in 3 quarts water and 1 tablespoon salt for 10 minutes or until tender; drain. Rinse in cold water and dry. Combine Ricotta, egg, 2 tablespoons parsley and ½ teaspoon salt; mix well. In a 13x9-inch baking dish, place 1½ cups sauce, a layer of noodles, ½ of Ricotta mixture and top with ½ of Mozzarella, 1½ cups sauce over cheese, ¼ cup Parmesan cheese, noodles. Repeat. End with sauce, Mozzarella and Parmesan. Cover with foil. Bake at 375° for 25 minutes. Uncover. Bake 25 minutes more.

Patricia Gregg

Lasagna II

Oven: 350° - 20 minutes   **Yield:** 8 servings

1 (8-ounce) package
  lasagna noodles
3 tablespoons olive oil,
  divided
1 pound ground beef
½ cup onion, chopped
½ teaspoon garlic powder
2 teaspoons parsley,
  minced
2 teaspoons oregano

2 (6-ounce) cans tomato
  paste
2½ cups water
1½ teaspoons salt
½ teaspoon black pepper
1 pound Ricotta cheese
½ pound Mozzarella cheese,
  sliced
¾ cup Parmesan cheese,
  grated

Boil noodles in water with 1 tablespoon salt for 12 minutes. Stir gently; drain. Add 1 tablespoon olive oil to prevent sticking. Cool. Sauté beef and onion in 2 tablespoons olive oil until meat is browned; drain. Add seasonings, tomato paste, 2½ cups water, salt and pepper; simmer 25 minutes. Spread several spoonfuls of sauce onto bottom of a greased 13x9-inch baking dish. Alternate layers of noodles, sauce, Ricotta, Mozzarella and Parmesan cheese. Top layer is sauce and Parmesan. Bake at 350° for 20 minutes.
Freezes well.

Pat Gold

Zucchini Beef Lasagna

Oven: 350° - 40-45 minutes   **Yield:** 6 servings

½ pound lean ground
  beef
⅓ cup onion, chopped
1 (15-ounce) can tomato
  sauce
½ teaspoon whole oregano
¼ teaspoon whole basil
¼ teaspoon pepper
1 cup lowfat cottage
  cheese

1 egg
4 medium zucchini, cut
  lengthwise in ¼-inch
  slices
1 tablespoon all-purpose
  flour
1 cup Mozzarella cheese,
  shredded

Cook ground beef and onions until meat is browned; drain. Add tomato sauce, oregano, basil and pepper. Bring to a boil. Reduce heat and simmer, uncovered, for 5 minutes, stirring occasionally. Combine cottage cheese and egg; set aside. Arrange half of zucchini in an 8x12-inch baking dish. Sprinkle with flour. Spread cottage cheese mixture evenly over zucchini. Top with half of meat mixture. Sprinkle evenly with cheese. Cover with remaining zucchini. Top with remaining meat mixture. Bake at 350° for 40-45 minutes until zucchini is tender. Let stand 10 minutes before serving.

Debbie Perry

Meatballs in Sour Cream Gravy

Yield: 6-8 servings

2 pounds ground beef
  Salt and pepper to taste
2 eggs; beaten
1 cup onion, chopped
3 tablespoons all-purpose
  flour

½-1 cup water
2 cups sour cream
1 teaspoon dill seed
¼ teaspoon salt
  Cooked noodles

Combine meat, salt, pepper, eggs and onion; mix well. Shape into meatballs. Brown in large skillet. Remove meatballs from skillet; keep hot. Reserve 3 tablespoons fat in skillet; blend in flour. Add water; cook until thickened. Add sour cream, dill seed and ¼ teaspoon salt. Pour over meatballs. Serve over cooked broad noodles.

Dorothy Densmore

Aunt Sue's Spaghetti Sauce

Yield: 4 servings

1 small onion, chopped
1 small green pepper,
  chopped
2 tablespoons butter
1 pound ground beef
1 (14½-ounce) can tomatoes,
  undrained
1 (10¾-ounce) can tomato
  soup

1 (8-ounce) can water
  chestnuts, drained and
  chopped
1 (4-ounce) can sliced
  mushrooms, drained
  Salt and pepper to taste
  Worcestershire to taste
4 ounces Velveeta cheese
  Cooked spaghetti

Sauté onion and green pepper in butter. Add ground beef and brown; drain. Add tomatoes; simmer at least 1 hour. Add tomato soup, water chestnuts and mushrooms. Season with salt, pepper and Worcestershire. Continue to simmer, adding cheese just before serving. Stir until cheese melts. Serve over spaghetti.

Cissy Cloud

Screwy Spaghetti

Oven: 350° - 30 minutes

Yield: 8 servings

12 ounces twisted macaroni,
  cooked and drained
1 (32-ounce) jar prepared
  spaghetti sauce or
  favorite recipe

1 (8-ounce) package
  Mozzarella cheese
1 (3½-ounce) package
  sliced pepperoni

Layer macaroni, spaghetti sauce, half of cheese and half of pepperoni in a large casserole dish; mix well. Top with remaining cheese and pepperoni. Bake at 350° for 30 minutes or until cheese is melted.
Easy to prepare.

Jo Bishop

Spaghetti Pie

Oven: 350° - 25 minutes   Yield: 6 servings

- 1 (8-ounce) package spaghetti, cooked and drained
- 2 tablespoons butter or margarine
- 1/3 cup Parmesan cheese, grated
- 2 eggs, well beaten
- 1 cup cottage cheese
- 1 pound ground beef or bulk pork sausage
- 1/2 cup onion, chopped
- 1/4 cup green pepper, chopped
- 1 (8-ounce) can tomatoes, undrained and cut up
- 1 (6-ounce) can tomato paste
- 1 teaspoon sugar
- 1 teaspoon oregano, crushed
- 1/2 teaspoon garlic salt
- 1/2 cup Mozzarella cheese, shredded

Stir butter into hot spaghetti, Parmesan cheese and eggs. Form spaghetti mixture into a crust in a buttered 10-inch pie plate. Spread cottage cheese over bottom of spaghetti crust. Cook ground beef or pork sausage, onion and green pepper until vegetables are tender and meat is browned; drain. Stir in undrained tomatoes, tomato paste, sugar, oregano and garlic salt. Heat through. Place meat mixture into spaghetti crust. Bake, uncovered, at 350° for 20 minutes. Sprinkle the Mozzarella cheese on top. Bake 5 minutes longer or until cheese melts.

Brenda Burgess

Spaghetti Casserole

Oven: 350° - 30-40 minutes   Yield: 6-8 servings

- 1 pound ground beef
- 1 medium onion, chopped
- 1 small green pepper, chopped
- 1 (28-ounce) can tomatoes
- 1 (6-ounce) can tomato paste
- 1 (4-ounce) can mushrooms, sliced
- 1 (8-ounce) package spaghetti, cooked and drained
- Salt and pepper to taste
- 1 teaspoon chili powder
- 1/4 teaspoon curry powder
- 1/4 teaspoon oregano
- 1 teaspoon sugar or more to taste
- 1/2 pound Cheddar cheese, grated

Combine ground beef, onion and pepper. Cook until meat is browned; drain. Add remaining ingredients except cheese. Layer ground beef mixture with cheese, ending with cheese on top. Bake, uncovered, at 350° for 30-40 minutes or until bubbly and slightly browned.

Lillian Thomason

Moussaka Dubrounik

Oven: 375° - 1 hour **Yield:** 8-10 servings

Meat Filling

3 large onions, finely
  chopped
1 clove garlic, minced
¼ cup margarine
1 pound lean lamb ground
  with ½ pound each lean
  pork and beef or 2
  pounds ground beef

2 eggs
½ teaspoon salt
¼ teaspoon pepper
¼ cup seasoned bread
  crumbs

Sauté onions and garlic in margarine until transparent. Mix together meat, eggs, salt, pepper and bread crumbs; add to onions. Cook over medium heat until meat is crumbled and browned; set aside.

Eggplant

3 medium-sized eggplants,
  peeled and cut lengthwise
  into ¼-inch thick slices
Salt to taste
All-purpose flour

5 eggs, beaten
⅔ cup vegetable oil
  or margarine
Sauce

Sprinkle eggplant slices with salt. Let stand for 15 minutes. Dust slices with flour; dip into beaten eggs. Brown a few slices at a time in the oil. Place a layer of eggplant in a shallow 3½ or 4-quart baking dish. Place a layer of meat mixture. Repeat layers until all used up, ending with a top layer of eggplant. Pour Sauce over eggplant. Bake, uncovered, at 375° for 1 hour.

Sauce

¼ cup margarine
6 tablespoons all-purpose
  flour
2 cups milk
½ teaspoon salt

⅛ teaspoon nutmeg
3 egg yolks or 2 egg
  yolks + 1 egg
  white, beaten

Melt margarine, blend in flour. Stir in milk, salt and nutmeg. Cook, stirring constantly, until thickened. Mix a little hot mixture into egg yolks, beat back into sauce.

Ann Ruppel

Mi Casa Casserole

Oven: 350° - 30 minutes   **Yield:** 8 servings

1 pound ground beef
1 medium onion, chopped
1 clove garlic, minced
3 (8-ounce) cans tomato
  sauce
1 cup ripe olives,
  sliced
1 (8-ounce) carton sour
  cream

1 (8-ounce) carton small-
  curd cottage cheese
1 (4-ounce) can green
  chilies, chopped
1 (7-ounce) package
  tortilla corn chips,
  crushed
8 ounces Monterey Jack
  cheese, shredded

Cook ground beef until browned, stirring often to crumble; drain off drippings. Add onion, garlic, tomato sauce and olives. Cook over low heat until onion is transparent. Combine sour cream, cottage cheese and chilies. Layer half the chips, meat mixture, sour cream mixture, and cheese in a 3-quart round baking dish; repeat the layers. Bake at 350° for 30 minutes.

Florence Cauble

Beef-Cheese Casserole

Oven: 350° - 35-40 minutes   **Yield:** 8-10 servings

1½ pounds ground chuck
1 medium onion, chopped
1 teaspoon salt
⅛ teaspoon pepper
2 (8-ounce) cans tomato
  sauce
1 cup fine cottage
  cheese
1 (8-ounce) package cream
  cheese

¼ cup sour cream
⅓ cup green pepper,
  chopped
⅓ cup green onion
  or chives, chopped
1 (8-ounce) box egg noodles,
  cooked and drained

Combine ground chuck and onion in skillet. Cook until beef is browned; drain, if necessary. Add salt, pepper and tomato sauce; simmer slowly while preparing remaining ingredients. Combine cottage cheese, cream cheese, sour cream, green pepper, green onion or chives. Place half of cooked noodles in the bottom of a buttered 2-quart baking dish. Top with cheese mixture, then the remaining noodles. Pour meat mixture over top. Bake at 350° for 35-40 minutes.
Easy; very good!

Anne Huey

Hearty Beef 'n Beans

Oven: 375° - 18-23 minutes   **Yield:** 4-6 servings

1 pound ground beef
¼ cup green pepper,
  chopped
1 (15-ounce) can kidney
  beans, undrained
1 (10½-ounce) jar pizza
  or spaghetti sauce
1 (4-ounce) can mushrooms,
  stems and pieces,
  drained

¼ teaspoon garlic powder
1 (10-count) can
  refrigerated flaky
  biscuits
  Cheddar cheese
1-2 tablespoons sesame seeds

Brown ground beef and green pepper in a 10-inch skillet; drain. Stir in kidney beans, pizza or spaghetti sauce, mushrooms and garlic powder. Heat until hot and bubbly. Pour into a greased baking dish; set aside. Separate can of biscuits into individual biscuits. Place a ½-inch cube of Cheddar cheese in center of each biscuit. Fold dough over cheese, covering well, and shape into balls. Arrange filled biscuit balls on hot meat mixture. Sprinkle with sesame seeds. Bake at 375° for 18-23 minutes until deep golden brown.

Connie Turner

Barbecue Beefies

Oven: 350° - 1 hour   **Yield:** 6-8 servings

1½ pounds ground beef
1½ cups milk
1 cup rolled oats
2 tablespoons onion,
  grated

1½ teaspoons salt
⅛ teaspoon pepper
½ teaspoon chili powder
  Barbecue Sauce

Mix all ingredients. Shape mixture into 16 patties. Place in an ungreased 9x13-inch baking dish. Pour Barbecue Sauce over patties. Bake, uncovered, at 350° for 1 hour.

Barbecue Sauce

3 medium onions,
  finely chopped
¾ cup catsup
¾ cup water

2 tablespoons vinegar
2 tablespoons Worcestershire
1 teaspoon chili powder
½ teaspoon paprika

Combine all ingredients in a saucepan. Simmer, uncovered, for 30 minutes. *Can be made ahead.*

Barbara Gentry

Easy Chili

Yield: 5-6 servings

1½ tablespoons margarine
1 medium onion, coarsely
  chopped
1 pound ground beef
1 teaspoon salt
3-4 tablespoons chili
  powder

1 teaspoon cumin powder
4 cups stewed tomatoes,
  puréed
1 (16-ounce) can kidney
  beans, drained

Melt margarine; sauté onions until soft. Add ground beef; stir until browned. Drain. Add salt, chili powder, cumin, tomatoes and beans. Stir to a boil, then reduce heat. Simmer for 1 hour, stirring occasionally.
For a thicker chili, simmer uncovered.

Jackson Harris

Great Hamburgers

Yield: 8 servings

2 pounds chopped sirloin
2 cups soft bread crumbs
4 tablespoons onion,
  finely chopped
2 eggs, slightly beaten
2½ tablespoons sugar

4 tablespoons soy sauce
4 tablespoons water
2 cloves garlic,
  crushed
Dash of ginger

Combine all ingredients; mix well. Shape into 8 patties. Cook on grill over charcoal and hickory chips until desired degree of doneness is reached. Serve in hamburger buns.

Florence Cauble

Chili Top Meat Loaf

Oven: 350° - 1 hour   **Yield:** 6 servings

1½ pounds ground beef
1 cup Parmesan cheese,
  grated
½ cup green pepper,
  chopped
½ cup onion, chopped

1 cup cracker crumbs
1 egg, beaten
¾ cup milk
1 teaspoon salt
Chili sauce

Mix all ingredients, except chili sauce. Place in a greased 9x5-inch loaf pan. Bake at 350° for 45 minutes. Turn out loaf onto a baking sheet. Spread chili sauce over top and sides of loaf. Bake for 15 minutes more.

Wanda Roach

Ultimate Homemade Pizza

Oven: 375° - 25-30 minutes   **Yield:** 6 servings

 1 cup lukewarm water
 1 package active dry yeast
 1 tablespoon butter, melted
 1 tablespoon sugar
 1 teaspoon salt
 2½ cups all-purpose flour
 1 (16-ounce) can tomato
   sauce
   Italian seasoning or
   oregano

Pepperoni slices
Ground beef, browned
  and drained
Onions, sliced
Mushrooms, sliced
Green pepper, chopped
 2 cups Mozzarella cheese,
   grated

Mix the first 6 ingredients. Knead several times until easy to handle. Form into large ball; let rise in floured bowl, covered, 2-3 hours. Grease a round pizza pan; press dough into pan, forming a thick edge. Pour tomato sauce over crust. Sprinkle with Italian seasoning. Add pepperoni, ground beef, onions, mushrooms or green peppers, according to taste. Top with cheese. Bake at 375° for 25-30 minutes.

Christi Kook

Veal Scallops with Mustard Sauce

Yield: 3-4 servings

 8 veal scaloppine,
   about ¾ pound
 ⅓ cup all-purpose flour
   Salt and pepper to taste
 4 tablespoons butter
 2 tablespoons shallots,
   finely minced

 ¼ cup dry white wine
 ½ cup heavy cream
 1 tablespoon Dijon
   mustard
   Cooked buttered noodles

Place the scaloppine on a flat surface. Pound thin with a flat mallet or the bottom of a clean skillet. Blend flour, salt and pepper. Dredge the scaloppine on all sides. Heat the butter in a large, heavy skillet until quite hot, but not brown. Add the scaloppine (shrinks some while cooking). Cook quickly for 2 minutes or until golden on each side. Place on a warmed dish. Cover with foil to keep warm. Add shallots to skillet. Cook briefly, stirring constantly. Add the wine. Cook, stirring constantly, until liquid has almost totally evaporated. Add cream. Bring to a boil, stirring constantly. Cook about 30 seconds. Remove from heat. Stir in mustard. Spoon sauce over meat. Serve with fine buttered noodles.

Holly Wulfing
Chef for Georgia Governor's
Mansion

Veau á la Campagne

Yield: 4 servings

1½ pounds veal cutlets,
   sliced thin
1 teaspoon garlic salt
½ cup all-purpose flour
½ cup butter
½ pound fresh mushrooms,
   sliced

Salt and pepper to taste
½ cup dry white wine
1 teaspoon fresh lemon
   juice
Snipped fresh parsley
2 lemons

Flatten veal as thin as possible with a wooden mallet. Sprinkle both sides of cutlets with garlic salt. Dip in flour, coating well. Heat butter in skillet. Add veal; sauté until golden on both sides. Place mushrooms over veal. Sprinkle with salt and pepper. Add wine. Cover skillet. Cook over very low heat 15-20 minutes, checking occasionally to make certain meat is not sticking to pan. Add water in small amounts to keep veal moist. Before serving, sprinkle with lemon juice and parsley. Garnish with very thinly sliced lemon curls.

Anne Harris

Stuffed Pork Tenderloin

Oven: 325° - 1 hour 30 minutes - 2 hours   **Yield:** 8-10 servings

1 (6-ounce) package long
   grain wild rice mix
½ cup boiling water
½ cup dried apricots,
   chopped
2 green onions,
   finely chopped
½ cup fresh mushrooms,
   chopped
¼ cup green pepper,
   chopped
2 tablespoons butter
3 tablespoons pecans,
   chopped

1 tablespoon fresh
   parsley, chopped
⅛ teaspoon salt
⅛ teaspoon pepper
   Dash of cayenne pepper
   Dash of garlic powder
4 (1½-pound) boneless pork
   tenderloins
4 slices bacon
   Canned apricot halves
   Fresh parsley

Cook rice according to package directions; set aside. Pour boiling water over apricots; let stand 20 minutes to soften; drain. Sauté green onions, mushrooms and green pepper in butter until tender. Add rice, apricots, pecans, parsley and seasonings. Stir until combined. Cut a lengthwise slit on top of each tenderloin being careful not to cut through bottom and sides. Spoon half of stuffing into the opening of one tenderloin; place cut side of 2nd tenderloin over it. Tie together securely with string. Place on rack in roasting pan with 2 bacon slices on top. Repeat with remaining tenderloins. Place aluminum foil tent over tenderloins. Bake at 325° for 1 hour 30 minutes - 2 hours or until meat thermometer registers 170°. Remove foil the last 30-40 minutes. Remove from oven: Let stand 5 minutes. Remove string. Slice. Garnish with apricot halves and parsley.
Long, but worth the effort.

Linda Hasty

Cantonese Sweet-Sour Pork

Crock Pot: 5-7 hours **Yield:** 4-6 servings

2 pounds lean pork
   shoulder, cut into
   strips
1 green pepper, cut
   into strips
½ medium onion,
   thinly sliced
¼ cup brown sugar,
   firmly packed

2 tablespoons cornstarch
2 cups pineapple chunks,
   drained, reserving juice
¼ cup cider vinegar
¼ cup water
1 tablespoon soy sauce
½ teaspoon salt
   Chow Mein noodles

Place pork strips in crock pot. Add green pepper and onion. Mix brown sugar and cornstarch. Add 1 cup reserved pineapple juice, vinegar, water, soy sauce and salt; blend until smooth. Pour over meat and vegetables. Cover; cook on low setting for 5-7 hours. One hour before serving, add pineapple chunks; stir into meat and sauce. Serve over chow mein noodles.

Sue Wood

Sweet-Sour Kraut and Chops

Oven: 350° - 90 minutes **Yield:** 6 servings

4 medium baking potatoes,
   peeled and thinly
   sliced
½ cup onion, chopped
¼ cup water
6 pork rib chops,
   ¾-inch thick
2 tablespoons vegetable
   oil

1 (27-ounce) can sauerkraut,
   rinsed and drained
1 (20-ounce) can crushed
   pineapple, undrained
2 tablespoons brown sugar
½ teaspoon salt
   Dash of pepper

Combine potato slices and onion in a 12x7-inch baking dish. Add water. Cover; bake at 350° for 45 minutes or until nearly tender. Brown chops on both sides in hot oil. Combine sauerkraut, pineapple and brown sugar. Spoon sauerkraut mixture over potatoes. Place chops on top. Season with salt and pepper. Bake, covered, for 45 minutes.

Betty McDaniel

Sweet-Sour Pork Chops

Yield: 6-8 servings

8 thick pork chops
2 tablespoons margarine
  or vegetable oil
1½ cups chicken broth
¼ cup cornstarch
¼ cup soy sauce
¼ cup brown sugar,
  firmly packed

2 tablespoons vinegar
1 green pepper, sliced
8 small white onions,
  quartered
1 (15-ounce) can pineapple
  chunks, drained

Brown chops on both sides in margarine. Add broth. Cover; simmer 20-30 minutes or until tender. Blend together cornstarch, soy sauce, brown sugar and vinegar; add to pan juices with the chops, stirring until thickened. Add the green pepper, onions and pineapple. Cook, covered, about 10 minutes until vegetables are tender.

Ann Ruppel

Pork Chops and Rice

Yield: 4-6 servings

6-8 pork chops
2 cups water
2 cups instant rice,
  uncooked
¾ teaspoon salt

Pepper to taste
1 tablespoon marjoram
1 (11-ounce) can mandarin
  orange slices, drained
  (optional)

Brown pork chops; set aside. Add water to skillet; loosen drippings. Add rice and salt. Layer pork chops on top of rice. Sprinkle pepper to taste, and marjoram. Reduce heat to medium-low; simmer 20 minutes or until all water is absorbed. Can be garnished after cooking with mandarin oranges, if desired.

Joan McFather

Batter Baked Pork Chops

Oven: 350° - 40 minutes

Yield: 6 servings

6 loin pork chops
  Salt and pepper to taste
1 egg

½ cup milk
1 cup corn flake crumbs

Trim excessive fat from chops; season with salt and pepper. Beat egg and milk in a shallow dish. Dip pork chops into egg mixture, then into corn flake crumbs; place chops on a rack in a shallow baking pan or casserole. Bake at 350° for about 20 minutes; turn pork chops; bake an additional 20 minutes or until done.

Jerry Land

Honey BBQ Pork Chops

Oven: 300° - 1 hour 30 minutes   **Yield:** 6 servings

½ cup honey
3 tablespoons soy sauce
1 teaspoon prepared mustard
  Dash of garlic
1 cup chicken broth

¼ cup catsup
½ teaspoon salt
¼ teaspoon pepper
6 pork chops

Mix all ingredients in blender. Pour over pork chops. Marinate 1 hour at room temperature. Bake, uncovered, at 300° for 1 hour 30 minutes or until done.

Mandy Mills

Smoked Ham

Oven: 400° - 30 minutes per pound   **Yield:** 8 servings

6-7 pound ham roast
4 tablespoons liquid smoke

1 (20-ounce) can sliced
  pineapple, drained

Rub liquid smoke on the ham. Arrange pineapple slices on the ham. Wrap securely in foil. Place in roasting pan. Bake at 400° for 30 minutes per pound.

Brenda Lawson

Ham Puff

Oven: 425° - 25-30 minutes   **Yield:** 6-8 servings

1 (10-ounce) package frozen
  asparagus, thawed and
  diced
2 cups cooked ham, diced
¼ cup margarine
1¼ cups all-purpose flour,
  divided
1 teaspoon salt, divided
½ teaspoon nutmeg
¼ teaspoon pepper

3¼ cups milk, divided
1 teaspoon lemon juice
1 teaspoon Dijon mustard
2 cups Swiss cheese,
  shredded
2 eggs
1 teaspoon vegetable oil
½ cup sliced almonds
2 green onions, sliced

Combine asparagus and ham in 13x9-inch pan. Melt margarine. Stir in ¼ cup flour, ½ teaspoon salt, nutmeg and pepper. Cook, stirring constantly, until smooth and bubbly. Remove from heat. Stir in 2¼ cups milk. Heat, stirring constantly. Boil and stir 1 minute. Stir in lemon juice and mustard. Pour over ham and asparagus in dish. Sprinkle with cheese. Beat eggs, 1 cup milk, oil, 1 cup flour and ½ teaspoon salt until smooth. Pour over cheese. Sprinkle with almonds and green onions. Cook, uncovered, at 425° for 25-30 minutes or until puffy and golden.

Elly Hobgood

Hot Baked Ham Salad

Oven: 400° - 20-25 minutes   Yield: 4-6 servings

3 cups cooked ham, diced
1 cup celery, diced
½ cup pimiento-stuffed
   olives, chopped
2 hard-cooked eggs,
   diced
2 teaspoons onion,
   minced

1 tablespoon lemon juice
2 teaspoons prepared mustard
Dash of pepper
¾ cup mayonnaise
1 cup potato chips,
   crushed

Combine all ingredients except chips. Pour into an 8x2-inch round baking dish. Sprinkle with chips. Bake at 400° for 20-25 minutes.

Betty Barrett

Peachtree Ribs

Oven: 350° - 1 hour 30 minutes   Yield: 6 servings

1 (7¾-ounce) jar baby
   food peaches
⅓ cup catsup
½ cup vinegar
2 tablespoons Worcestershire

½ cup brown sugar,
   firmly packed
2 teaspoons garlic salt
1 teaspoon ginger
Spare ribs for 6

Mix all ingredients. Pour over ribs. Bake at 350° for 1 hour 30 minutes.

Mandy Mills

Dijon Lamb Chops

Oven: 500° - 4 minutes   Yield: 4 servings
      350° - 15 minutes

4 lamb chops
1 lemon, cut in half
   Garlic powder
   Freshly ground pepper
1 cup fresh parsley,
   chopped

⅓ cup Dijon mustard
1 tablespoon + 1 teaspoon
   wheat bran
Vegetable cooking spray
Lemon slices (optional)
Lime slices (optional)

Trim fat from lamb chops. Rub both sides with lemon; sprinkle lightly with garlic powder and pepper. Combine parsley, mustard and bran; mix well. Press on all sides of chops. Put in a baking dish sprayed with vegetable cooking spray. Cook at 500° for 4 minutes. Reduce heat to 350°. Cook an additional 15 minutes. Garnish with lemon or lime slices, if desired.

Frances Gober

Leg of Lamb

Yield: 10-12 servings

1 (6-pound) boneless
   Western leg of lamb
   Lemon juice
3 cloves garlic
   Salt and pepper to taste
1/3 cup Worcestershire
1 cup water, divided

1 onion, sliced thin
1/4 cup Worcestershire
2 tablespoons catsup
1 teaspoon dry mustard
1/2 cup wine
   Cooked rice

Rub lamb all over with lemon juice and garlic. Sprinkle with salt and pepper. Cut garlic into small pieces and stick into little holes cut in lamb. In a Dutch oven with a little vegetable oil, brown lamb on fat side first over medium heat. Continue browning and turning until browned all over. Mix the 1/3 cup Worcestershire with the 1/2 cup water. Pour over the lamb. Let simmer for 3 hours on very low heat. After about 1 hour, place onion slices on the top of the lamb. Mix remaining 1/2 cup water, 1/4 cup Worcestershire, catsup, mustard and wine. Pour over the lamb. Continue simmering for the remaining 2 hours (for a total of 3 hours). Let cool slightly before slicing. Use gravy in pan over rice, if desired.

Florence Cauble

Lamb Pilaf

Yield: 8 servings

1 pound ground lamb
2 large onions, chopped
2 cloves garlic, minced
3 (14½-ounce) cans chicken
   broth
2 (28-ounce) cans whole
   tomatoes, undrained
2 cups brown rice,
   uncooked

1 teaspoon dried whole
   oregano
1 (10-ounce) package frozen
   English peas
1/2 cup raisins
1 (4-ounce) jar pimiento,
   diced
1/2 teaspoon salt
1/2 teaspoon pepper

Combine lamb, onion and garlic in a large Dutch oven. Cook until lamb is browned and onion is tender. Stir in remaining ingredients; bring to a boil. Reduce heat and simmer 4-5 minutes. Stir. Simmer an additional 30 minutes, stirring often.
Great casual meal for family.

Frances Gober

Rice and Sausage Casserole

Oven: 350° - 35-40 minutes   **Yield:** 8 servings

1 pound sausage
4½ cups boiling water
2 boxes (4 envelopes) chicken
    noodle soup
½ cup rice, uncooked

1 large green pepper,
    chopped
1 large onion, chopped
2 stalks celery, chopped
½ cup slivered almonds

Brown sausage; drain well. Set aside. Combine boiling water, soup mix and rice. Bring to boil; cook 7 minutes. Remove from heat. Add onion, celery, green pepper, sausage and almonds. (This can be put in the refrigerator at this point until later.) Pour into a 2-quart baking dish. Bake at 350° for 35-40 minutes. *Can be prepared the day before.*

Cissy Cloud

Sausage and Cheese Bake

Oven: 425° - 20-25 minutes   **Yield:** 6-8 servings

1 (8-ounce) can refrigerated
    crescent or Italian
    crescent dinner rolls
1 (8-ounce) package sausage
2 cups Monterey Jack cheese
    or Swiss cheese, shredded
4 eggs, beaten
¾ cup milk

2 tablespoons green pepper,
    chopped
½ teaspoon salt
¼ teaspoon pepper
¼ teaspoon oregano

Line a 9x13-inch baking dish with the crescent rolls. Crumble the uncooked sausage over the dough. Place the cheese over the sausage. Mix remaining ingredients; pour over cheese. Bake at 425° for 20-25 minutes. Cut into squares. Serve immediately.

Pat Stewart

Easy Parmesan Chicken

Oven 350° - 1 hour   **Yield:** 6 servings

1 cup dry bread crumbs
½ cup Parmesan cheese,
    grated
¼ teaspoon oregano
¼ teaspoon pepper
    Salt to taste

¾ cup + 2 tablespoons
    butter, melted, divided
1 clove garlic, minced
6 chicken breasts,
    skinned

Combine bread crumbs, cheese, oregano, pepper and salt; set aside. Melt 2 tablespoons butter; sauté garlic. Add remaining ¾ cup butter; melt. Dip chicken in butter; roll in bread crumb mixture. Place in a large greased shallow baking dish. Cook, covered, at 350° for 45 minutes. Remove cover. Bake 15 minutes more.
A quick and easy recipe; a favorite with children.

Helen Spears

Crabmeat Stuffed Chicken Breasts

Oven: 350° - 1 hour

Yield: 4-6 servings

6 chicken breasts,
   skinned and boned
½ cup onion, chopped
½ cup celery, chopped
5 tablespoons margarine
   or butter, divided
3 tablespoons dry white
   wine
1 (7½-ounce) can crabmeat,
   drained

1 (4-ounce) can water
   chestnuts, drained and
   chopped
½ cup herbed stuffing
   mix
2 tablespoons all-purpose
   flour
½ teaspoon paprika
   Cooked rice
   Sauce

Roll chicken between waxed paper until thin. Sauté onion and celery in 3 tablespoons margarine. Add wine. Combine with stuffing mix, crabmeat and water chestnuts. Divide stuffing on each piece of rolled chicken. Roll and tuck chicken around mixture. Place in greased shallow pan. Mix flour and paprika. Pat on chicken. Drizzle with 2 tablespoons melted margarine. Bake at 350° for 1 hour. Serve over cooked rice. Top with Sauce.

Sauce

1 envelope Hollandaise
   sauce mix
¾ cup milk

2 tablespoons white wine
½ cup Swiss cheese,
   shredded

Cook sauce mix according to package directions. Add wine and cheese. Stir; add more wine if too thick.
After preparation, can be refrigerated and baked later.

Betty Barrett

Coq au Vin

Yield: 4 servings

2 medium onions, chopped
½ pound mushrooms, sliced
1 cup butter
1½ teaspoons salt, divided
1 teaspoon pepper, divided
2 (2½-pound) fryers, cut up

   Paprika
1 teaspoon fresh parsley,
   chopped
1 cup burgundy wine
1 tablespoon all-purpose
   flour

Sauté the onions and mushrooms in the butter. Add half of the salt and pepper. Remove onions and mushrooms; set aside. Season the chicken with remaining salt and pepper; sprinkle heavily with paprika. Brown the chicken in the butter remaining in the pan on both sides; add the onions and mushrooms. Add the parsley and the wine. Simmer, covered, for 45 minutes or until chicken is tender. Remove chicken, onions and mushrooms to heated serving platter. Blend flour into sauce. Simmer for 3 minutes. Pour over chicken.

Cookbook Committee

Party Chicken and Shrimp

Yield: 6 servings

4 tablespoons butter
1 medium onion, diced
3 whole large chicken
   breasts, cut in half,
   skinned and boned
3 tablespoons parsley,
   minced
1 (8-ounce) can tomato
   sauce

⅓ cup port wine
¼ cup water
¾ teaspoon salt
1 teaspoon basil
¼ teaspoon pepper
1 pound medium shrimp,
   shelled and deveined
Parsley sprigs

Melt butter in a 12-inch skillet. Cook onion until tender, stirring occasionally. Remove onion to bowl. Cook chicken breasts in drippings remaining in skillet over medium heat until browned on both sides. Add minced parsley; stir in onion, tomato sauce, wine, water, salt, basil and pepper. Heat to boiling. Reduce heat to low. Cover; simmer 10 minutes. Add shrimp; simmer, covered, for 5 minutes or until chicken and shrimp are tender. Skim fat from mixture in skillet. Spoon mixture onto warm platter. Garnish with parsley sprigs. *Can do ahead and reheat.*

Mary Sparks

Baked Chicken Rosé

Oven: 350° - 45-60 minutes
         325° - 25-30 minutes

Yield: 6-8 servings

2½ pounds chicken breasts
   All purpose flour
   Salt and pepper to taste
6 tablespoons butter,
   divided
2 tablespoons all-purpose
   flour
¾ cup chicken stock

½ cup Rosé wine
¼ cup green onions,
   sliced with tops
½ pound mushrooms, sliced
   and sautéed in butter
1 (6-ounce) jar marinated
   artichoke hearts,
   undrained

Dust chicken with flour mixed with salt and pepper. Melt 4 tablespoons butter in shallow baking dish. Put chicken in dish, skin side down. Bake, uncovered, at 350° for 45-60 minutes or until almost tender. Melt remaining butter in saucepan. Stir in flour; cook 2 minutes. Add stock and wine. Cook until thickened. Remove chicken from oven. Turn pieces over. Sprinkle with onions, mushrooms and artichokes (including oil). Pour sauce over chicken. Return to oven. Reduce heat to 325°. Bake 25-30 minutes longer.
Variations: Sliced water chestnuts or tomatoes may be substituted or used in any preferred combination.

Linda Hasty

Sweet and Sour Chicken I

Yield: 4-5 servings

2½ cups cooked chicken,
    cut into bite-sized
    pieces
1 egg, beaten
½ cup + 2 tablespoons
    cornstarch, divided
    Vegetable oil
1 (15¼-ounce) can pineapple
    chunks

½ cup vinegar
½ cup sugar
1 green pepper, cut in
    1-inch chunks
¼ cup water
1 teaspoon soy sauce
1 (16-ounce) can sliced
    carrots, drained
    Cooked rice

Combine chicken and egg, to coat, then dredge in ½ cup cornstarch. Fry in hot oil until golden brown. Drain; set aside. Drain pineapple; reserve juice. Add enough water to pineapple juice to measure 1 cup. Combine juice, vinegar and sugar in large skillet. Stir; bring to boil. Add green pepper; simmer for 2 minutes. Combine water and 2 tablespoons cornstarch; mix well; add to skillet. Cook, stirring until thick. Stir in pineapple, soy sauce, carrots and chicken. Heat thoroughly. Serve over rice.

Joan Satterfield

Sweet and Sour Chicken II

Yield: 4 servings

4 chicken breasts, skinned,
    boned and cut into
    bite-sized pieces
1 large onion, cut into
    large pieces
1 stalk celery, chopped
1 large carrot, sliced
1 green pepper, cut into
    bite-sized pieces
4 tablespoons vegetable oil
1 (8-ounce) bottle Russian
    salad dressing

¼ cup honey
3 teaspoons Worcestershire
1 teaspoon salt
¼ teaspoon pepper
6-7 fresh mushrooms,
    sliced
1 cucumber, peeled and
    cut into 1-inch pieces
2 tomatoes, peeled and
    cut into wedges
    Cooked white or fried rice

Sauté chicken, onion, celery, carrot and green pepper in vegetable oil in an electric skillet until chicken loses its color; drain. Add salad dressing, honey, Worcestershire, salt, pepper and mushrooms. Bring to a boil. Reduce heat; simmer for 40 minutes. Add cucumber and tomatoes; simmer 6-8 minutes. Serve over white or fried rice.

Susan Roach
Jackson, Georgia

Chicken Cordon Bleu

Yield: 6 servings

6 chicken breasts,
    skinned and boned
1 (8-ounce) package Swiss
    cheese, sliced
1 (6-ounce) package cooked
    ham
3 tablespoons all-purpose
    flour

1 teaspoon paprika
6 tablespoons butter
1 cup water
1 chicken bouillon cube
1 cup heavy cream
1 tablespoon cornstarch
Cooked rice

1¼ hours before serving, spread chicken breasts flat; fold cheese and ham slices to fit on top. Fold breast over filling; fasten edges with toothpick. Mix flour and paprika; coat chicken. Melt butter in a skillet, over medium heat. Cook chicken until browned on all sides. Add water and bouillon cube; heat to boiling. Reduce heat to low; simmer, covered, 30 minutes or until tender. Remove chicken with a slotted spoon to a warm platter; remove toothpicks. Blend cream into cornstarch until smooth. Add to drippings; stir until sauce is thickened. Pour over chicken. Serve with rice.

Jeannie Adams

Stuffed Chicken Breast

Oven: 325° - 1 hour 20 minutes

Yield: 6-8 servings

8 chicken breasts,
    skinned and boned
1 (12-ounce) package herb
    dressing mix
1 (15¼-ounce) can chicken
    broth
1 (4-ounce) can mushrooms,
    stems and pieces

Salt and pepper to taste
30 ripe olives, chopped
1 cup white wine
1 (10¾-ounce) can cream
    of chicken soup
Orange slices for garnish

Flatten chicken breasts with a mallet. Mix dressing with chicken broth to moisten; place about 2 tablespoons on flattened chicken breast. Fold chicken breast around dressing mixture; secure with a toothpick. Lay chicken seam side down in pan. Sprinkle with salt and pepper. Cover with chopped olives. Add white wine. Bake, covered, at 325° for 1 hour. Remove from oven. Mix together pan sauces with soup. Mix well. Pour over chicken breasts. Bake for 20 minutes more. Garnish with orange slices.
Very elegant and tasty.

Van Fell
Director, Food Services
Gulf Coast Hospital

Aspar Chick au Gratin

Oven: 350° - 30 minutes   **Yield:** 6-8 servings

4 cups bread crumbs
1 cup sharp Cheddar cheese,
    grated
¼ cup butter, melted
1 (10-ounce) package frozen
    asparagus, cooked
¼ cup butter
⅓ cup all-purpose flour

½ teaspoon salt
1 teaspoon pepper
1½ cups chicken broth
1½ cups milk
3 cups chicken, cooked
    and diced

Toss the bread crumbs, cheese and butter lightly. Line a greased 9x13-inch baking dish with ½ bread crumb mixture. Place asparagus over crumb crust. Melt butter in a saucepan; stir in flour. Add salt, pepper, chicken broth and milk. Stir until thickened. Add chicken. Pour over asparagus. Top with remaining crumb mixture. Bake at 350° for 30 minutes.

Jeweldine Chambers

Chicken with Stir-Fry Vegetables

Yield: 2 servings

¼ cup vegetable oil,
    divided
2 chicken breasts, skinned,
    boned and cut into
    bite-sized pieces
1 medium zucchini, sliced
1 medium green pepper,
    cut into strips
1 small onion, cut
    into eighths

1 cup fresh mushrooms,
    sliced
2 tablespoons dry sherry
1 tablespoon cornstarch
3 tablespoons water
1 tablespoon soy sauce
1 cup cooked rice

Pour 3 tablespoons oil in wok or large skillet; heat 2 minutes on medium heat. Add chicken; stir-fry 2-3 minutes until lightly browned. Remove chicken; set aside. Pour remaining oil in wok; heat at medium high for 2 minutes. Add vegetables and sherry. Cook, covered, for 2-3 minutes. Combine cornstarch, water, and soy sauce. Stir well. Add mixture and chicken to vegetables. Reduce heat. Simmer, stirring constantly, until thickened. Serve over rice with additional soy sauce, if desired.

Judy Bishop

Chicken with Chipped Beef

Oven: 350° - 1 hour 30 minutes   **Yield:** 6-8 servings

6-8 **chicken breasts,**
     skinned and boned
6-8 **slices bacon**
  1 **(8-ounce) jar chipped**
     beef
1½ **(10¾-ounce) cans cream**
     of mushroom soup

1 **pint sour cream**
1 **cup white wine**
½ **pound fresh mushrooms,**
   sliced
Paprika
Slivered almonds

Wrap each piece of chicken with slice of bacon. Secure with a toothpick. Lightly grease a 9x13-inch baking dish. Line with chipped beef. Place chicken on top of beef. Combine soup, sour cream, wine and mushrooms. Pour over chicken. Sprinkle with paprika. Bake, uncovered, at 325° for 1 hour. Add almonds. Bake an additional 30 minutes.
Easy. Do Ahead.

Linda Hasty

Cantonese Chicken

Yield: 6 servings

¾ **cup soy sauce**
2 **tablespoons honey**
½ **cup brown sugar,**
   firmly packed
1½ **cups water**
2 **tablespoons ginger**
   root, chopped

3 **cloves garlic, crushed**
¼ **cup green onions,**
   chopped
3 **pounds chicken breasts,**
   skinned and boned
2 **tablespoons cornstarch**
4 **tablespoons water**

Bring soy sauce, honey, brown sugar, water, ginger root, garlic and green onions to a boil. Simmer for 2 minutes. Add chicken. Simmer for 40 minutes or until tender. Remove chicken; cut into pieces. Arrange on a serving platter. Combine cornstarch and water. Add to sauce, stirring constantly, until thickened. Pour sauce over chicken.

Brenda Lawson

Spicy Chicken Pieces

Yield: 4 servings

1 **pound chicken breasts,**
   skinned, boned and cut
   into 1-inch pieces
1½ **cups buttermilk**
3 **tablespoons lemon juice**

1½ **tablespoons Worcestershire**
   All-purpose flour
   Vegetable oil for frying
   Salt to taste

Place chicken in a shallow dish. Combine buttermilk, lemon juice and Worcestershire. Pour over chicken. Refrigerate overnight. Coat each piece, without rinsing, with flour. Fry, uncovered, until brown. Sprinkle with salt while cooking. Drain on paper towels.

Myra Ramsey

Chicken Oregano

Oven: 375° - 1 hour

Yield: 6 servings

2½-3 pounds chicken
    pieces
½ cup olive oil or
    vegetable oil
¼ cup lemon juice
2 teaspoons dried oregano
    leaves

1 teaspoon salt
½ teaspoon pepper
1 clove garlic, chopped
    Lemon slices

Place chicken in an ungreased 9x13-inch baking dish. Mix remaining ingredients, except lemon slices. Pour over chicken. Cook, uncovered, at 375° for 30 minutes, spooning oil mixture over chicken occasionally. Turn chicken .Bake 30 minutes more. Garnish with lemon slices.

Cathy Lacy

Lemon Fried Chicken

Yield: 4-6 servings

1 (2½-3-pound) fryer, cut up
1 teaspoon salt, divided
¾ teaspoon pepper, divided
¼ cup shortening, melted
⅓ cup lemon juice

¼ cup vegetable oil
½ teaspoon sugar
¼ teaspoon paprika
¼ teaspoon prepared mustard
⅛ teaspoon garlic powder

Rinse and pat chicken dry. Season with ½ teaspoon salt and ¼ teaspoon pepper. Brown chicken in melted shortening. Combine lemon juice, oil, sugar, ½ teaspoon salt, ½ teaspoon pepper, paprika, mustard and garlic powder. Pour over chicken. Cover; simmer 40-50 minutes or until tender.

Virginia Spears

Chicken Paprika

Yield: 6 servings

12 chicken pieces
1 tablespoon margarine
1 tablespoon vegetable oil
1 large onion, chopped
2 teaspoons paprika
1½ teaspoons salt
¼ teaspoon black pepper
¼ teaspoon garlic powder

1½ cups tomato juice
3 cups cooked rice
2 tablespoons parsley,
    chopped
½ cup sour cream
2 tablespoons all-purpose
    flour

Brown chicken in margarine and oil in a skillet. Add onion; sauté until tender. Add seasonings and tomato juice. Simmer, covered, for 30 minutes or until fork tender. Toss rice with parsley. Mound on hot serving platter. Arrange chicken on rice. Blend sour cream and flour. Stir into liquid remaining in skillet. Cook until thickened, but do not boil. Pour over chicken.

Nancy Moore

Buttermilk Chicken

Oven: 425° - 1 hour   **Yield:** 6 servings

- 6 chicken breasts, skinned
- 1½ cups buttermilk, divided
- ¾ cup all-purpose flour
- ½ teaspoon salt
- ¼ teaspoon pepper
- ¼ cup margarine
- 1 (10¾-ounce) can cream of mushroom soup
- Parsley

Dip chicken in ½ cup buttermilk; then roll chicken in mixture of flour, salt and pepper. Melt margarine in a 9x13-inch baking dish. Place chicken in dish. Bake, uncovered, at 425° for 30 minutes. Turn chicken. Bake 15 minutes longer. Turn chicken again; pour mixture of 1 cup buttermilk and soup over chicken. Bake 15 minutes longer. Remove chicken to platter. Garnish with parsley. Serve with pan gravy.

Anne Huey

Chicken Boneless

Yield: 4-6 servings

- 1 (8-ounce) package cream cheese
- ½ cup green onions, chopped
- Tarragon leaves
- 6 chicken breasts, skinned and boned
- 12 slices bacon

Roll a tablespoon of cream cheese in the green onion and tarragon leaves. Wrap chicken around the cream cheese. Place 2 slices bacon around chicken. Secure with a toothpick. Cook on a charcoal grill for 20-30 minutes or until tender. *Do ahead and refrigerate.*

David Cannon

Hawaiian Sesame Chicken

Yield: 6 servings

- 1 (2½-3 pound) fryer, cut up
- 1 tablespoon sesame seeds
- 2 tablespoons vegetable oil
- ¼ cup sugar
- 2 tablespoons cornstarch
- ⅛ teaspoon ginger
- 1 (15-ounce) can crushed pineapple, undrained
- 1 cup water
- ⅓ cup soy sauce
- 1 clove garlic, pressed
- Cooked rice

Brown chicken and sesame seeds in oil in large skillet. Combine sugar, cornstarch and ginger in medium saucepan. Mix well. Add pineapple, water, soy sauce and garlic. Cook over medium heat, stirring constantly, until thick and bubbly. Pour sauce over chicken. Cover; simmer 45 minutes or until tender. Serve on rice.

Elly Hobgood

Baked Chicken

Oven: 350° - 1 hour   **Yield:** 8 servings

8 chicken breasts   Garlic salt
¼ cup lemon juice   ½ cup margarine

Wash and dry chicken breasts, leaving skin on breast. Place chicken breasts in a shallow baking dish. Pour lemon juice over chicken. Sprinkle each piece liberally with garlic salt. Put a pat of butter on each piece. Bake, uncovered, at 350° for 1 hour.

Barbara Manous

Chicken with Cherries

Oven: 350° - 1 hour   **Yield:** 6 servings

⅓ cup all-purpose flour   ¼ cup butter or
1½ teaspoons salt   margarine
¼ teaspoon garlic salt   1 (16-ounce) can pitted dark
½ teaspoon paprika   sweet cherries, drained
6 chicken breasts,   1 cup Sauterne or any
    skinned   dry white wine

Combine flour, salt, garlic salt and paprika in a paper bag. Add chicken pieces one at a time; shake. Melt butter in a skillet; brown chicken. Place in a greased 9x13-inch baking dish. Pour cherries over chicken. Pour Sauterne over all. Bake, covered, at 350° for 1 hour or until tender.
Easy.

Cookbook Committee

Chicken Chow Mein

Yield: 6 servings

2 cups cooked chicken,   1 (16-ounce) can mixed
    chopped   Chinese vegetables
2 tablespoons butter or   1 (4-ounce) can mushrooms,
    margarine, melted   sliced and drained
2 cups celery, sliced   2 tablespoons cornstarch
1½ cups onion, sliced   3 tablespoons soy sauce
    Pepper to taste   Cooked rice
1 teaspoon salt
2 cups chicken or
    beef broth

Lightly brown chicken in butter. Add celery, onion, pepper, salt and chicken broth; cook, covered, 5-10 minutes until celery is tender. Add Chinese vegetables and mushrooms; simmer 1-2 minutes. Dissolve cornstarch in soy sauce; add to chicken mixture. Cook, stirring constantly, until slightly thickened. Serve over rice.

Joan Satterfield

Hawaiian Chicken

Oven: 350° - 1 hour 15 minutes   **Yield:** 4-6 servings

¾ cup unsweetened
   pineapple juice
⅓ cup catsup
¼ cup brown sugar,
   firmly packed
¼ cup butter
¼ cup vinegar

2 tablespoons cornstarch
1 teaspoon salt
1 teaspoon chili powder
1 teaspoon soy sauce
½ teaspoon Worcestershire
4-6 chicken pieces

Combine first 10 ingredients in a saucepan. Bring to a boil; cook for 1 minute. Place chicken in a shallow baking dish. Pour sauce over chicken. Bake, covered, at 350° for 45 minutes. Bake, uncovered, for 30 minutes, basting occasionally.

Cathy Conway

Chicken Parmesan

Oven: 350° - 55 minutes   **Yield:** 4-6 servings

2 pounds chicken pieces
¼ cup all-purpose flour
1¼ teaspoons salt
¼ teaspoon pepper
3 tablespoons shortening
1 (14½-ounce) can tomatoes,
   cut up
⅓ cup Heinz 57 sauce

⅓ cup Parmesan cheese,
   grated
1 tablespoon sugar
¼ teaspoon oregano
   leaves
¼ pound Mozzarella cheese,
   cut into strips
Cheddar cheese, grated

Coat chicken with mixture of flour, salt and pepper; brown well in shortening. Place chicken in baking dish. Blend any remaining flour mixture with tomatoes; add Heinz 57 sauce, Parmesan cheese, sugar and oregano. Pour over chicken. Bake, covered, at 350° for 30 minutes. Remove cover; top with cheeses. Bake, uncovered, 25 minutes longer or until chicken is tender. Skim excess fat from sauce.

Janice Ingram

Elegant Chicken Livers

Yield: 4 servings

1 pound chicken livers
1 orange, sliced
¾ cup green seedless
   grapes
White Sauce (page 122)

4 tablespoons brandy
Cooked rice
Artichoke hearts

Batter chicken livers; fry as desired. Remove from pan. Add orange slices and grapes to pan drippings; simmer slightly. Add White Sauce and brandy to pan. Ignite. Arrange livers on bed of rice. Pour sauce over livers. Add artichoke hearts.
Makes an elegant meal in a jiffy.

Eugenia Reid

Broiled Chicken

Oven: Broil - 25 minutes

Yield: 4 servings

1 (2-2½-pound) fryer, cut into pieces
½ cup vegetable oil
3 tablespoons vinegar

¼ teaspoon dry mustard
½ teaspoon salt
¼ teaspoon paprika
½ clove garlic, minced

Place chicken in a shallow baking dish. Combine remaining ingredients to make a marinade. Pour over chicken. Refrigerate at least 1 hour; turn chicken once. Remove from marinade. Place skin side down on broiler rack. Broil 4-5 inches from heat for 12 minutes, basting often with marinade. Turn; broil 15 minutes or until tender, continuing to baste.

Betty McDaniel

Jack's Barbecue Chicken

Yield: 10-12 servings

10-12 chicken breasts
5 ounces chicken drippings, including fat
1 medium onion, finely chopped
3 tablespoons butter
2 cups catsup
1½ cups red wine

1½-2 tablespoons black pepper
4 ounces Worcestershire
1 lemon, sliced and seeded
Pinch of cayenne pepper (optional)
Salt to taste

Parboil chicken breasts inside zip-lock bag in boiling water for 30 minutes. Remove 5 ounces chicken drippings from bag; set aside. Sauté the onion in butter until translucent. Add catsup, wine, pepper, Worcestershire, lemon and seasonings. Stir in chicken drippings. Simmer 20-30 minutes. Adjust seasonings to taste. Cook chicken over grill 15-20 minutes or until meat is done, basting with sauce.
Especially good when grilled over Mesquite wood.

Jack Goodwin

Easy Chicken Delight

Oven: 350° - 2 hours

Yield: 6 servings

1 (8-ounce) jar apricot or peach preserves
1 (8-ounce) bottle Russian dressing

1 package dry onion soup mix
6 chicken breasts

Mix preserves, dressing and soup mix. Pour over chicken. Bake, covered, at 350° for 2 hours or 400° for 1½ hours.
Easy, but so good.

Carole Haley

Overnight Chicken Sandwich

Oven: 325° - 1 hour　　　　　　**Yield:** 6 servings

12　slices white bread,
　　crusts removed
2　tablespoons butter
1　cup sharp Cheddar
　　cheese, grated
1　cup cooked chicken,
　　chopped
6　slices sandwich ham
　　(optional)

4　eggs, beaten
3　cups milk
　　Salt and pepper to taste
1　(10¾-ounce) can cream
　　of mushroom soup
1　(2-ounce) jar pimiento
　　Hard-cooked eggs,
　　chopped (optional)

Place 6 slices buttered bread into a greased 9x13-inch baking dish. Sprinkle with grated cheese, chicken, then slice of ham, if desired. Top with remaining 6 slices buttered bread. Blend eggs, milk, salt and pepper. Pour over sandwiches. Cover tightly. Refrigerate overnight. Bake, uncovered, at 325° for 1 hour. Combine soup and pimiento; heat. Pour a little sauce over each sandwich when serving. Garnish with eggs, if desired.
This recipe is excellent for brunches and luncheons. Easy, do ahead recipe.

Judy Bishop

Chicken and Wild Rice

Oven: 350° - 50 minutes　　　　**Yield:** 6-8 servings

1　(3-pound) fryer
1　large onion, thinly
　　sliced and separated
　　into rings
½　teaspoon salt
1　teaspoon curry powder
⅛　teaspoon pepper
1　cup cooking sherry
1　(6-ounce) package long
　　grain and wild rice
　　mix

2　tablespoons butter or
　　margarine
½　pound fresh mushrooms,
　　sliced
1　(10¾-ounce) can cream
　　of mushroom soup
1　cup sour cream
　　Slivered almonds (optional)

Place chicken, onion, salt, curry powder, pepper and sherry in a large pan; add enough water to cover chicken. Heat to boiling; cover. Reduce heat. Simmer 1 hour. Remove chicken; let cool. Bone chicken and dice meat. Reserve 2½ cups chicken broth. Cook rice according to package directions, using reserved chicken broth for liquid. Set aside. Melt butter in a small skillet; add mushrooms; cook until tender. Place mushrooms and chicken in a large bowl. Stir in rice, soup, and sour cream, mixing well. Spoon mixture into a greased 13x9-inch baking dish. Top with almonds, if desired. Bake, covered, at 350° for 50 minutes.
This freezes well.

Dot Patterson

Chicken Valenciana

Yield: 12-14 servings

1 (5-pound) hen
3 large onions, chopped
  medium coarse
  (about 2 cups)
2 cups celery, chopped
  medium coarse
1 green pepper, chopped
  medium coarse
½ cup butter
2 cups chicken stock

1 tablespoon Worcestershire
1 tablespoon horseradish
1 (28-ounce) can tomatoes
1 (6-ounce) can tomato
  paste
Salt and pepper to taste
1½ cups raw rice,
  cooked until tender
1 (4-ounce) can mushrooms
1 (16-ounce) can early peas

Boil hen. Season stock highly; reserve stock. Set chicken aside to cool. Cook onion, celery and green pepper in butter until tender. Add 2 cups chicken stock. Cook 15 minutes. Add Worcestershire and horseradish. Add tomatoes and paste. Simmer until tomatoes have cooked to pieces and a thick Creole sauce is formed. Thirty minutes before serving, add chicken which has been cut into large pieces, rice and mushrooms. Add more stock if necessary. Cook until rice absorbs liquid. Add peas 10 minutes before serving.
Freezes well.

Martha Nichols

Chicken Enchiladas

Oven: 450° - 8 minutes

Yield: 6-8 servings

3½ cups sour cream,
  divided
2 cups cooked chicken,
  broken into pieces
2 (4-ounce) cans mushrooms,
  stems and pieces,
  drained
1 (4-ounce) can green
  chilies, drained

⅓ cup onion flakes
1 teaspoon chili powder
½ teaspoon salt
½ teaspoon garlic powder
¼ teaspoon pepper
12 flour tortillas
⅓ pound Cheddar cheese,
  shredded

Spread 1 cup sour cream in bottom of 9x13-inch baking dish. Mix chicken, mushrooms, chiles, onion flakes, chili powder, salt, garlic powder, pepper and ½ cup sour cream in a saucepan. Cook over low heat until hot. To soften tortillas: either put salad oil in pan, frying tortilla for 1 second on each side or dip each tortilla in hot chicken broth. Put ¼ cup chicken mixture in each tortilla. Roll and place in pan. Spread top with remainder of sour cream. Sprinkle with Cheddar cheese. Bake at 450° for 8 minutes or until cheese is melted.

Janis Farr

Chicken and Mushroom Gravy

Oven: 350° - 1 hour

Yield: 10 servings

10 chicken breasts, skinned
Salt and pepper to taste
2 (10¾-ounce) cans cream of mushroom soup
2 soup cans milk

2 (4½-ounce) jars mushrooms, sliced
1 medium onion, sliced
Butter

Place chicken breasts in a large shallow baking dish. Sprinkle with salt and pepper. Combine soup and milk; pour over chicken. Place mushrooms and onions over breasts. Dot each breast with butter. Bake, covered, at 350° for 1 hour or until tender.

Beverly Madden

Chicken Tetrazzini

Oven: 350° - 30-45 minutes

Yield: 10-12 servings

1 (4-pound) hen
1 (16-ounce) package spaghetti
4 (10¾-ounce) cans mushroom soup
3 tablespoons butter
1 cup celery, chopped

4 small garlic cloves, minced
4 small onions, chopped
½ cup slivered almonds
Grated Cheddar cheese

Cover hen with water; boil until tender. Reserve broth. Cut chicken into bite-sized pieces; set aside. Cook spaghetti in chicken broth. Drain. Melt butter; sauté celery, garlic and onion. Mix all ingredients. Place in a greased 3-quart baking dish. Sprinkle with cheese. Bake at 350° for 30-45 minutes.

Virginia Jones

Oven-Baked Chicken Salad

Oven: 450° - 12 minutes

Yield: 6 servings

2 cups cooked chicken, cubed
2 cups celery, diced
1 cup bread cubes, toasted
½ cup almonds, toasted
2 teaspoons onion, grated
½ teaspoon salt

1 cup mayonnaise
2 tablespoons lemon juice
1 cup bread crumbs
½ cup Cheddar cheese, grated

Combine chicken, celery, bread cubes, almonds, salt and onions. Add mayonnaise and lemon juice. Mix well. Pile lightly in individual baking dishes. Sprinkle with bread crumbs and Cheddar cheese. Bake at 450° for 12 minutes.

Judy McClure

First Place Chicken Casserole

Oven: 350° - 40-45 minutes   **Yield:** 8 servings

2-3 cups chicken,
     cooked and diced
  4 hard-cooked eggs,
     finely chopped
  2 cups cooked rice
1½ cups celery, chopped
  1 small onion, chopped
  1 cup mayonnaise

2 (10¾-ounce) cans cream
     of mushroom soup
1 (3-ounce) package slivered
     almonds
1 teaspoon salt
2 tablespoons lemon juice
1 cup bread crumbs
2 tablespoons margarine

Combine all ingredients, except bread crumbs and margarine. Place mixture into a greased 9x13-inch baking dish. Brown bread crumbs lightly in margarine. Sprinkle over casserole. Refrigerate overnight. Remove from refrigerator 1 hour before cooking. Bake at 350° for 40-45 minutes.

Doris Thacker

Chicken Pot Pie

Oven: 400° - 40 minutes   **Yield:** 6 servings

  1 cup onion, chopped
  1 cup celery, chopped
  1 cup carrot, chopped
⅓ cup butter or
     margarine, melted
½ cup all-purpose flour
2½ cups chicken broth
1½ cups half and half

1 teaspoon salt
¼ teaspoon pepper
1 (8½-ounce) can early
     peas, drained
4 cups cooked chicken,
     chopped
Basic Pastry
Parsley (optional)

Sauté onion, celery and carrot in butter over low heat for 10 minutes. Add flour, stirring well. Cook 1 minute, stirring constantly. Combine broth and half and half; gradually stir into sautéed mixture. Cook over medium heat, stirring constantly, until thickened and bubbly. Add salt, pepper, chicken and peas; stir gently. Pour mixture into a shallow 2½-quart baking dish. Top with pastry; cut slits to allow steam to escape. Bake at 400° for 40 minutes or until golden brown. Garnish with parsley, if desired.

Basic Pastry

  1 cup all-purpose flour
½ teaspoon salt
⅓ cup + 1 tablespoon
     shortening

2-3 tablespoons cold water

Combine flour and salt; cut in shortening until mixture resembles coarse meal. Sprinkle cold water evenly over surface; stir with fork until all dry ingredients are moistened. Shape into a ball; chill. Roll pastry to fit baking dish.

Susan Roach
Jackson, Georgia

Curried Chicken Casserole

Oven: 350° - 30 minutes   **Yield:** 6-8 servings

2 (10¾-ounce) cans cream
   of chicken soup
1 cup mayonnaise
1 teaspoon lemon juice
½ teaspoon curry powder
   Salt and pepper to taste

2 (10-ounce) packages frozen
   chopped broccoli, cooked
   and drained
4 cups chicken, cooked
   and diced
   Buttered bread crumbs

Combine chicken soup, mayonnaise, lemon juice, curry powder, salt and pepper; mix well. Layer half of broccoli, chicken and soup mixture in a lightly greased shallow baking dish. Repeat layers. Sprinkle with buttered bread crumbs. Bake at 350° for 30 minutes.

Elly Hobgood

Chicken Casserole

Oven: 350° - 30 minutes   **Yield:** 4-6 servings

4 chicken breasts, cooked
   and diced, reserve broth
1½-2 cups chicken broth
1 (10¾-ounce) can cream
   of chicken soup

1 (10¾-ounce) can cream
   of celery soup
1 (8-ounce) package
   cornbread stuffing mix

Combine chicken, broth and soups. Pour into a greased 1½-quart baking dish. Top with stuffing mix. Bake at 350° for 30 minutes or until browned.

Sara Lathem

Chicken Rotel

Oven: 350° - 30-45 minutes   **Yield:** 10-12 servings

2 (3-pound) fryers or
   equivalent pieces
1 (8-ounce) package vermicelli
6 cups chicken broth
1 pound Velveeta cheese,
   chopped or sliced
1 medium onion, chopped
2 green peppers, chopped
½ cup butter

1 (10-ounce) can Rotel
   tomatoes
1 (8-ounce) can English
   peas, drained
1 cup mushrooms, chopped
¼ cup sherry
   Grated Cheddar cheese
   or crushed potato chips
   Paprika

Boil chicken until tender; reserve broth. Chop chicken; set aside. Boil vermicelli in 6 cups broth according to package directions. Do not drain. Add cheese; mix until melted. Sauté onion and peppers in butter. Add Rotel tomatoes, peas and mushrooms. Add to cheese mixture, along with chicken and sherry. Pour into a greased 9x13-inch baking dish. Top with cheese or crushed potato chips and paprika. Bake at 350° for 30-45 minutes or until bubbly.

Pat Contino

Chicken-Green Noodle Casserole

Oven: 350° - 20 minutes   **Yield:** 15 servings

1 hen or 2 fryers
½ cup butter or
  margarine
1 cup celery, chopped
1 cup green pepper,
  chopped
1 cup onion, chopped
1 (16-ounce) package
  Velveeta cheese, cut
  into pieces

1 (10¾-ounce) can cream
  of mushroom soup
1 (4-ounce) can mushrooms,
  sliced
1 (2-ounce) jar pimiento-
  stuffed olives, chopped
1 (12-ounce) package green
  spinach noodles
Cheese crackers, crushed

Boil chicken in water to cover until tender. Reserve stock. Cut chicken in large-sized pieces. Set aside. Melt butter; sauté celery, green pepper and onion. Add cheese; stir until melted and smooth. Add soup, mushrooms and olives. Cook noodles in chicken broth; drain, saving stock. Combine chicken, sauce and noodles. Mixture should be soupy. If too thick, add some stock. Pour into a large baking dish. Top with crackers and some olives slices. Bake at 350° for 20 minutes or until hot and bubbly.
Will keep uncooked in refrigerator for several days. Freezes well.

Lane Towers

Chicken á la King

Yield: 4-6 servings

3 tablespoons butter
5 tablespoons all-purpose
  flour
1 cup chicken broth
1 cup heavy cream
1 teaspoon salt
¼ teaspoon paprika
2 cups cooked chicken,
  diced
1 cup fresh mushrooms,
  sliced and sautéed
  in butter

⅓ cup ripe olives,
  sliced
2 tablespoons pimiento,
  diced
1 teaspoon lemon juice
Cooked rice or
  chow mein noodles

Melt butter in a saucepan. Add flour, mixing to a smooth paste. Add broth, cream, salt and paprika. Cook over low heat until thickened, stirring constantly. Add chicken, mushrooms, olives, pimiento and lemon juice. Heat for 5 minutes. Serve over rice or chow mein noodles.
Easy; do ahead.

Wanda Roach

Crunchy Chicken'n Rice Bake

Oven: 350° - 40 minutes **Yield:** 5-6 servings

1 (10¾-ounce) can cream
   of mushroom soup
2 cups milk
2 cups chicken, cooked
   and diced
1 cup rice, uncooked
1 (16-ounce) can cut
   green beans, drained

1 (4½-ounce) jar sliced
   mushrooms, drained
2 tablespoons pimiento,
   chopped
1 cup Cheddar cheese,
   grated, divided
1 (2.8-ounce) can French
   fried onions, divided

Combine soup and milk; heat just to boiling, stirring constantly. Remove from heat. Stir in chicken, rice, beans, mushrooms, pimiento, ½ cup cheese and ½ can French fried onions. Pour into a greased 2-quart baking dish. Stir. Bake, covered, at 350° for 40 minutes. Top with remaining cheese and onions. Return to oven, uncovered, for 5-10 minutes, until cheese is bubbly.

Louise Roach

Chicken Pie

Oven: 350° - 1 hour **Yield:** 4-6 servings

1 (2½-3 pound) fryer
1 (10¾-ounce) can cream
   of celery soup
1¾ cups chicken broth

Salt and pepper to taste
1 cup self-rising flour
¾ cup milk
½ cup margarine, melted

Boil chicken in enough water to cover until tender. Reserve broth. Chop chicken. Place in a greased 9x13-inch baking dish. Spread soup over chicken. Pour broth over soup. Sprinkle with salt and pepper to taste. Mix flour, milk and margarine; pour over chicken mixture. Bake, uncovered, at 350° for 1 hour.

Tissie Jones

Hot Chicken Salad

Oven: 325° - 25 minutes **Yield:** 6-8 servings

2 cups chicken, cooked and
   diced
1 cup celery, diced
½ cup slivered almonds
½ teaspoon salt
2 tablespoons onions,
   grated
1 small green pepper,
   chopped

½ cup mayonnaise
2 teaspoons pimiento,
   chopped
2 teaspoons lemon juice
1 (10¾-ounce) can cream
   of chicken soup
½ cup sharp Cheddar
   cheese, grated

Combine all ingredients, except cheese. Pour into a greased 2-quart baking dish. Top with cheese. Bake at 325° for 25 minutes.
Easy. May do ahead of time and refrigerate.

Nancy Stackhouse

Chicken Curry

Yield: 8 servings

4 large chicken breasts,
   skinned and boned
½ cup butter
2 medium onions, finely
   chopped
2 large cloves garlic,
   finely minced
2 large apples, peeled
   and chopped
2 cups celery, chopped
6 tablespoons curry
2 teaspoons ginger
8 tablespoons all-purpose
   flour
¼ cup brown sugar,
   firmly packed

2 cups cream
1 (8½-ounce) can pineapple
   chunks, undrained
5 cups chicken broth
2 tablespoons lemon juice
1 teaspoon monosodium
   glutamate
1 teaspoon salt
½ teaspoon black pepper
4 tablespoons Major Grey's
   chutney
½ cup seedless raisins
Condiments

Cut chicken breasts into bite-sized chunks. Melt butter in large cooking pan. Sauté the onions, garlic and apples until soft, but not browned. Add celery. Blend curry, ginger, flour and brown sugar. Add mixture to pan gradually, stirring thoroughly. Mix cream, pineapple, chicken broth and lemon juice. Add to mixture, cooking until thickened. Add monosodium glutamate, salt, pepper, chicken, chutney and raisins. Mix thoroughly. Cook, covered, for about 20 minutes. Serve with Condiments.

Condiments

Crisp fried bacon,
   chopped
Hard-cooked eggs,
   chopped
Green onions, chopped
Grated coconut

Whole or crushed peanuts
Raisins
Green pepper, chopped
Macadamia nuts
Candied ginger

Arrange condiments to provide color, each in its own separate bowl. Serve the curry on white rice or alongside it or layer condiments on top of the curry or around it, as your taste dictates.

Bob Stubbs

Saumon Poche Sauce St. Jacques

Yield: 6-8 servings

10 tablespoons unsalted
  butter, divided
3 shallots, finely
  chopped
½ pound bay scallops
1 cup dry white wine
  Salt and freshly ground
  pepper to taste

2 cups whipping cream
10-15 mushrooms, sliced
¼ pound small shrimp,
  cooked and shelled
2-3 cups Court Bouillon
6-8 (6-ounce) salmon
  fillets, skinned
  and boned

Melt 2 tablespoons butter in 10-inch skillet over medium heat. Add shallots; stir until softened. Add scallops, wine, salt and pepper; cook 2-3 minutes. Remove scallops from skillet using slotted spoon; set aside. Cook remaining liquid over medium-high heat until reduced by half. Reduce heat to medium; add cream. Cook, stirring until sauce is thickened, about 7-10 minutes. Whisk in 6 tablespoons butter, 1 tablespoon at a time. Remove sauce from heat; set aside and keep warm. Melt remaining 2 tablespoons butter in large skillet over medium-high heat; add mushrooms; sauté until cooked and liquid has evaporated, about 5 minutes. Blend into sauce. Slice reserved scallops; add to sauce with shrimp, mixing well. Bring Court Bouillon to simmer in a large skillet over high heat. Reduce heat to low; add salmon and poach until cooked, 6-7 minutes. Drain fillets well. Transfer to warmed plates. Reheat scallop mixture. Spoon over fillets. Serve immediately.

A long process, but worth every minute of effort. A seafood lover's delight.

Court Bouillon

6 cups water
3 small onions, finely
  chopped
3 carrots, finely chopped
3 celery stalks, finely
  chopped

Bouquet garni (1 bay leaf,
  1 parsley sprig, 1 teaspoon
  dried thyme, 2 whole
  peppercorns)
1 cup dry white wine
  Salt to taste

Combine water, vegetables and bouquet garni in saucepan. Bring to simmer over medium heat. Simmer, uncovered, 20 minutes. Add wine and salt; continue simmering until reduced to 3 cups. Remove from heat; strain before using.
Can be made ahead. Refrigerate.

Wanda Roach

Salmon Loaf with White Sauce

Oven: 350° -30 minutes   **Yield:** 4-6 servings

2 cups salmon, flaked
½ cup bread crumbs
¼ cup butter
2 eggs
Salt and pepper to taste
1 tablespoon lemon juice

1 tablespoon green pepper, minced
1 tablespoon onion, minced
1 tablespoon Worcestershire
White Sauce

Combine all ingredients, mixing well. Pour into a greased 9x5-inch loaf pan. Bake at 350° for 30 minutes. Pour White Sauce over salmon loaf. Serve.

White Sauce

2 tablespoons butter
2 tablespoons all-purpose flour

1 cup milk
Salt and pepper to taste

Combine all ingredients. Cook 2 minutes, or until thickened.

Renay Carnes

Crispy Baked Fillets

Oven: 500° - 10 minutes   **Yield:** 4 servings

⅓ cup cornflake crumbs, crushed
Salt and pepper to taste

1 pound fish fillets
2 tablespoons vegetable oil

Mix crumbs, salt and pepper. Dip fillets in oil, then in crumb mixture. Place in a shallow baking pan. Bake at 500° for 10 minutes.
Low calorie taste of deep frying.

Christi Kook

Fish and Chips

Oven: 500° - 12-15 minutes   **Yield:** 6 servings

2 pounds frozen fish fillets, thawed
¼ cup milk
1 cup potato chips, crushed

¼ cup Parmesan cheese, grated
½ teaspoon thyme

Dip fillets in milk, then in mixture of remaining ingredients. Place in buttered baking dish; sprinkle with extra chips. Place foil loosely over top to prevent chips burning. Remove foil during the last few minutes of cooking time. Bake at 500° for 12-15 minutes.

Joan McFather

Hawaiian Fish Fillets

Oven: 350° - 20-25 minutes　　　　**Yield:** 4-6 servings

　1　**pound fish fillets**
　½　**cup pineapple tidbits,**
　　　drained
　2　**tablespoons honey**

　1　**tablespoon Worcestershire**
　¼　**cup catsup**
　½　**teaspoon salt**

Arrange fillets in shallow baking dish; top with pineapple. Combine honey, Worcestershire, catsup and salt. Pour over fish. Bake, uncovered, at 350° for 20-25 minutes, or until fish flakes easily.

Julia Dennis

Tuna Casserole

Oven: 350° - 25-30 minutes　　　　**Yield:** 4-6 servings

　¼　**cup shortening**
　⅓　**cup onion, chopped**
　2　**tablespoons green pepper,**
　　　chopped
　1　**(11-ounce) can Cheddar**
　　　cheese soup
　½　**cup milk**
　1　**tablespoon pimiento**

　1　**teaspoon salt**
　⅛　**teaspoon pepper**
　1　**(7-ounce) can tuna,**
　　　drained
　4　**ounces noodles, cooked**
　　　and drained
　½　**cup cracker or**
　　　bread crumbs

Melt shortening in skillet. Brown onion and green pepper. Combine with remaining ingredients except crumbs. Pour in a greased 1½-quart baking dish. Top with crumbs. Bake at 350° for 25-30 minutes.

Jeweldine Chambers

Oyster Supreme

Oven: 300° - 1 hour　　　　**Yield:** 8 servings

　1　**pint oysters,**
　　　fresh or frozen
　6　**slices white bread**
　2　**teaspoons butter**
　2　**eggs, beaten**
　½　**pound Longhorn cheese,**
　　　grated

　½　**teaspoon black pepper**
　1　**teaspoon salt**
1½　**cups milk**
　½　**teaspoon paprika**

Drain oysters, reserving liquid. Spread bread with butter; tear bread into small pieces. Combine eggs, bread, oysters, cheese, pepper and salt in baking dish. Pour milk and oyster liquid over all; stir lightly. Sprinkle with paprika. Bake, covered, at 300° for 1 hour.
Delicious with turkey and dressing.

Randall Bagwell

Creamed Oysters

Yield: 4-6 servings

½ cup onion, chopped
½ cup celery, chopped
¼ cup margarine or
   butter
1 pint fresh oysters,
   undrained
2 tablespoons all-purpose
   flour
1 teaspoon prepared mustard

1 teaspoon anchovy paste
½ teaspoon salt
⅛ teaspoon lemon pepper
   seasoning
   Dash of cayenne
1 cup light cream
1 tablespoon dry sherry
4 English muffins,
   split and toasted

Cook onion and celery in butter or margarine until tender. Add undrained oysters. Cook until edges curl. Stir in flour, mustard, anchovy paste, salt, lemon pepper and cayenne. Add cream. Cook until bubbly. Stir in sherry; heat thoroughly. Serve over muffins.

Gus White

Cedar Creek Boiled Shrimp

Yield: 4 servings

1 gallon water
⅓ cup salt
⅓ cup prepared mustard
1 bay leaf

1 clove garlic
2 pounds fresh shrimp
   in shells

Bring first 5 ingredients to boil; add as many shrimp as will comfortably fit into container. Maintain the boil until shrimp float to top, approximately 2 minutes. Immediately plunge shrimp into ice water to stop cooking process. Chill and eat with favorite cocktail sauce.
Several batches may be done with same boiling mixture. Be careful when bringing mixture to boil; it foams up and over quickly!

Ed McFather

Marinated Shrimp, Cloister Style

Yield: 6-8 servings

3 cups creamy French
   dressing
2 cups onions, minced
1 cup green pepper,
   minced
   Juice of 1 lemon
2 tablespoons mustard

2 tablespoons Worcestershire
¼ cup chopped fresh or
   dehydrated chives
   Salt and white pepper
   to taste
2 pounds cooked shrimp,
   shelled and deveined

Mix all ingredients, except shrimp in mixing bowl. Add shrimp. Marinate for several hours in refrigerator.

Ann Ruppel

Fried Shrimp

1 cup all-purpose flour
¼ cup cornstarch
⅛ cup corn meal
¼ teaspoon baking powder
½ teaspoon salt
1 egg, beaten

½ cup water
¼ cup milk
1 quart shrimp, peeled
  and deveined
Vegetable oil

Combine all ingredients except shrimp. Add shrimp. Mix gently. Fry in hot oil.

Debbie Perry

Shrimp Rolls

Yield: 12-15 rolls

Crêpes

1 cup all-purpose flour
1 teaspoon salt

3 eggs, beaten
1 cup water

Mix all ingredients until smooth. Make crêpes (about 12-15) using a crêpe pan. *Egg roll wrappers can be used instead of crêpes.*

Filling

1 stalk celery, shredded
1 carrot, shredded
1 small onion, shredded
  Bean sprouts to taste
1 teaspoon sugar
½-1 cup cooked chicken,
  chopped

½-1 cup cooked shrimp,
  chopped
Salt and pepper to taste
Soy sauce to taste
Vegetable oil

Combine all ingredients except oil. Place small amount in center of each crêpe. Fold sides in and roll. Fry in oil on both sides until browned. Serve with Hot Mustard Sauce or Sweet and Sour Sauce.

Hot Mustard Sauce

3 tablespoons dry mustard

2 tablespoons hot water

Mix. Let stand at least 10 minutes. Yield: ¼ cup.

Sweet and Sour Sauce

½ cup vinegar
½ cup water
¼ cup brown sugar,
  firmly packed

¼ cup sugar
¼ cup cornstarch
½ cup pineapple juice

Combine vinegar, water and sugars. Bring to a boil. Combine cornstarch and pineapple juice, blending well. Add to sugar mixture. Cook, stirring constantly, until thick. Yield: ¼ cup.

Ruth Gramling

Shrimp and Crabmeat Medley

Oven: 350° - 30 minutes   **Yield:** 8 servings

1 green pepper, chopped
1 small onion, grated
1 cup celery, chopped
1 pound flaked crabmeat
2 pounds cooked shrimp,
    shelled and deveined
½ teaspoon salt

Pepper to taste
2 teaspoons Worcestershire
1 cup mayonnaise
Almonds (optional)
Water chestnuts (optional)
1 cup bread crumbs,
    buttered

Combine all ingredients, except bread crumbs. Place in individual sea shells or in 1 large baking dish. Sprinkle with buttered bread crumbs. Bake at 350° for 30 minutes.
Delicious and easy!

Ann Cullens

Shrimp and Crabmeat Casserole

Oven: 325° - 30 minutes   **Yield:** 6 servings

1 (6-ounce) package long
    grain and wild
    rice mix
3 tablespoons onion, diced
½ cup green pepper,
    chopped
½ cup celery, chopped
2 tablespoons butter or
    margarine, melted

1 (6-ounce) can crabmeat,
    drained and flaked
2 (4½-ounce) cans shrimp,
    drained
1 (10¾-ounce) can cream
    of mushroom soup
1 (2-ounce) jar diced
    pimiento, drained
1 tablespoon lemon juice

Prepare rice according to package directions. Sauté onion, pepper and celery in butter until tender. Combine rice, sautéed vegetables and remaining ingredients. Mix well. Spoon mixture into a greased 2-quart baking dish. Bake at 325° for 30 minutes

James Coleman

Shrimp Scampi

                                          Yield: 4 servings

¼ cup butter, melted
2 tablespoons olive oil
24 jumbo shrimp,
    shelled and deveined
3 cloves garlic, crushed
2 tablespoons parsley,
    chopped

2 tablespoons dry white
    wine
1 tablespoon lemon juice
    Salt and pepper to taste

Heat butter and oil in large skillet; add shrimp. Sauté on both sides about 5 minutes until done. Pour off pan drippings into small pan. Add remaining ingredients. Cook over high heat for 1 minute. Pour sauce over shrimp. Serve.

Donna Priestley

Fettucine with Shrimp in Garlic Butter

Yield: 6 servings

Shrimp and Noodle Mixture

4 tablespoons unsalted butter
2 tablespoons olive oil
1 pound medium shrimp,
   peeled and deveined
½ cup dry white wine
1 (12-ounce) package
   fettucini noodles

Garlic Butter
3-4 tablespoons heavy
   cream
⅔ cup Parmesan cheese,
   or more if desired
⅔ cup parsley, chopped
Salt and pepper to taste

Melt butter and olive oil until hot, but not burning, in a medium skillet. Add shrimp and turn while cooking until shrimp become pink and curl up, approximately 2-3 minutes. Add white wine; cook 2 minutes more. Set aside. Cook the fettucine noodles in 4-5 quarts of boiling water to which 2½ tablespoons salt have been added. Cook until just tender. Remove and drain well. Place in large bowl; toss with shrimp and wine mixture. Stir in the Garlic Butter. Mix well until all butter has melted. Add the heavy cream. Stir in the Parmesan cheese and the parsley. Toss well. Adjust salt and pepper to taste. Serve immediately with additional Parmesan cheese, if desired.

Garlic Butter

¾ cup unsalted butter,
   softened
2 teaspoons garlic, finely
   chopped
3 tablespoons shallots,
   finely chopped

½ cup parsley, chopped
⅛ teaspoon salt
   Fresh ground pepper
   to taste

Mix all ingredients in a bowl.

Anne Huey

Cheese Shrimp Luncheon Casserole

Oven: 350° - 25 minutes

Yield: 4 servings

¼ pound fresh mushrooms,
   sliced
2 tablespoons butter or
   margarine
1 pound cooked shrimp,
   shelled and deveined
1½ cups cooked rice
1½ cups Cheddar cheese,
   grated

½ cup cream or half
   and half
½ teaspoon Worcestershire
2 tablespoons catsup
½ teaspoon salt
   Dash of pepper

Sauté mushrooms in butter until tender. Mix lightly with shrimp, rice and cheese. Combine cream, Worcestershire, catsup and seasonings. Add to shrimp mixture. Pour into lightly greased 1½-quart baking dish. Bake at 350° for approximately 25 minutes.
Can be refrigerated for baking the next day.

Grace Hyatt

Shrimp and Artichoke Casserole

Yield: 8 servings

Cedar Creek Shrimp Boil
(page 190)

2 pounds fresh shrimp,
shelled and deveined

Bring Cedar Creek Shrimp Boil to a boil; add shrimp; cook 1 minute. Plunge into cold water to stop cooking process. Drain after 2-3 minutes.

Sauce

3 tablespoons butter
3 tablespoons all-purpose
flour
2 cups warm milk or
2 cups half and half
for richer sauce
1 teaspoon salt
¼ teaspoon white pepper
3 tablespoons sherry
1 (14-ounce) can artichoke
hearts, drained and
quartered

1 pound fresh mushrooms,
sliced and quartered
and sautéed briefly
in butter
4 tablespoons Parmesan
cheese, grated
⅛ teaspoon paprika

Melt butter in a skillet over low heat. Add flour; blend with wire whisk. Slowly stir in heated milk. Add salt and pepper. Cook and stir until sauce is smooth and boiling. Remove from heat. Add sherry. Place artichoke hearts in a buttered 9x13-inch baking dish. Scatter shrimp and mushrooms over hearts. Cover all with sauce. Sprinkle with Parmesan and paprika. Bake at 350° for 30 minutes or until sauce bubbles.

May be prepared day before and kept refrigerated. Especially good with saffron rice and salad.

Joan McFather

Shrimp Stroganoff

Yield: 4-6 servings

3 tablespoons butter
½ cup onion, chopped
1 small clove garlic,
minced
¼ cup all-purpose flour
1 teaspoon salt
½ teaspoon dill weed
1 (10½-ounce) can beef broth

1 (2-ounce) can mushrooms,
sliced
2 cups cooked shrimp,
shelled and deveined
1 cup yogurt, at room
temperature
Cooked rice or noodles

Melt butter in a saucepan on low heat. Add onion and garlic. Sauté until onion is tender. Stir in flour, salt and dill weed. Remove from heat; stir in beef broth and mushrooms gradually. Cook over medium heat, stirring constantly, until thickened. Add shrimp. Cook over low heat for 5-10 minutes. Stir in yogurt, heat but do not boil. Serve shrimp mixture over rice or noodles.

Ann Hopkins

Shrimp Supreme

Yield: 4 servings

3 tablespoons butter
2 (7-ounce) packages frozen
    shrimp or 1 pound cooked
    fresh shrimp, shelled
    and deveined
½ pound fresh mushrooms,
    sliced

¼ cup butter
¼ cup all-purpose flour
3 tablespoons sherry
¼ teaspoon dry mustard
2 cups half and half
¼ cup Parmesan cheese
   Cooked rice

Melt butter in skillet. Sauté shrimp and mushrooms for 5 minutes. Drain and set aside. Melt butter; stir in flour. Add sherry and dry mustard; stir in half and half. Cook until thickened, stirring constantly. Add shrimp, mushrooms and Parmesan cheese. Heat thoroughly. Serve over rice.

Wanda Roach

Sourdough Shrimp Casserole

Oven: 350° - 25-30 minutes

Yield: 6-8 servings

6 slices sourdough bread
1 pound cooked shrimp,
    shelled and deveined
½ pound old English or
    sharp Cheddar cheese,
    cut into cubes

¼ cup butter, melted
3 eggs, beaten
½ teaspoon dry mustard
   Salt to taste
1 pint milk

Break bread into cubes. Combine bread cubes, shrimp and cheese; toss lightly. Place in a buttered 2-quart baking dish. Pour butter over all. Mix eggs, dry mustard, salt and milk. Pour over shrimp mixture. Refrigerate 3 hours or overnight. Bake, covered, at 350° for 25-30 minutes.

Anne Harris

Linguini with Clam Sauce

Yield: 4 servings

1 large onion, chopped
3 cloves garlic, minced
¼ cup margarine
¼ cup olive oil
1 cup parsley, minced
½ cup dry white wine
⅛ teaspoon oregano

2 (6½-ounce) cans chopped
    clams with juice
6 ounces mushrooms, sliced
   Salt and pepper to taste
8 ounces linguine,
    cooked and drained
¼ cup Romano cheese

Sauté onion and garlic in margarine and oil until tender. Stir in parsley, oregano, wine, clams with juice and mushrooms. Simmer, uncovered, for 5 minutes. Season with salt and pepper. Serve over hot linguine. Sprinkle with Romano cheese.
Quick, easy, low-calorie - 384 calories per serving.

Ann Fincher

Scallops Parisienne Duchess

Oven: Broil - 5-10 minutes   **Yield:** 4-6 servings

1 pound scallops, cut
   in bite-sized pieces
²/₃ cup dry white wine
¹/₃ cup water
¼ teaspoon salt
Dash of white pepper
2 tablespoons shallots,
   chopped
1 bay leaf
1 celery leaf
2 sprigs parsley
2½ tablespoons sweet butter

Juice of 1 small lemon
½ pound fresh mushrooms,
   sliced
2 tablespoons butter
4 tablespoons all-purpose
   flour
½ cup milk
2 egg yolks
¹/₃ cup heavy cream
Potato Duchess
5 tablespoons Gruyére
   cheese, grated

Combine wine, water, salt and pepper. Tie the next 4 ingredients in cheese-cloth. Add to liquid. Simmer, uncovered, for 10 minutes. Add scallops, and, if necessary, enough water to cover them. Simmer, covered, for about 5 minutes. Set aside. Melt 2½ tablespoons sweet butter. Add lemon juice and mushrooms. Simmer, covered with buttered waxed paper, for about 4-5 minutes, shaking once or twice. Strain liquid into scallop liquid. Set mushrooms aside. Strain mushroom-scallop liquid into non-aluminum pan. Reduce, by boiling liquid to 1¼ cups. Melt 2 tablespoons butter. Add flour, blending until smooth. Stir in scallop-mushroom liquid and milk. Boil for 1 minute, stirring constantly until thick. Mix egg yolks and cream together. Put a spoonful of hot mixture into yolks. Add to remaining hot mixture. Cook, stirring constantly, over low heat for 3 minutes. Combine scallops, mushrooms and sauce. Fill individual scallop shells, leaving a 1-inch border. Pipe Potato Duchess as border. Sprinkle each with Gruyére cheese. Place 8 inches under broiler. Broil for 5-10 minutes until tops are browned.

These can be made ahead to broiling step and refrigerated overnight. These freeze well for up to 2 months. Really worth the effort!

Potato Duchess

1 pound boiling potatoes
2 egg yolks
6 tablespoons soft sweet
   butter

Salt and white pepper
   to taste
Nutmeg to taste

Boil potatoes in salted water until tender; drain. Peel and pat dry. Mash into the butter. Beat in the egg yolks one at a time. Season to taste. Fill large pastry bag with half-inch star tip.

Sara Jones

Scallops in Lemon Sauce

Yield: 4 servings

1½ pounds scallops,
   washed and dried,
   divided
3 tablespoons butter,
   divided
¼ cup lemon juice
1 clove garlic, crushed

¼ teaspoon dill weed
⅛ teaspoon freshly ground
   pepper
3 tablespoons fresh parsley,
   chopped

Sauté ½ the scallops in 2 tablespoons butter for 4 minutes or until opaque. With slotted spoon, transfer to warm serving dish. Sauté remaining scallops in 1 tablespoon butter until opaque. Transfer to serving dish; keep warm. Reduce heat. Add lemon juice, garlic, dill weed and pepper. Cook briefly, stirring to scrape up brown bits. Pour over scallops. Garnish with parsley. Serve immediately.

Ann Fincher

Seafood Kabobs

Yield: 6-8 servings

2 pounds large shrimp,
   shelled and deveined
2 pounds scallops
   Oil and vinegar dressing
   for marinade
   Wooden sticks or skewers
2-3 fresh lemons, cut
   into wedges

Green peppers, cut
   into chunks
1 small basket cherry
   tomatoes
¼ cup butter, melted
   Cooked rice

Marinate shrimp and scallops overnight in enough oil and vinegar dressing to cover in refrigerator. Using wooden sticks or skewers, thread marinated shrimp, wedge of lemon, scallops, piece of green pepper, cherry tomato and repeat. Place kabobs on prepared charcoal grill. Brush with butter. Cook for 1½ minutes on each side. Serve on bed of rice.
Great light summer meal.

Van Fell
Director, Food Services
Gulf Coast Hospital

Maryland Lady Crab Cakes

Yield: 4-6 servings

1 pound backfin crabmeat
1 cup Italian seasoned
   bread crumbs
1 egg
¼ cup mayonnaise
¼ teaspoon pepper

1 teaspoon Worcestershire
1 teaspoon dry mustard or
   spicy brown mustard
Margarine, butter or
   vegetable oil for
   frying

Remove any shells from crabmeat. Combine bread crumbs, egg, mayonnaise and seasonings; add crabmeat; mix gently but thoroughly. Add a little more mayonnaise if mixture is too dry. Shape into 6 crab cakes. Fry in just enough fat to prevent sticking, about 5 minutes on each side until browned. If desired, crab cakes can be deep fried at 350° 2-3 minutes.

Ann Ruppel

Crab Casserole

Oven: 350° - 20 minutes

Yield: 8 servings

2 (6-ounce) cans crabmeat,
   drained and flaked
1 cup mayonnaise
1 teaspoon salt
4 tablespoons lemon juice
4 hard-cooked eggs,
   sliced

1 onion, grated
2 cups Ritz cracker
   crumbs, divided
White Sauce

Mix crabmeat, mayonnaise, salt, lemon juice, eggs, onion and 1 cup cracker crumbs. Add this mixture to White Sauce. Pour into a greased 2-quart casserole; top with remaining 1 cup cracker crumbs. Bake at 350° for 20 minutes. Let stand about 10 minutes before serving.

White Sauce

½ cup margarine
5 heaping tablespoons
   all-purpose flour

2 cups milk

Melt margarine. Stir in flour. Heat until bubbly. Gradually add milk, cooking until thickened.

Doris Thacker

Okra Shrimp Creole

Yield: 8-10 servings

¾ cup green pepper,
  chopped
1 cup celery, diced
1 large onion, chopped
½ cup butter, melted
½ teaspoon sugar
2 teaspoons salt
¼ teaspoon hot sauce
¼ teaspoon black pepper
¼ teaspoon cayenne pepper
2 teaspoons Worcestershire
2 tablespoons all-purpose
  flour
1 cup water

1 cup tomato sauce
1 (12-ounce) can cocktail
  vegetable juice
1 (16-ounce) can okra
  and tomatoes
1 (8-ounce) can tomatoes,
  puréed
2 pounds cooked shrimp,
  shelled and deveined
½ cup water chestnuts,
  sliced
Cooked rice
Parsley

Sauté green pepper, celery and onion in butter. Add seasonings and flour, blending well. Stir in water, tomato sauce, vegetable juice, okra and tomatoes, and puréed tomatoes; simmer 20 minutes. Stir in shrimp and water chestnuts. Simmer 10-15 minutes longer. Serve over rice. Garnish with parsley.

Sylvia Peterson

Seafood Gumbo I

Yield: 6-8 servings

6 tablespoons vegetable
  oil, divided
4 tablespoons all-purpose
  flour
3 cups okra, chopped
2 onions, chopped
1 (14-ounce) can tomatoes
1 quart shrimp,
  shelled and deveined
Crabmeat to taste
½ pint oysters

2 quarts water
1 bay leaf
1 teaspoon salt
  (to taste)
3 cloves garlic
Red and black pepper
  to taste
Tabasco to taste
Worcestershire to taste
Green pepper to taste
Cooked rice

Mix 4 tablespoons oil and flour to make a dark roux. Set aside. Smother okra and onions in 2 tablespoons oil. Add tomatoes when done. Add shrimp, crabmeat, oysters, water and bay leaf. Add roux. Add seasonings to taste. Cook, covered, slowly at least 30 minutes. Serve over rice.

Dean Hunter

Seafood Gumbo II

Yield: 12 servings

1 cup vegetable oil
1 cup all-purpose flour
2 large onions, diced
2 stalks celery, diced
1 large green pepper,
   diced
6 cloves garlic, minced
3 tomatoes, peeled and
   chopped
1 gallon warm water

2 tablespoons salt
  Red and black pepper
   to taste
1 pint oysters
1 pound crabmeat
2 pounds shrimp,
   shelled and deveined
  Cooked rice
½ cup green onions,
   chopped

Brown flour in oil. Add onions, celery, green pepper, garlic and tomatoes. Cook until tender. Add water; simmer. Add seafood. Cook for 1 hour. Serve over rice with chopped green onions.

Sue Carver

Quail in a Chafing Dish

Yield: 8 servings

8 quail
  Salt and pepper to taste
½ cup butter
3 ounces sherry
  Juice of 1½ lemons

4 tablespoons Worcestershire
2 tablespoons all-purpose
   flour
1 cup cream

Split birds or leave whole. Season to taste. Brown birds, breast side down, lightly in butter in a Dutch oven. Add enough water to keep birds from burning. Cover; cook for about 1 hour. When almost done, add sherry, lemon juice and Worcestershire. Cook about 20 minutes longer; remove birds. Combine flour and cream; add to gravy, stirring until thickened. Put birds and gravy in a chafing dish. Let stand until ready to serve. Light dish to reheat about ½ hour before serving.

Doves are delicious cooked this way also. This recipe is famous in my family and a seasonal favorite.

Martha Nichols

Doves Cooked with Wine and Mushrooms

Yield: 6 servings

12 doves, split
Butter
Juice of 1 lemon
½ cup + 1 teaspoon
sherry, divided
3-4 (4-ounce) cans
button mushrooms

½ cup butter
½ cup all-purpose flour
½ teaspoon salt
Dash of pepper
Milk
Cooked rice

Place birds, breast side down, in a Dutch oven. Place a liberal pat of butter on each. Add the juice of the lemon and 1 teaspoon sherry. Add enough water to keep birds from burning. Drain mushrooms; reserve liquid. Add to birds. Cover. Cook gently for 1 hour or until well done, adding small amounts of boiling water as needed. After birds have cooked, melt ½ cup butter in a saucepan; add flour, stirring to a smooth paste. Add salt and pepper. Combine mushroom liquid, pan juices, ½ cup sherry and enough milk to equal 4 cups. Add to paste, stirring until thickened. Pour over birds; simmer a few minutes. Serve with rice.

Equally good for quail or pheasant.

Margaret Logan

Delicious Doves in Foil

Oven: 325° - 1 hour 30 minutes

Yield: 6 servings

6 doves, cleaned and
washed
3 slices bacon, halved
4 medium potatoes,
quartered
4 small onions, quartered

4 carrots, cut into
lengths
2 green peppers, cut
into pieces
Salt and pepper to taste
12 tablespoons Worcestershire

Place doves, breast side up, on aluminum foil 12 inches square. Place bacon around each breast. Arrange vegetables around each dove. Season to taste. Sprinkle 2 tablespoons Worcestershire over each dove. Fold foil to seal. Bake at 325° for 1 hour 30 minutes.

Frances Gober

Venison Steaks

Yield: 4 servings

⅓ cup soy sauce
2 tablespoons butter, melted

1½ teaspoons lemon juice
4 Venison steaks

Combine soy sauce, butter and lemon juice. Place steaks in a shallow dish. Pour soy sauce mixture over steaks. Marinate for 1-2 hours. Cook slowly on a charcoal grill, basting with marinade, for about 10 minutes. Turn steaks twice during cooking time.

Best when steaks are rare to medium rare.

Jack Fincher

Desserts

Lemon Cheese Cake

Oven: 350° - 25 minutes   **Yield:** 1 (9-inch) 3-layer cake

1 cup butter or margarine	¾ cup milk
2 cups sugar	6 egg whites, stiffly beaten
3 cups cake flour, sifted	Lemon Filling
1 tablespoon baking powder	Seven Minute Frosting

Cream butter and sugar. Sift together flour and baking powder; add to creamed mixture alternately with milk. Fold in egg whites. Pour into 3 greased and floured 9-inch cake pans. Bake at 350° for 25 minutes or until surface springs back when gently pressed. Cool in pans 5 minutes; turn out on wire racks to cool. Spread Lemon Filling between layers and in center of top of cake. Frost sides and top edges with Seven Minute Frosting.

Lemon Filling

½ cup butter or margarine	Grated rind of 2 large lemons
1 cup sugar	Juice of 2 large lemons
6 eggs yolks, beaten	

Combine all ingredients in a saucepan. Cook over low heat until thickened. Cool.

Seven Minute Frosting

2 egg whites	⅓ cup water
1½ cups sugar	1 teaspoon vanilla extract
1 tablespoon light corn syrup or ¼ teaspoon cream of tartar	

Place all ingredients except vanilla in top of double boiler. Beat 1 minute with electric mixer. Cook over boiling water for 7 minutes or until stiff peaks form when beater is raised. Remove from boiling water; add vanilla; beat for 2 minutes.

Linda Merrell

Frost on the Pumpkin Cake

Oven: 350° - 35-40 minutes   **Yield:** 1 (9-inch) 2-layer cake

2 cups sugar
1 cup vegetable oil
4 eggs
2 cups all-purpose flour
2 teaspoons baking soda
2 teaspoons cinnamon

1 teaspoon baking powder
½ teaspoon salt
2 cups pumpkin, cooked
    and mashed
Cream Cheese Frosting
½ cup pecans, chopped

Combine sugar, oil and eggs; mix well. Combine dry ingredients; add to oil mixture, beating well. Stir in pumpkin. Pour into 2 greased and floured 9-inch cake pans. Bake at 350° for 35-40 minutes. Cool. Fill and frost with Cream Cheese Frosting. Sprinkle pecans on top.
Moist and delicious.

Cream Cheese Frosting

¼ cup butter, softened
1 (8-ounce) package cream
    cheese, softened

1 (16-ounce) box
    confectioners' sugar
2 teaspoons vanilla extract

Combine all ingredients; beat until smooth.

Joan Satterfield

Old-Fashioned Chocolate Cake

Oven: 375° - 30-40 minutes   **Yield:** 24 servings

3 eggs
1½ cups sugar
1 cup vegetable oil
2 cups self-rising flour

1 cup buttermilk
1 teaspoon vanilla extract
Chocolate Icing

Cream eggs and sugar. Add oil; mix well. Add flour and buttermilk alternately. Add extract. Pour into a greased and floured 9x13-inch baking pan. Bake at 375° for 30-40 minutes. Do not remove cake from pan. Cut into squares. Pour Chocolate Icing immediately over cake.
Easy to make. Delicious served hot.

Chocolate Icing

¼ cup cocoa
½ cup margarine
2 cups sugar

½ cup milk
1 teaspoon vanilla extract

Combine cocoa, margarine, sugar and milk in a saucepan. Boil for 2 minutes. Remove from heat; add vanilla.

Linda Lowery

Rikes Fudge Cake

Oven: 350° - 40 minutes   **Yield:** 1 (9-inch) 2-layer cake

½ cup shortening
3 eggs, separated
2½ cups sugar
1½ cups milk
2½ cups all-purpose flour

2 (1-ounce) squares
    unsweetened chocolate,
    melted
2 teaspoons vanilla extract
2 teaspoons baking powder
    Chocolate Icing

Cream shortening; add egg yolks, sugar, milk and flour. Beat until well blended. Add chocolate. Beat egg whites until stiff but not dry. Fold egg whites, vanilla and baking powder into creamed mixture. Pour into 2 greased and floured 9-inch cake pans. Bake at 350° for 40 minutes. Fill and frost with Chocolate Icing.

Chocolate Icing

2 cups sugar
1½ (1-ounce) squares
    unsweetened chocolate,
    cut up
½ cup shortening

⅔ cup milk
½ teaspoon salt
2 tablespoons butter
1 teaspoon vanilla extract

Combine all ingredients in a saucepan. Bring to a boil; cook on medium high for 3 minutes, stirring constantly. Remove from heat. Cool until spreading consistency, stirring often.

Nellie Holcomb

Candy Bar Cake

Oven: 325° - 1 hour-1 hour 15 minutes   **Yield:** 1 (10-inch) cake

6 (1.45-ounce) chocolate
    candy bars
1 cup chocolate syrup
1 cup butter
2 cups sugar
4 eggs

2½ cups all-purpose flour
¼ teaspoon salt
½ teaspoon baking soda
1 cup buttermilk
1 cup pecans, chopped
    (optional)

Melt candy bars with syrup; cool; set aside. Cream butter and sugar. Add 1 egg at a time, blending well. Sift together flour, salt and baking soda; add alternately with buttermilk. Add chocolate mixture and nuts, if desired. Pour into a greased and floured 10-inch tube pan. Bake at 325° for 1 hour - 1 hour 15 minutes. Cool. Remove from pan.

Susan Roach
Jackson, Georgia

Mocha Cake

Oven: 350° - 30 minutes

Yield: 1 (9-inch) 2-layer cake

1⅔ cups sugar
⅔ cup margarine, softened
3 eggs
2 teaspoons instant coffee
   granules
1⅓ cups water
⅔ cup cocoa

2 cups all-purpose flour
1½ teaspoons baking soda
½ teaspoon baking powder
½ teaspoon salt
1 teaspoon vanilla extract
Mocha Frosting

Combine sugar and margarine; beat until smooth. Add eggs, beating after each addition. Dissolve coffee into water. Combine dry ingredients; add to creamed mixture alternately with water. Stir in vanilla. Grease 2 9-inch cake pans; lightly coat with cocoa. Pour batter into prepared pans. Bake at 350° for 30 minutes or until toothpick inserted in center comes out clean. Cool. Fill and frost with Mocha Frosting.
Cake can be baked in a 9x13-inch baking pan.

Mocha Frosting

1 (16-ounce) box
   confectioners' sugar
½ cup margarine, softened
¼ cup cocoa
¼ cup milk

1 teaspoon instant coffee
   granules
1 teaspoon vanilla extract
⅛ teaspoon salt

Combine all ingredients. Beat on high speed for 3 minutes until light and fluffy.

Elly Hobgood

Carolina Fudge Cake

Oven: 375° - 20 minutes

Yield: 32-36 servings

1 cup margarine
4 tablespoons cocoa
1 cup water
2 eggs
½ cup buttermilk
1 teaspoon vinegar
1 teaspoon baking soda

1 teaspoon vanilla extract
2 cups all-purpose flour,
   sifted
2 cups sugar
1 teaspoon salt
Chocolate Icing (page 209)

Combine margarine, cocoa and water in a saucepan; bring to a boil. Mix together eggs, buttermilk, vinegar, baking soda and vanilla. Sift together flour, sugar and salt; add to milk mixture. Add cocoa mixture; mix well. Pour batter into a greased and floured 15½x10½x1-inch jelly roll pan. Bake at 375° for 20 minutes. Spread Chocolate Icing on cake while warm.
Freezes well.

Ruth Denney

Pat's Chocolate Cinnamon Cake

Oven: 350° - 30-35 minutes   **Yield:** 15-20 servings

½ cup margarine
½ cup shortening
1 cup water
4 tablespoons cocoa
2 cups self-rising flour
1 teaspoon baking soda
½ teaspoon baking powder

2 cups sugar
2 eggs, beaten
½ cup buttermilk
1 teaspoon cinnamon
1 teaspoon vanilla extract
Chocolate Icing

Combine margarine, shortening, water and cocoa in a saucepan. Bring to a boil, stirring until mixture is smooth. Remove from heat. Add remaining ingredients. Pour into a greased and floured 9x13-inch baking pan. Bake at 350° for 30-35 minutes. Remove from oven. Pour Chocolate Icing over cake while hot. *Great for covered dish suppers.*

Chocolate Icing

½ cup margarine
4 tablespoons cocoa
6 tablespoons milk
1 (16-ounce) box
   confectioners' sugar

1 teaspoon vanilla extract
1 cup nuts, chopped

Combine margarine, cocoa and milk in a saucepan; boil until margarine is dissolved. Remove from heat. Beat in confectioners' sugar and vanilla. Stir in nuts.

Elly Hobgood

Chocolate Pudding Cake

Oven: 400° - 20 minutes   **Yield:** 6-8 servings

¼ cup margarine, softened
1¼ cups sugar, divided
7 tablespoons cocoa, divided
1 tablespoon vanilla extract
1¼ cups self-rising flour
¾ cup milk

⅓ cup nuts, chopped
   (optional)
1 cup brown sugar,
   firmly packed
2 cups boiling water
Vanilla ice cream (optional)

Combine margarine, ¾ cup sugar, 4 tablespoons cocoa, vanilla, flour, milk and nuts, if desired. Mix until well blended. Pour into a greased 9x13-inch baking dish. Combine brown sugar, ½ cup sugar and 3 tablespoons cocoa. Sprinkle over creamed mixture. Pour boiling water over all. Bake at 400° for 20 minutes. Serve warm. Top with vanilla ice cream, if desired.

Janice Ingram

Southern Apple Cake

Oven: 325° - 45 minutes   Yield: 10-12 servings

1 cup corn oil
2 cups sugar
3 eggs, beaten
3 cups all-purpose flour
1 teaspoon baking soda
1 teaspoon salt

1 cup pecans, chopped
3 cups fresh apples,
　　peeled and chopped
1 teaspoon vanilla extract
Topping
Whipped cream (optional)

Combine oil and sugar, blending well; add eggs. Sift together flour, baking soda and salt; add to creamed mixture. Stir in pecans, apples and vanilla. Pour into a greased and floured 9x13-inch baking pan. Start in cold oven; turn on to 325°. Bake for 45 minutes. Pour Topping over warm cake. Cut into squares. Top with whipped cream, if desired.

Topping

½ cup butter
½ cup light brown sugar,
　　firmly packed

½ cup sugar
¼ cup evaporated milk
1 teaspoon vanilla extract

Combine butter, sugars and milk in a saucepan. Cook over low heat until butter melts; then boil 2 minutes. Stir in vanilla; beat until smooth.

Elizabeth Harris
First Lady of Georgia

Apple Cake

Oven: 300° - 1 hour   **Yield:** 1 (10-inch) cake

1 cup shortening
2 cups sugar
4 eggs, beaten
1 teaspoon nutmeg
1 teaspoon cloves
½ teaspoon salt
1 teaspoon cinnamon
3½ - 4 cups all-purpose
　　flour

4 tablespoons cocoa
1 teaspoon baking soda
1 cup cold water
1 cup black walnuts,
　　chopped
2 cups raisins
2 cups apples, peeled
　　and diced

Cream shortening and sugar well. Add eggs, beating after each addition. Combine nutmeg, cloves, salt, cinnamon, flour and cocoa. Stir soda into water. Add dry ingredients to creamed mixture alternately with soda and water. Stir in walnuts, raisins and apples. Pour into a greased and floured 10-inch tube pan. Bake at 300° for 1 hour or until toothpick comes out clean.
This recipe has been in my family for 5 generations.

Nancy Moore

Apple Cinnamon Funnel Cakes

Yield: 7 cakes

Vegetable oil
1¼ cups all-purpose flour
¾ cup apple cider
   or apple juice
1 teaspoon baking powder
1 teaspoon almond extract

⅛ teaspoon salt
1 egg
¾ teaspoon cinnamon,
   divided
2 tablespoons confectioners'
   sugar

Thirty minutes before serving: Pour ¾-inch oil into a 12-inch skillet (nonstick works best). Heat to 325° on deep fat thermometer. Mix flour, apple cider, baking powder, almond extract, salt, egg and ½ teaspoon cinnamon. Holding a narrow spout funnel, close spout with finger, pour ¼ cup batter into funnel. Over hot oil, move finger to let batter run out in a stream, making a spiral about 6 inches in diameter. Fry 3-5 minutes, turning once. Repeat using remaining batter, stirring well before pouring. Add more oil as needed. Drain on paper towels. Mix confectioners' sugar and ¼ teaspoon cinnamon until blended. Sprinkle or sift over cakes to taste.

Peggy Rutledge

Pumpkin Roll

Oven: 375° - 15 minutes

Yield: 8-10 servings

3 eggs
1 cup sugar
⅔ cup canned pumpkin
1 teaspoon lemon juice
½ teaspoon salt
1 teaspoon baking powder
¾ cup all-purpose flour

2 teaspoons cinnamon
1 teaspoon ginger
½ teaspoon nutmeg
½ cup nuts, chopped
   (optional)
Confectioners' sugar
Filling

Beat eggs, sugar, pumpkin and lemon juice. Sift salt, baking powder, flour and spices. Add to pumpkin mixture; beat well. Grease a 15½x10½x1-inch jelly roll pan. Line with waxed paper; grease waxed paper. Spread batter evenly in pan. Sprinkle nuts over batter. Bake at 375° for 15 minutes. Sprinkle linen towel with confectioners' sugar. Remove cake from oven. Turn out hot cake onto towel. Peel off waxed paper. Roll cake in towel starting at narrow end. Cool on wire rack, seam side down. Unroll cake. Spread with Filling. Reroll. Refrigerate. *Can be frozen. Slicing is easier when frozen.*

Filling

4 tablespoons margarine,
   softened
1 (3-ounce) package cream
   cheese, softened

1 cup confectioners' sugar
½ teaspoon vanilla extract

Beat margarine and cream cheese until smooth. Add sugar and vanilla; beat well.

Cathy Conway

Elegant Lemon Cake Roll

Oven: 350° - 10-12 minutes   **Yield:** 8-10 servings

4 eggs, separated
¾ cup sugar, divided
1 teaspoon lemon extract
1 tablespoon vegetable oil
⅔ cup cake flour, sifted
1 teaspoon baking powder
¼ teaspoon salt

Confectioners' sugar
Creamy Lemon Filling
½ cup flaked coconut
½ teaspoon water
1-2 drops yellow food
      coloring

Beat egg yolks until light and lemon colored; gradually add ¼ cup sugar, beating constantly. Stir in lemon extract and oil; set aside. Beat egg whites until foamy; add ½ cup sugar, beating until stiff but not dry. Fold yolk mixture into whites. Combine flour, baking powder and salt; fold into egg mixture. Grease a 15x10x1-inch jelly roll pan; line with waxed paper; grease and flour waxed paper. Spread batter evenly in pan. Bake at 375° for 10-12 minutes. Sift confectioners' sugar in a 15x10-inch rectangle on a linen towel. When cake is done, immediately loosen from sides of pan; turn out on towel. Peel off waxed paper. Roll up cake and towel together, starting at narrow end; cool on a wire rack, seam side down. Unroll cake; spread with half of Creamy Lemon Filling; reroll. Place on serving plate, seam side down; spread remaining filling on all sides. Combine coconut, water and food coloring in a plastic bag; shake well. Sprinkle colored coconut over cake roll. Refrigerate overnight.

Creamy Lemon Filling

1 (14-ounce) can sweetened
    condensed milk
⅓ cup lemon juice
1-2 teaspoons lemon rind,
      grated

5 drops yellow food
    coloring
1 (4-ounce) carton frozen
    whipped topping, thawed

Combine sweetened condensed milk, lemon juice, lemon rind and food coloring; mix well. Fold in whipped topping.

Wanda Roach

Coconut Pound Cake with Lemon Filling and Orange Glaze

Oven: 300° - 1 hour 30 minutes   **Yield:** 1 (10-inch) cake

1½ cups unsalted butter,
    softened
3 cups sugar
6 eggs, room temperature
3 cups all-purpose flour
¼ teaspoon salt
¼ teaspoon baking soda

1 cup sour cream
4 ounces frozen coconut,
    thawed
2 teaspoons vanilla extract
Lemon Filling
Orange Glaze

Cream butter; gradually add sugar, beating until light and fluffy. Beat in eggs one at a time. Sift dry ingredients. Blend into butter mixture alternately with sour cream. Mix in coconut and vanilla. Pour into a greased and floured 10-inch tube pan. Bake at 300° for 1 hour 30 minutes or until it tests done. Cool in pan 30 minutes; invert onto rack and cool completely. Cut cake in half to make 2 layers. Fill with 1¼ cups Lemon Filling; spread ½ cup on top. Pour Orange Glaze over cake and filling. (Cake can be completely assembled a day ahead. Cake and filling can be made 2 days ahead.)

Lemon Filling

Yield: 3½ cups

6 large lemons
2 cups sugar
¾ cup unsalted butter,
    cut into pieces

6 eggs, room temperature
    and beaten

Remove zest from lemons in thin strips using vegetable parer. Chop finely in food processor. Squeeze 1 cup lemon juice. Heat juice with peel or zest, sugar and butter in double boiler over water until blended. Strain in eggs. Cook until very thick, about 20 minutes. Do not boil. Chill. (One half of lemon filling recipe is enough for cake. Additional filling keeps 1 month in refrigerator for use in other desserts.)

Orange Glaze

⅓ cup orange juice
¼ cup sugar

2 teaspoons fresh lemon juice
¼ teaspoon almond extract

Combine all ingredients in a saucepan; cook over low heat until sugar dissolves. Increase heat; boil 5 minutes.

Elly Hobgood

Chocolate Pound Cake

Oven: 325° - 1 hour 20 minutes   **Yield:** 1 (10-inch) cake

1 cup butter
½ cup shortening
3 cups sugar
5 eggs
3 cups all-purpose flour

½ teaspoon baking powder
½ teaspoon salt
½ cup cocoa
1 cup milk
1 teaspoon vanilla extract

Cream butter and shortening. Add sugar and eggs. Sift dry ingredients together. Add dry ingredients alternately with milk to creamed mixture. Add vanilla. Pour into a greased and floured 10-inch tube pan. Bake at 325° for 1 hour 20 minutes.
Sprinkle with confectioners' sugar or frost with Chocolate Icing (page 230).

Jeannie Adams

Confectioners' Sugar Pound Cake

Oven: 350° - 45 minutes   **Yield:** 1 (10-inch) cake
          375° - 30 minutes

1 (16-ounce) box
   confectioners' sugar
¼ teaspoon salt
1 cup margarine, softened
½ cup shortening
1 teaspoon vanilla extract

1 teaspoon almond, lemon
   or orange extract
6 eggs
3½ cups all-purpose flour,
   sifted
⅔ cup milk

Combine sugar, salt, margarine, shortening, extracts and eggs; blend well. Add flour alternately with milk. Pour into a greased and floured 10-inch tube pan. Bake at 350° for 45 minutes. Increase oven to 375°; bake 30 minutes more.

Lois Cloud

Pound Cake I

Oven: 325° - 1 hour   **Yield:** 16-18 servings

1½ cups margarine
2¼ cups sugar
8 eggs
2 tablespoons rum or
   2 teaspoons any desired
   extract

3 cups all-purpose flour,
   sifted
1 teaspoon baking powder

Cream margarine. Add sugar; beat well. Alternately add eggs and flour. Add extract. Pour into a greased and floured 10-inch tube pan. Bake at 325° for 1 hour.
This cake has earned Estelle the title locally as "The Pound Cake Lady."

Estelle Lurwig

Pound Cake II

Oven: 300° - 1 hour 25 minutes

Yield: 1 (10-inch) cake

1 cup shortening
3 cups sugar
6 eggs
3 cups + 3 tablespoons
  all-purpose flour

½ pint whipping cream,
  unwhipped
1 teaspoon vanilla extract

Cream shortening and sugar well; add eggs, one at a time, beating well after each. Add flour and whipping cream alternately; add vanilla. Pour into a greased and floured 10-inch tube pan. Put in cool oven; turn oven to 300°. Bake for 1 hour 25 minutes.

This cake is different because using the cream gives a good buttery flavor.

Betty Johnson

Cream Cheese Pound Cake

Oven: 325° - 1 hour 30 minutes

Yield: 1 (10-inch) cake

1 (8-ounce) package cream
  cheese, softened
1½ cups margarine, softened
3 cups all-purpose flour

3 cups sugar
6 eggs
1 teaspoon vanilla extract
Cream Cheese Frosting

Beat cream cheese, margarine and sugar until fluffy. Add flour and eggs alternately, beating well. Add vanilla; beat well. Pour into a lightly greased and floured 10-inch tube pan. Bake at 325° for 1 hour 30 minutes. Cool. Spread Cream Cheese Frosting on cake.

Cream Cheese Frosting

1 (8-ounce) package cream
  cheese, softened
½ cup margarine, softened

1 (16-ounce) box
  confectioners' sugar
1 teaspoon vanilla extract

Beat cream cheese and margarine until light and fluffy. Add confectioners' sugar gradually, beating well. Add vanilla; beat well.

Patsy Neese

Pineapple Pound Cake

Oven: 325° - 1 hour 30 minutes   **Yield:** 1 (10-inch) cake

3 cups sugar
1½ cups shortening
10 eggs
3 cups all-purpose flour
½ teaspoon salt

1 (8-ounce) can crushed
  pineapple, drained
  (reserve juice for
  Glaze)
Glaze

Cream sugar and shortening. Add eggs one at a time, beating well after each addition. Add flour and salt, beating until well mixed. Stir in pineapple. Pour into a greased and floured 10-inch tube pan. Bake at 325° for 1 hour 30 minutes. Pour Glaze over warm cake.
This is an old family recipe.

Glaze

1 cup sugar
¼ cup butter

Reserved pineapple juice

Combine all ingredients. Bring to a boil over medium heat. Boil for 5-10 minutes.

Essie Lowery

Sour Cream Pound Cake

Oven: 350° - 1 hour 30 minutes   **Yield:** 1 (10-inch) cake

3 cups all-purpose flour
½ teaspoon salt
¼ teaspoon baking soda
1 cup butter or margarine,
  softened
2¾ cups sugar

6 eggs
½ teaspoon lemon extract
½ teaspoon orange extract
½ teaspoon vanilla extract
1 cup sour cream

Stir together flour, salt and soda; set aside. Beat butter on medium speed until fluffy; gradually add sugar, beating until light and fluffy. Add eggs one at a time, beating 1 minute after each. Scrape bowl frequently. Add extracts; beat well. Add dry ingredients and sour cream alternately, beating after each addition. Pour into a greased and floured 10-inch tube pan. Bake at 350° for 1 hour 30 minutes. Cool on wire rack 15 minutes before removing from pan.

Lynn Payne

Coconut Pound Cake

Oven: 300° - 1 hour 20 minutes   **Yield:** 1 (10-inch) cake

1½ cups shortening	1 teaspoon baking powder
2½ cups sugar	1 cup milk
5 eggs	2 teaspoons coconut extract
3 cups all-purpose flour	1 (6-ounce) package frozen
¼ teaspoon salt	coconut, thawed

Cream shortening and sugar until light and fluffy. Add eggs one at a time, beating well after each. Sift flour, salt and baking powder. Add alternately with milk and extract to creamed mixture; beat well. Stir in coconut; beat until smooth. Pour into a greased and floured 10-inch tube pan. Bake at 300° for 1 hour 20 minutes.

Mandy Mills

Greek Honey-Walnut Cake

Oven: 350° - 35-40 minutes   **Yield:** 1 (9-inch) square cake

1¼ cups all-purpose flour	¾ cup milk
¾ cup sugar	⅓ cup shortening
1 teaspoon baking powder	1 egg, beaten
1 teaspoon cinnamon	1 cup walnuts, finely chopped
½ teaspoon salt	Honey Syrup
¼ teaspoon cloves	

Combine all ingredients except walnuts; beat on low speed until blended. Beat on high speed for 1 minute. Stir in walnuts. Pour into a greased and floured 9-inch square baking pan. Bake at 350° for 35-40 minutes or until wooden pick inserted in center comes out clean. Pour Honey Syrup evenly over cake.

Honey Syrup

¼ cup sugar	¼ cup honey
¼ cup water	1 teaspoon lemon juice

Combine sugar and water in a saucepan; bring to a boil. Reduce heat and simmer 5 minutes. Stir in honey and lemon juice.

Cathy Lacy

Apricot Nectar Pound Cake

Oven: 350° - 1 hour   **Yield:** 1 (10-inch) cake

    1 package lemon cake mix   4 eggs, beaten
    ½ cup corn oil   1 cup apricot nectar
    ½ cup sugar   Lemon Glaze

Combine all ingredients. Pour into a greased and floured 10-inch tube pan. Bake at 350° for 1 hour. Pour Lemon Glaze over hot cake.

Lemon Glaze

    1 (6-ounce) can frozen   2 cups confectioners' sugar
      lemonade concentrate,
      thawed

Combine all ingredients, mixing well.

Gayle Anderson

Easy Cake Layers

Oven: 350° - 30 minutes   **Yield:** 2 (9-inch) layers

    2 cups sugar   1 cup milk
    1 cup shortening   2 cups self-rising flour
    4 eggs   2 teaspoons vanilla extract

Combine shortening, sugar and eggs; add milk and flour. Beat until creamy. Add vanilla. Pour into 2 greased and floured 9-inch cake pans. Bake at 350° for 30 minutes. Use favorite frosting.

Grace McClure

Basic Yellow Cake Layers

Oven: 350° - 40-45 minutes   **Yield:** 4 (9-inch) layers

    1 cup butter (no   1 teaspoon vanilla extract
      substitute), softened   1 teaspoon baking powder
    1 cup shortening   5 eggs
    2⅔ cups sugar   3 cups all-purpose flour
    ½ teaspoon salt   1 cup milk

Beat butter and shortening until light and fluffy. Add sugar gradually, beating continuously. Add salt, vanilla and baking powder; blend well. Add eggs one at a time, beating after each addition. Add flour and milk alternately, beginning and ending with flour. Pour batter into 4 greased and floured 9-inch cake pans. Bake at 350° for 40-45 minutes. Frost with Pineapple Icing, (page 230); Coconut Icing, (page 229) or favorite frosting.

Sylvia Peterson

White Cake Layers

Oven: 350° - 30 minutes

Yield: 2 (9-inch) layers

⅔ cup shortening
2 cups sugar
3 cups all-purpose flour
¼ teaspoon salt
2 teaspoons baking powder, divided

1 cup water
1 teaspoon vanilla extract
4 egg whites, stiffly beaten

Cream shortening and sugar. Combine flour, salt and 1 teaspoon baking powder. Add to creamed mixture alternately with water. Stir in vanilla. Fold in beaten egg whites and remaining 1 teaspoon of baking powder. Pour into 2 greased and floured 9-inch cake pans. Bake at 350° for 30 minutes. Use favorite frosting.
Makes a great birthday cake.

Cindy Holcomb

Orange Cake

Oven: 350° - 30-35 minutes

Yield: 1 (9-inch) 2-layer cake

2½ cups all-purpose flour
1½ teaspoons baking soda
¾ teaspoon salt
1½ cups sugar
1½ cups buttermilk
½ cup butter or margarine, softened
¼ cup shortening

3 eggs
1½ teaspoons vanilla extract
1 cup golden raisins, cut up
½ cup pecans, finely chopped
1 tablespoon orange rind, grated
Orange Frosting

Sift together flour, soda and salt; set aside. Cream sugar, buttermilk, butter, shortening, eggs and vanilla; gradually add dry ingredients. Stir in raisins, nuts and orange rind. Pour into 2 greased and floured 9-inch cake pans. Bake at 350° for 30-35 minutes. Cool. Fill and frost with Orange Frosting. Decorate with thin ribbons of orange peel arranged in bow pattern, if desired.

Orange Frosting

4½ cups confectioners' sugar
½ cup butter, softened
4-5 tablespoons orange juice

1 tablespoon orange rind, grated

Blend together sugar and butter; stir in orange juice and orange rind. Beat until smooth.

Joy Owen

Italian Cream Cake

Oven: 350° - 25-30 minutes

Yield: 1 (9-inch) 3-layer cake

½ cup margarine
½ cup shortening
2 cups sugar
5 eggs, separated
2 cups all-purpose flour
1 teaspoon baking soda
1 cup buttermilk

1 teaspoon vanilla extract
1 (3½-ounce) can flaked
   coconut
1½ cups nuts, chopped,
   divided
Cream Cheese Frosting
   (page 206)

Cream margarine, shortening and sugar. Add egg yolks one at a time, beating until blended. Combine flour and soda. Add to creamed mixture, alternating with buttermilk. Stir in vanilla. Add coconut and 1 cup nuts. Beat egg whites until stiff; fold into mixture. Pour into 3 greased and floured 9-inch cake pans. Bake at 350° for 25-30 minutes. Cool. Fill and frost with Cream Cheese Frosting. Sprinkle ½ cup pecans on top.

Jane Wofford

Banana Cake

Oven: 350° - 45 minutes

Yield: 1 (8-inch) 2-layer cake

½ cup shortening
3 cups sugar
3 eggs
1½ cups bananas, mashed
½ teaspoon baking soda
½ teaspoon vanilla extract

¼ cup buttermilk
2½ cups cake flour
2 teaspoons baking powder
½ teaspoon salt
Banana Frosting

Cream shortening and sugar. Add eggs, one at a time, beating well after each. Combine bananas, soda, vanilla and buttermilk; add to creamed mixture. Sift flour with baking powder and salt; add to banana mixture. Pour into 2 greased and floured 8-inch cake pans. Bake at 350° for 45 minutes. Cool. Frost with Banana Frosting.

Banana Frosting

½ cup bananas, mashed
½ teaspoon lemon juice
½ cup flaked coconut

¼ cup butter, softened
3½ cups confectioners' sugar,
   divided

Mix bananas, lemon juice and coconut together. Cream butter with 1 cup confectioners' sugar; add to banana mixture. Beat in remaining confectioners' sugar until spreading consistency is reached.

Brenda Lawson

Carrot Cake

Oven: 325° - 1 hour 10 minutes   Yield: 1 (10-inch) cake

1¼ cups vegetable oil
4 eggs
2 cups sugar
2 teaspoons cinnamon
1 teaspoon salt
3 cups raw carrots,
     sliced

1 cup pecans, finely
     chopped
2 cups all-purpose flour
1 teaspoon baking soda
2 teaspoons baking powder
   Confectioners' sugar

Mix oil, eggs, sugar, cinnamon and salt in a food processor or blender; blend thoroughly. Gradually add carrots; blend until grated. Pulse in pecans, flour, soda and baking powder. Pour into a greased and floured 10-inch tube pan. Bake at 325° for 1 hour 10 minutes. Sprinkle with confectioners' sugar. *Good with a cream cheese, coconut-pecan or butter frosting.*

Linda Hasty

Sweet Potato Cake with Coconut Filling

Oven: 350° - 25-30 minutes   Yield: 1 (8-inch) 3-layer cake

1½ cups vegetable oil
2 cups sugar
4 eggs, separated
4 tablespoons hot water
2½ cups cake flour
3 teaspoons baking powder
¼ teaspoon salt

1 teaspoon cinnamon
1 teaspoon nutmeg
1½ cups raw sweet
     potato, grated
1 cup pecans, chopped
1 teaspoon vanilla extract
   Coconut Filling

Combine oil and sugar; beat until smooth. Add egg yolks, beating well. Stir in hot water. Combine flour, baking powder, salt and spices; blend into sugar mixture. Stir in sweet potato and pecans. Beat egg whites until stiff; fold into batter. Pour into 3 greased and floured 8-inch cake pans. Bake at 350° for 25-30 minutes. Remove from pans; cool on wire racks. Spread Coconut Filling between layers and on top of cake.

Coconut Filling

1 (13-ounce) can evaporated
     milk
1 cup sugar
½ cup butter or margarine

3 tablespoons all-purpose
     flour
1 teaspoon vanilla extract
1⅓ cups flaked coconut

Combine all ingredients except coconut in saucepan. Cook, stirring constantly, over medium heat until thickened, about 12 minutes. Remove from heat; stir in coconut.

Joan Satterfield

Plum Cake

Oven: 350° - 1 hour 10 minutes   **Yield:** 1 (10-inch) cake

1 cup vegetable oil	½ teaspoon cloves
2 cups sugar	2 (4½-ounce) jars plum
3 eggs	baby food
2 cups self-rising flour	1 cup pecans, chopped
½ teaspoon cinnamon	Glaze
¼ teaspoon nutmeg	

Mix all ingredients together. Pour into a greased and floured 10-inch tube pan. Bake at 350° for 1 hour 10 minutes. Pour Glaze on cake while warm.

Glaze

1 cup confectioners' sugar   Juice of 2 lemons

Mix confectioners' sugar and lemon juice.

Marie Moore

Oatmeal Cake

Oven: 350° - 30-40 minutes   **Yield:** 1 (11x15-inch) cake

1¼ cups boiling water	1 teaspoon cinnamon
1 cup quick oatmeal	1 teaspoon nutmeg
1 cup brown sugar, firmly packed	1⅓ cups all-purpose flour
1 cup sugar	1 teaspoon vanilla extract
½ cup margarine	Coconut-Pecan Topping
2 eggs	
1 teaspoon baking soda	

Pour boiling water over oatmeal; let stand 20 minutes. Cream sugars, margarine and eggs. Add dry ingredients; mix well. Stir in oatmeal and vanilla. Spread batter into a greased and floured 11x15-inch baking pan. Sprinkle Coconut-Pecan Topping over batter. Bake at 350° for 30-40 minutes.

Coconut-Pecan Topping

1 cup flaked coconut	3 tablespoons milk
¾ cup brown sugar, firmly packed	3 tablespoons margarine, melted
1 cup pecans, chopped	1 egg

Combine all ingredients. Mix until blended.

Debra Goodwin

Bourbon Pecan Cake

Oven: 275° - 3 hours

Yield: 1 (10-inch) cake

1½ teaspoons baking soda
2 tablespoons water
2 cups all-purpose flour, sifted
2 teaspoons baking powder
1 teaspoon nutmeg
1 teaspoon cinnamon

1 pound pecans, chopped
2 pounds golden raisins
2 cups sugar
1 cup butter, melted
4 eggs, separated
1 cup bourbon

Dissolve soda in water; set aside. Sift flour with baking powder and spices. Dust nuts and raisins well with part of dry ingredients. Mix sugar and butter; add beaten egg yolks and the soda water. Add flour alternately with bourbon. Stir in raisins and nuts. Beat egg whites until stiff but not dry; fold into mixture. Pour into a greased and floured 10-inch tube pan. Bake at 275° for 3 hours with a pan of water placed on lower rack to prevent premature browning.
A good alternative to fruit cake for Christmas. Will keep several weeks stored in an airtight container.

Sara Jones

Light Fruit Cake

Oven: 275° - 3 hours

Yield: 1 (10-inch) cake

1 cup butter or margarine, softened
2¼ cups sugar
6 eggs
4 cups all-purpose flour
1 teaspoon cinnamon
½ teaspoon cloves
½ teaspoon allspice
½ teaspoon nutmeg

1 teaspoon salt
4 cups pecan halves
1 pound candied pineapple, chopped
1 pound whole candied cherries
½ pound dates, chopped
½ pound golden raisins

Cream butter, adding sugar gradually; beat until light and fluffy. Add eggs, one at a time. Sift together flour, spices and salt; add to creamed mixture. Add pecans and all fruits; mix into batter with spoon or hands. Pour into a 10-inch tube pan which has been lined with foil. Bake at 275° for 3 hours. (Cake can be decorated by removing from oven ½ hour before done. Brush with light corn syrup. Press reserved nuts and fruits into cake to make them stick. Return to oven to finish baking.) When cake has cooled, remove from pan and peel off foil. Wrap cake in cheesecloth dampened with wine or apple juice. Store in airtight container in a cool place. Make cake 3 weeks or more ahead so flavors can blend and cake mellows.

Linda Merrell

Candied Fruit Cake

Oven: 275° - 1 hour 15 minutes   **Yield:** 2 loaves

3 **(8-ounce) packages pitted dates**	2 **teaspoons baking powder**
1 **pound candied pineapple**	½ **teaspoon salt**
1 **pound candied cherries**	1 **cup sugar**
8 **cups pecan halves**	4 **eggs, beaten**
2 **cups all-purpose flour, sifted**	

Cut dates and pineapple into coarse pieces. Mix with whole cherries and pecan halves. Sift together flour, baking powder and salt; mix with fruit. Beat sugar and eggs together. Combine with first mixture. Grease and line with waxed paper 2 9x5-inch loaf pans. Pack each with mixture. Bake at 275° for 1 hour 15 minutes.

Ann Ponder

Japanese Fruit Cake

Oven: 300° - 1 hour   **Yield:** 1 (9-inch) 3-layer cake

1 **cup butter or margarine**	1 **teaspoon cinnamon**
2 **cups sugar**	1 **teaspoon allspice**
4 **eggs**	1 **teaspoon cloves**
3 **cups all-purpose flour**	1 **cup raisins**
½ **teaspoon salt**	1 **cup nuts, chopped**
1 **teaspoon baking soda**	**Filling**
1 **cup buttermilk**	

Cream butter and sugar. Add eggs, one at a time, beating well after each addition. Sift flour, salt and baking soda together; add alternately with buttermilk. Grease and flour 3 9-inch cake pans. Pour batter into 2 pans, leaving batter for 1 pan in bowl. Add to this batter the spices, raisins and nuts. Pour into remaining cake pan. Bake at 300° for 1 hour or until cake leaves sides of pan. Spread Filling between layers and on top of cake.

Filling

2 **cups flaked coconut**	**Juice of 2 lemons**
2½ **cups sugar**	**Grated rind of 2 lemons**
2 **tablespoons all-purpose flour**	1½ **cups hot water**

Combine all ingredients in a saucepan. Cook until thick. Cool slightly.

Ann Benzel

Turtle Cake

Oven: 350° - 25-30 minutes   Yield: 12 servings

1 package German chocolate
   cake mix
¾ cup margarine, melted
1 cup evaporated milk,
   divided

1 (7¼-ounce) package
   caramels
1 cup pecans, chopped
1 cup semi-sweet chocolate
   chips

Mix cake mix, margarine and ⅔ cup milk together. Pour ½ batter into a greased 9x13-inch baking pan. Bake at 350° for 10-15 minutes. Melt caramels and remaining ⅓ cup milk in a saucepan. Remove cake from oven. Pour caramel mixture over cake. Sprinkle pecans and chocolate chips over caramel mixture. Spread remaining batter over top. Bake for 15 minutes.
A very moist and chewy cake.

Anne Huey

Chocolate Chip Cake

Oven: 350° - 55-60 minutes   Yield: 1 (10-inch) cake

4 eggs
½ cup vegetable oil
1 package yellow cake mix
1 (3½-ounce) package instant
   vanilla pudding
1 (8-ounce) carton sour cream

1 (4-ounce) bar German sweet
   chocolate, grated
1 (12-ounce) package semi-
   sweet chocolate chips
Coconut-Pecan Frosting

Beat eggs well. Fold in oil, cake mix, pudding and sour cream; mix well. Add chocolate and chocolate chips. Pour into a greased and floured 10-inch tube pan or Bundt pan. Bake at 350° for 55-60 minutes. Cool. Frost with Coconut-Pecan Frosting.

Coconut-Pecan Frosting

1 cup evaporated milk
1 cup sugar
3 egg yolks, slightly beaten
½ cup butter

1 teaspoon vanilla extract
1½ cups flaked coconut
1 cup pecans, chopped

Combine milk, sugar, egg yolks and butter in a saucepan. Cook on medium heat for 12 minutes or until thick, stirring constantly. Add vanilla, coconut and pecans. Cool until thick enough to spread, beating occasionally.

Florence Cauble

Five Flavor Cake

Oven: 325° - 1 hour 15 minutes   **Yield:** 1 (10-inch) cake

1 cup butter or margarine
½ cup shortening
3 cups sugar
5 eggs, well beaten
3 cups all-purpose flour
½ teaspoon baking powder
1 cup milk

1 teaspoon coconut extract
1 teaspoon rum extract
1 teaspoon butter flavoring
1 teaspoon lemon extract
1 teaspoon vanilla extract
  Glaze (optional)

Cream butter, shortening and sugar until light and fluffy. Add eggs. Combine flour and baking powder; add to creamed mixture alternately with milk. Stir in extracts. Spoon mixture into a greased and floured 10-inch Bundt or tube pan. Bake at 325° for 1 hour 15 minutes or until cake tests done. Add Glaze, if desired. Pour ½ of Glaze while cake is in pan. Cool in pan about 10 minutes; remove. Pour remaining Glaze over cake.

Glaze

1 cup sugar
½ cup water
1 teaspoon coconut extract
1 teaspoon rum extract

1 teaspoon lemon extract
1 teaspoon vanilla extract
1 teaspoon almond extract

Combine all ingredients in a saucepan; bring to a boil, stirring until sugar is melted.

Edna Ivy

Orange Slice Cake

Oven: 250° - 2 hours 30 minutes-3 hours   **Yield:** 1 (10-inch) cake

1 cup butter
2 cups sugar
4 eggs, slightly beaten
1 teaspoon baking soda
½ cup buttermilk
3½ cups all-purpose flour
1 pound dates, chopped

1 pound candy orange
  slices, chopped
2 cups nuts, chopped
1 (3½-ounce) can flaked
  coconut
1 cup fresh orange juice
2 cups confectioners' sugar

Cream butter and sugar; add eggs. Dissolve soda in buttermilk; add to creamed mixture. Mix flour, dates, orange slices and nuts; add to creamed mixture. Stir in coconut. Pour into a greased and floured 10-inch tube pan. Bake at 250° for 2 hours 30 minutes - 3 hours. Combine orange juice and confectioners' sugar. Pour over hot cake. Let stand in pan overnight.

Betty McDaniel

Sweetmilk Cake

Oven: 350° - 25 minutes   **Yield:** 10 servings

2¼ cups self-rising flour
1½ cups sugar
 1 cup milk
 ¾ cup shortening

2 eggs
1 teaspoon vanilla extract
   Vanilla Frosting

Sift together flour and sugar. Add milk and shortening; blend thoroughly. Add eggs and vanilla. Beat for 1 minute on medium speed. Pour into 2 greased and floured 9-inch cake pans. Bake at 350° for 25 minutes. Cool. Fill and frost with Vanilla Frosting.
My grandmother's basic recipe.

Vanilla Frosting

2 egg whites
1 cup light corn syrup

1 teaspoon vanilla extract

Beat egg whites until stiff, but not dry; gradually add corn syrup and vanilla. Beat at high speed for 3 minutes.
This icing will not set but will be soft and easy to spread.

June Howell

Strawberry Cake

Oven: 325° - 25 minutes   **Yield:** 1 (8-inch) 3-layer cake

1 package butter cake mix
½ cup vegetable oil
4 eggs, beaten

1 (10-ounce) package frozen
   strawberries, thawed
   Strawberry Frosting

Mix cake mix, oil and eggs. Add strawberries. Pour into 3 greased and floured 8-inch cake pans. Bake at 325° for 25 minutes. Cool. Fill and frost with Strawberry Frosting. Chill before serving. Store in refrigerator.
Can be made the day before.

Strawberry Frosting

1 (16-ounce) package frozen
   strawberries, thawed
1 (3½-ounce) package instant
   vanilla pudding

1 (12-ounce) carton frozen
   whipped topping

Mix strawberries and pudding. Fold in frozen whipped topping.

Marjean Morris

"Public House" Torte Cake

Oven: 300° - 1 hour 15 minutes   **Yield:** 1 (10-inch) 7-layer cake

2¾ cups sugar
1 cup whipped butter
1 cup shortening
5 eggs
3 cups all-purpose flour

1 cup milk
1 teaspoon vanilla extract
1 teaspoon almond extract
Filling
Chocolate Frosting

Cream sugar, butter and shortening. Add eggs one at a time, beating after each addition. Add flour alternately with milk. Stir in vanilla and almond extracts. Pour into a greased and floured 10-inch tube pan. Bake at 300° for 1 hour 15 minutes. Cool cake completely. Slice into 7 layers. Spread Filling on each layer. Frost top and sides with Chocolate Frosting. Chill at least 24 hours before serving. Bring to room temperature before serving.

This recipe is from the Public House, Roswell, Georgia

Filling

1 (16-ounce) carton Ricotta or cream-style cottage cheese
2 tablespoons cream
½ cup sugar
3 tablespoons Strega (Italian orange liqueur) (optional)

3 tablespoons candied fruit, chopped
2 ounces mini semi-sweet chocolate chips

Sieve and cream Ricotta, beating constantly. Add cream, sugar and Strega, if desired. Fold in fruit and chocolate chips.

Chocolate Frosting

1 (12-ounce) package semi-sweet chocolate chips

¾ cup coffee granules
1 cup butter, cut into pieces

Melt chocolate and coffee, stirring constantly. Remove from heat. Beat in butter, one piece at a time. Chill to spreading consistency.

Carole Haley

Hummingbird Cake

Oven: 350° - 25-30 minutes   **Yield:** 1 (9-inch) 3-layer cake

- 3 cups all-purpose flour
- 2 cups sugar
- 1 teaspoon baking soda
- 1 teaspoon salt
- 1 teaspoon cinnamon
- 3 eggs, beaten
- 1 cup vegetable oil
- 1½ teaspoons vanilla extract

- 1 (8-ounce) can crushed pineapple, undrained
- 1½ cups pecans, chopped, divided
- 2 cups bananas, chopped
- Cream Cheese Frosting (page 206)

Combine flour, sugar, baking soda, salt and cinnamon. Add eggs and oil, stirring until dry ingredients are moistened. Do not beat. Stir in vanilla, pineapple, 1 cup pecans and bananas. Pour into 3 greased and floured 9-inch cake pans. Bake at 350° for 25-30 minutes. Cool. Spread Cream Cheese Frosting between layers and on sides and top. Top with ½ cup pecans.

Mary Winslow

Caramel Cake Frosting

- 2 cups sugar
- ½ cup light brown sugar, firmly packed
- 1 teaspoon baking soda

- ½ cup butter
- 1 cup buttermilk
- 1 teaspoon vanilla extract

Mix all ingredients in a heavy saucepan. Cook to soft ball stage. Remove from heat. Cool. Beat or stir until creamy. Fills and frosts a 2-layer cake.

Linda Merrell

Coconut Icing

- 1 fresh coconut, peeled and finely grated
- Milk from coconut
- 3 tablespoons all-purpose flour

- ¼ cup butter
- 1 cup sugar

Combine all ingredients in a saucepan. Boil until thick, stirring constantly. Will frost top and fill 4 9-inch cake layers.

Sylvia Peterson

Lemon Cheese Cake Filling

¾ cup sugar
2 tablespoons cornstarch
Dash of salt
1 egg yolk, slightly beaten
¾ cup water

3 tablespoons lemon juice
1 teaspoon lemon rind, grated
1 tablespoon butter or margarine

Combine sugar, cornstarch and salt in double boiler. Stir in egg yolk, water and lemon juice. Cook over boiling water 5 minutes, stirring constantly. Cook 10 minutes longer or until mixture is thick, stirring occasionally. Remove from hot water; add lemon rind and butter. Fills an 8-inch or 9-inch layer cake.
This is good with a white cake and Seven Minute Frosting.

Louise Roach

Chocolate Icing

1½ cups sugar
½ cup cocoa
6 tablespoons butter

Pinch of salt
1 teaspoon vanilla extract
½ cup milk

Combine all ingredients in a saucepan. Bring to a boil; cook 1½ minutes. Remove from heat; cool. Beat until stiff. Fills and frosts a 2-layer cake.

Jeannie Adams

White Icing

1 cup sugar
1 teaspoon white vinegar
2 tablespoons light corn syrup

¼ cup water
2 egg whites, stiffly beaten

Combine sugar, vinegar, corn syrup and water in a saucepan. Boil until hard ball forms in cold water. Pour syrup into egg whites. Beat on medium speed until spreading consistency. Fills and frosts a 2-layer cake.

Myrtie Whidby

Pineapple Icing

1 (20-ounce) can crushed pineapple, undrained
3 tablespoons all-purpose flour

¼ cup margarine
1 cup sugar

Combine all ingredients together in a saucepan. Boil until thick, stirring constantly. Will frost top and fill 4 9-inch cake layers.

Sylvia Peterson

Apple Pie

Oven: 415° - 40-50 minutes   Yield: 1 (9-inch) pie

8 cups apples, thinly sliced	½ teaspoon lemon peel, grated
¼ cup sugar	¼ teaspoon salt
¼ cup brown sugar, firmly packed	2 teaspoons lemon juice
2 tablespoons all-purpose flour	1 tablespoon margarine
1 teaspoon cinnamon	Flaky Pastry

Toss apples, sugar, brown sugar, flour, cinnamon, lemon peel, salt and lemon juice together. Pour into 9-inch unbaked bottom crust. Dot with margarine. Seal with top crust. Bake at 415° for 40-50 minutes.

With less sugar than the traditional recipes and the hint of lemon, this makes a lighter pie.

Flaky Pastry

2 cups all-purpose flour	¾ cup vegetable shortening
1 teaspoon salt	5-6 tablespoons ice water

Combine flour and salt. Cut in shortening until mixture resembles crumbs. Slowly add ice water, blending well between additions. Press into 2 equal portions. Chill. Roll out for 2 9-inch pie crusts.

Elly Hobgood

Dutch Apple Pie

Oven: 375° - 50-55 minutes   Yield: 1 (9-inch) pie

⅛ teaspoon cloves	½ cup all-purpose flour
½ cup light brown sugar	1 teaspoon cinnamon
½ cup sugar	½ cup butter, softened
⅛ teaspoon nutmeg	6 medium apples, sliced
⅛ teaspoon lemon peel, grated	1 (9-inch) pie crust, unbaked

Mix first 8 ingredients together. Spoon ⅓ mixture on bottom of pie crust. Place sliced apples over mixture. Spoon remaining topping over apples. Bake at 375° for 50-55 minutes.

Linda Satterfield

Concord Grape Pie

Oven: 450° - 10 minutes
    350° - 25 minutes

Yield: 1 (9-inch) pie

3½ cups Concord grapes
 1 cup sugar
 ¼ cup all-purpose flour
 ⅛ teaspoon salt

1 tablespoon lemon juice
2 tablespoons butter, melted
1 (9-inch) pie crust, unbaked
  Crumb Topping

Wash grapes. Slip skins; set aside for later use. Cook pulp until soft; mash through a sieve to remove seeds. Combine sugar, flour and salt. Add grape skins. Add lemon juice, butter and grape pulp. Pour into pie crust. Sprinkle Crumb Topping over pie. Bake at 450° for 10 minutes. Reduce heat to 350°. Bake for 25 minutes. Cool to room temperature before serving.
This is a treat in the Fall when fresh grapes are in season.

Crumb Topping

½ cup sugar
¾ cup all-purpose flour

⅓ cup butter, softened

Combine all ingredients.

Elly Hobgood

Pumpkin Pie

Oven: 375° - 35-40 minutes

Yield: 1 (9-inch) pie

1 cup pumpkin, cooked
   and mashed
1 cup milk
1 cup sugar
2 tablespoons all-purpose
   flour

1 teaspoon cinnamon
2 eggs, beaten
2 tablespoons butter
1 (9-inch) pie crust,
   partially baked

Combine all ingredients in a saucepan. Bring to a slow boil, stirring constantly, until slightly thickened. Pour into pie crust. Bake at 375° for 35-40 minutes.

Hazel Hasty

Sweet Potato Custard Pie

Oven: 350° - 30 minutes

Yield: 2 (9-inch) pies

3 cups sweet potatoes,
   cooked and mashed
½ cup milk
1½ cups sugar
½ teaspoon salt

2 eggs, beaten
2 teaspoons vanilla extract
½ cup margarine, softened
2 (9-inch) pie crusts, unbaked

Combine all ingredients. Beat until smooth. Pour into pie crusts. Bake at 350° for 30 minutes or until filling is set.

Jennie Turner

Lemon Cake Pudding Pie

Oven: 350° - 40 minutes

Yield: 1 (9-inch) deep-dish pie

1 cup sugar
¼ cup all-purpose flour
¼ cup margarine, melted
⅛ teaspoon salt
2 eggs, separated
½ cup lemon juice

2 teaspoons lemon peel, grated
⅔ cup evaporated milk
⅓ cup water
1 (9-inch) deep-dish pie crust

Combine sugar, flour, margarine, salt and egg yolks. Mix well. Beat in lemon juice and peel. Gradually add milk mixed with water. Beat egg whites until stiff, but not dry. Fold into lemon mixture. Pour all into pie crust. Place on pre-heated cookie sheet. Bake at 350° for 40 minutes or until toothpick in center comes out clean. Cool. Refrigerate several hours.

Betty Barrett

Lemon Chiffon Pie

Yield: 1 (9-inch) pie

1 envelope unflavored gelatin
¼ teaspoon salt
⅓ cup + ½ cup sugar, divided
4 eggs, separated
⅓ cup water
1 tablespoon lemon peel, grated

¼ cup lemon juice
½ cup heavy whipping cream, whipped
1 (9-inch) pie crust, baked
Whipped cream
Shredded lemon peel for garnish

Combine gelatin, salt and ⅓ cup sugar in a saucepan. Beat egg yolks, water, lemon peel and lemon juice together; add to gelatin mixture. Cook over low heat, stirring constantly, until mixture thickens and coats spoon. Remove from heat. Cool. Beat egg whites until soft peaks form; gradually add in ½ cup sugar, beating until sugar is completely dissolved. Fold lemon mixture into egg whites just until blended. Spoon mixture into pie crust. Chill until firm. To serve, spoon whipped cream in mounds around pie edge or completely cover. Sprinkle with lemon peel.

Katherine Fincher

Lemon Meringue Pie

Oven: 400° - 8 minutes   **Yield:** 1 (9-inch) pie

Crust

1 package graham crackers
  (about 11 whole crackers),
  crushed fine

½ cup butter or margarine,
  melted
2 tablespoons sugar

Combine crumbs, butter and sugar. Press into a 9-inch pie plate.

Filling

1 (14-ounce) can sweetened
  condensed milk
1 (5-ounce) can evaporated
  milk

3 egg yolks, slightly beaten
Juice of 4 lemons

Combine condensed milk, evaporated milk and egg yolks. Blend in the lemon juice. Pour into pie crust. Top with meringue.

Meringue

3 egg whites   ⅓ cup sugar

Beat egg whites, gradually adding sugar, until stiff. Spread over outer edge of pie to seal. Bake at 400° for 8 minutes or until browned. Chill for 1 hour before serving.

Joy Owen

Key Lime Pie

Oven: 375° - 10-15 minutes   **Yield:** 1 (9-inch) pie

3 egg yolks
½ cup fresh lime juice
1 teaspoon lime peel, grated
1 (14-ounce) can sweetened
  condensed milk

Few drops green food
  coloring (optional)
1 (9-inch) pie crust, baked
Meringue

Beat egg yolks until light. Add lime juice and grated peel. Blend in condensed milk. Add food coloring, if desired. Pour into pie crust. Top with Meringue. Bake at 375° for 10-15 minutes or until lightly browned.

Meringue

4 egg whites
½ cup sugar

½ teaspoon lime juice

Beat egg whites until foamy; gradually add sugar and lime juice. Beat until stiff.

Linda Fowler

Lime Meringue Pie

Oven: 350° Yield: 1 (9-inch) pie

1½ cups hot water
1-1½ cups sugar, according
   to taste
½ cup fresh lime juice
1-2 drops green food
   coloring
¼ cup cornstarch
¼ cup all-purpose flour

¼ cup cold water
4 egg yolks, beaten
2 tablespoons margarine
1 tablespoon lime peel,
   grated
1 (9-inch) pie crust, baked
Meringue

Combine hot water, sugar, lime juice and food coloring in a saucepan. Dissolve cornstarch and flour in cold water. Add to lime mixture. Cook over medium heat until mixture begins to thicken, stirring constantly. Remove from heat. Gradually whisk in yolks. Return to heat. Whisk in butter and lime peel; cook, stirring constantly, for 5-7 minutes to melt butter and thicken. Cool. Pour into pie crust. Top with Meringue, spreading to seal edges. Bake at 350° until browned.

Meringue

4 egg whites
¼ teaspoon cream of tartar

⅓ cup sugar

Beat egg whites and cream of tartar until foamy. Gradually beat in sugar. Beat until stiff peaks form.

Ollie White

Icebox Blueberry Pie

Oven: 400° - 8-10 minutes Yield: 2 (9-inch) pies

2 (9-inch) pie crusts, unbaked
   Chopped pecans (optional)
1 (8-ounce) package cream
   cheese
1 (16-ounce) box
   confectioners' sugar

1 (9-ounce) carton frozen
   whipped topping
1 (21-ounce) can blueberry
   pie filling

Prick pie crusts with fork; cover bottom with pecans. Bake at 400° for 8-10 minutes. Beat cream cheese and confectioners' sugar until smooth; fold in frozen whipped topping. Pour into pie crusts. Top with blueberry filling. Chill well before serving.

Variation: Strawberry or cherry pie filling may be used instead of blueberry.

Ruth Denney

Creamy Pecan Pie

Oven: 325° - 20 minutes   **Yield:** 1 (10-inch) pie
350° - 10 minutes

1½ cups graham cracker   1 cup + 2 tablespoons sugar,
    crumbs   divided
½ cup margarine, softened   ¾ cup pecans, chopped
⅓ cup pecans, chopped   1 cup sour cream
2 (8-ounce) packages cream   2 teaspoons vanilla extract
    cheese, softened

Combine crumbs, margarine and ⅓ cup pecans. Reserve 2 tablespoons for top. Press crumbs in a 10-inch pie pan. Chill 20 minutes. Beat cream cheese until fluffy. Beat in 1 cup sugar. Stir in ¾ cup pecans. Spoon into crust. Bake at 325° for 20 minutes. Remove from oven. Increase oven to 350°. Blend sour cream, remaining 2 tablespoons sugar and vanilla. Spread over baked filling. Bake at 350° for 10 minutes. Chill until firm, about 3 hours.

Linda Satterfield

Butterscotch Pie

Oven: 350° - 10 minutes   **Yield:** 2 (9-inch) pies

1 cup sugar   3 tablespoons butter
½ cup brown sugar   1 tablespoon butter pecan
½ cup all-purpose flour   extract
¼ teaspoon salt   2 (9-inch) pie crusts, baked
5 egg yolks   Meringue
3 cups milk

Combine first 4 ingredients. Beat egg yolks well; add milk. Add dry ingredients into milk and egg mixture. Cook in double boiler until thick. Add butter and extract. Stir until smooth. Pour into pie crusts. Spread Meringue over filling. Bake at 350° for 10 minutes or until browned.

Meringue

5 egg whites   8 tablespoons sugar
⅓ teaspoon cream of tartar   1 teaspoon white vanilla
    Dash of salt   extract

Combine egg whites, cream of tartar and salt; beat until stiff. Add sugar and vanilla; beat until well combined.

Evelyn Turner

Buttermilk Pie

Oven: 350° - 35 minutes

Yield: 1 (9-inch) pie

2 eggs, beaten
1½ cups sugar
3 heaping tablespoons all-
    purpose flour

¼ cup butter, melted
1 cup buttermilk
  Juice of 1 lemon
1 (9-inch) pie crust, unbaked

Combine eggs, sugar and flour. Add butter; mix well. Add buttermilk and lemon juice. Pour into pie crust. Bake at 350° for 35 minutes.

Georgia Gold

Coconut Pie I

Oven: 350° - 30 minutes

Yield: 2 (8-inch) pies

1¾ cups sugar
¼ cup margarine, softened
½ cup self-rising flour
4 eggs, well beaten

2 cups milk
1 teaspoon vanilla extract
1 (7-ounce) package flaked
  coconut

Cream sugar and margarine. Add flour. Mix eggs, milk and vanilla together; add to creamed mixture. Stir in coconut. Pour into 2 well-greased 8-inch pie plates. Bake at 350° for 30 minutes.
This recipe forms its own crust.

Tissie Jones

Coconut Pie II

Oven: 325° - 20 minutes

Yield: 1 (9-inch) pie

2 tablespoons butter
¾ cup sugar
⅛ teaspoon salt
⅓ cup all-purpose flour
2 eggs, well-beaten
2 cups milk, scalded

½ teaspoon vanilla extract
1 (3½-ounce) can flaked
  coconut
1 (9-inch) pie crust, baked
  Meringue (page 235)

Combine butter, sugar, salt, flour and eggs. Add milk gradually, stirring constantly. Cook in a double boiler until thick and smooth. Add vanilla and coconut. Pour into pie crust. Cover with Meringue. Bake at 325° for 20 minutes. minutes.

Sadie Cole

Coconut Cream Pie

Yield: 1 (9-inch) pie

1 cup sugar
2 tablespoons cornstarch
Dash of salt
2 cups milk
2 egg yolks, slightly beaten

1 teaspoon vanilla extract
1 cup flaked coconut
1 (9-inch) pie crust, baked
Frozen whipped topping,
    thawed

Combine sugar, cornstarch and salt. Place in top of double boiler. Gradually stir in milk. Cook until mixture thickens. Add small amount of hot mixture to egg yolks. Stir egg yolks into cooked mixture. Cook 1 - 2 minutes longer, stirring constantly. Remove from heat. Stir in vanilla and coconut. Pour into pie crust. Cover with whipped topping.

Betty Johnson

Florence's Fudge Pie

Oven: 350° - 20-25 minutes

Yield: 1 (8-inch) pie

½ cup butter
2 (1-ounce) squares
    unsweetened chocolate
2 eggs, beaten

1 cup sugar
¼ cup all-purpose flour
Pinch of salt

Melt butter and chocolate in double boiler. Remove from heat. Add remaining ingredients, mixing well. Pour into an ungreased 8-inch pie plate. Bake at 350° for 20-25 minutes. Cool.

Pat Stewart

Chocolate Chess Pie

Oven: 350° - 40 minutes

Yield: 1 (9-inch) deep-dish pie

1½ cups sugar
3½ tablespoons cocoa
2 eggs, slightly beaten
¼ cup butter, melted and
    cooled
1 (5.33-ounce) can
    evaporated milk

1 teaspoon vanilla extract
1 (9-inch) deep-dish pie
    crust, unbaked
French vanilla ice cream
    or whipped cream

Combine sugar and cocoa. Add eggs and cooled butter. Stir in milk and vanilla. Pour into pie crust. Bake at 350° for 40 minutes. Serve with French vanilla ice cream or whipped cream on each slice.

Sara Jones

Chocolate Pie

Oven: 350° - 12 minutes   **Yield:** 2 (8-inch) pies

⅔ cup cornstarch
2 cups sugar
3 tablespoons cocoa
3 egg yolks
1 (5.33-ounce) can
     evaporated milk

1 cup water
¼ cup butter or margarine
1 teaspoon vanilla extract
2 (8-inch) pie crusts, baked
     Meringue

Sift together cornstarch, sugar and cocoa. Beat egg yolks, evaporated milk and water together. Add dry ingredients. Cook over low heat until mixture thickens. Add butter. Stir in vanilla. Pour into pie crusts. Top with Meringue. Bake at 350° for 12 minutes or until browned.

Meringue

3 egg whites
¼ teaspoon cream of tartar

6 tablespoons sugar

Beat egg whites with cream of tartar until glossy. Gradually add sugar, beating until stiff peaks form.

Karen Hames

Party Chocolate Pie

Oven: 200° - 40 minutes   **Yield:** 1 (9-inch) pie

Shell

3 egg whites
1 cup sugar
     Pinch of salt

1 tablespoon vinegar
1 teaspoon vanilla extract

Beat egg whites until stiff while gradually adding sugar for 20 minutes. Add salt, vinegar and vanilla. Shape with spoon to fit a greased 9-inch pie plate. Bake at 200° for 40 minutes. Cool.

Filling

2 (4-ounce) packages German
     chocolate
6 tablespoons water
1½ teaspoons bourbon
     Vanilla extract to taste

½ pint heavy cream, whipped
     Pinch of salt
¾ cup pecans, toasted and
     crushed

Put chocolate, water, bourbon and vanilla in top of double boiler, stirring to melt chocolate. Cool. Fold in whipped cream and salt. Pour into pie shell. Sprinkle with pecans. Chill at least 2 hours.

Doris Thacker

Chocolate Chip Pie

Oven: 350° - 45-50 minutes   **Yield:** 1 (9-inch) pie

2 eggs, slightly beaten
1 cup sugar
½ cup butter, melted
1 teaspoon vanilla extract
¼ cup cornstarch

1 cup pecans, chopped
1 (6-ounce) package semi-
    sweet chocolate chips
1 (9-inch) pie crust, unbaked
    Vanilla ice cream
    (optional)

Combine eggs and sugar. Add butter and vanilla; mix well. Blend in cornstarch. Stir in pecans and chocolate chips. Pour into pie crust. Bake at 350° for 45-50 minutes. Serve warm with vanilla ice cream, if desired.

Linda Satterfield

Chocolate Almond Pie

Oven: Crust, 350° - 10 minutes   **Yield:** 1 (9-inch) pie

Crust

1¼ cups cream-filled
      chocolate cookies, finely
      crushed

¼ cup butter, melted

Combine cookies and butter. Press into a 9-inch pie plate. Bake at 350° for 10 minutes. Cool.

Filling

1 (6-ounce) package semi
    sweet chocolate chips
⅓ stick butter
1 (8-ounce) package cream
    cheese, softened
3 eggs, separated
1 cup + 3 tablespoons sugar,
    divided

¾ cup almonds, toasted and
    chopped
1 cup whipping cream,
    whipped
1 teaspoon vanilla extract

Melt chocolate chips with butter over very low heat. Cool. Mix thoroughly cream cheese, egg yolks and 1 cup sugar. Combine cream cheese mixture with chocolate; add almonds. Whip egg whites with 3 tablespoons sugar until stiff, but not dry. Fold into chocolate mixture. Whip cream with vanilla. Fold into chocolate mixture. Pour into pie crust. Chill several hours before serving.

Wanda Roach

Blender Pecan Pie

Oven: 425° - 15 minutes
350° - 30 minutes

Yield: 1 (9-inch) pie

2 eggs
⅔ cup sugar
½ teaspoon salt
½ cup light corn syrup

2 tablespoons butter, melted
1 teaspoon vanilla extract
1 cup pecans
1 (9-inch) pie crust, unbaked

Put eggs, sugar, salt, corn syrup, butter and vanilla in blender; blend well. Add pecans; blend **just enough** to chop nuts coarsely. Pour into pie crust. Bake at 425° for 15 minutes. Reduce heat to 350°; bake for 30 minutes more.
A quick and easy pie to make.

Barbara Helton

Old Fashioned Pecan Pie

Oven: 350° - 45 minutes

Yield: 1 (9-inch) pie

1 cup sugar
3 eggs, beaten
1 cup pecan halves

½ cup light corn syrup
1 teaspoon vanilla extract
1 (9-inch) pie crust, unbaked

Mix all ingredients. Pour into pie crust. Bake at 350° for approximately 45 minutes.

Mandy Mills

Southern Pecan Pie

Oven: 350° - 50 minutes

Yield: 1 (9-inch) pie

3 eggs, beaten
⅔ cup sugar
¼ teaspoon salt
⅓ cup margarine, melted
¼ cup light corn syrup

¾ cup dark corn syrup
2 cups pecan halves
1 (9-inch) deep-dish pie
crust, unbaked

Combine eggs, sugar, salt, margarine, syrups and pecan halves. Pour into pie crust. Bake at 350° for 50 minutes or until custard sets.

Frances Gober

Orange Cream Pie

Yield: 2 (9-inch) pies

1 (14-ounce) can sweetened
   condensed milk
½ cup lemon juice
1 (12-ounce) carton frozen
   whipped topping
1 (11-ounce) can mandarin
   oranges, drained and
   chopped

½ cup nuts, chopped
2 (9-inch) graham cracker
   crusts

Combine condensed milk and lemon juice until smooth. Add remaining ingredients. Pour into graham cracker crusts. Chill.
This pie freezes well.

Marjean Morris

Rum Cream Pie

Oven: 375° - 6-8 minutes   Yield: 1 (10-inch) pie

Crust

2 cups graham cracker
   crumbs
2 tablespoons sugar

6 tablespoons butter or
   margarine, melted

Combine crumbs and sugar. Stir in melted butter. Press firmly on bottom and sides of 10-inch pie pan. Bake at 375° for 6-8 minutes or chill in refrigerator for 45 minutes.

Rum Filling

6 egg yolks
¾ cup sugar
2 envelopes unflavored
   gelatin
1 cup cold water

½ cup dark rum
1¾ cups heavy cream
   Whipped cream
   Chocolate curls
   (optional)

Beat egg yolks until light. Add sugar gradually; beat until well blended. Sprinkle gelatin over cold water in a small saucepan. Cook over low heat about 3 minutes or until dissolved, stirring constantly. Cool slightly. Briskly beat in egg mixture until well blended. Stir in rum. Whip heavy cream until fairly stiff. Gently fold into egg mixture. Chill in refrigerator until mixture begins to set. (It will mound when dropped from spoon. If chilled too long and mixture is too firm, beat with wire whisk until smooth.) Spoon into crust. Chill until firm. Garnish with additional whipped cream in middle; top with chocolate curls, if desired.

Chocolate Curls

Run potato peeler down edge of thick milk chocolate bar (warmed slightly by holding in hand) for desired number of curls. Lift gently; place on waxed paper. Chill.

Patricia Gregg

Million Dollar Pie

Yield: 2 (9-inch) pies

1 (14-ounce) can sweetened
  condensed milk
¼ cup lemon juice
1 (12-ounce) carton frozen
  whipped topping
1 (8-ounce) can crushed
  pineapple, drained

1 cup pecans, chopped
  (optional)
1 cup maraschino cherries,
  halved (optional)
2 (9-inch) pie crusts, baked

Combine condensed milk and lemon juice. Add whipped topping, crushed pineapple, pecans and cherries, if desired. Pour into pie crusts. Chill.

Janice Ingram

Chocolate-Amaretto Mousse Pie

Yield: 1 (9-inch) pie

2 (1.5-ounce) envelopes
  whipped topping mix
1½ cups milk
2 (4⅛-ounce) packages
  chocolate instant pudding
  mix

¼ cup Amaretto
1 (9-inch) pie crust,
  baked and cooled
1 (8-ounce) container frozen
  whipped topping, thawed
Chocolate shavings
  (optional)

Prepare topping mix according to package directions. Add milk, pudding mix and Amaretto. Whip with mixer on high. Spoon into pie crust. Chill. Top with whipped topping. Add chocolate shavings, if desired, before serving. *Best if made a day ahead. Makes an excellent fake mousse.*

Elly Hobgood

Crème de Menthe Pie

Yield: 1 (9-inch) pie

14 cream-filled chocolate
  wafers, finely crushed
2 tablespoons butter, softened
24 large marshmallows
½ cup milk

4 tablespoons green crème
  de menthe
2 tablespoons white crème
  de cacao
1 cup frozen whipped topping

Mix cookie crumbs with butter. Press into a 9-inch pie pan. Melt marshmallows and milk. Stir in crème de menthe and cacao. Fold in whipped topping. Pour into cookie crust. Chill for several hours.

Lila Stevens

Amelia Island Mud Pie

Yield: 1 (10-inch) pie

Shell

30 cream-filled chocolate wafers

3 tablespoons butter, softened

Chop cookies very fine. Mix with butter. Press into 10-inch pie plate. Place in freezer.

Filling

1 pint chocolate ice cream
2 tablespoons coffee, brewed
2 tablespoons Sanka, brewed
4 tablespoons whipping cream, whipped

2 tablespoons brandy
2 tablespoons Kahlúa
Kraft fudge topping
Whipped cream for garnish

Whip ice cream with coffee, Sanka, brandy and Kahlúa. Add whipped cream. Place in shell. Freeze until very hard. Cover top of pie with fudge topping. Garnish with whipped cream.

Linda Hasty

Frozen Chocolate Pecan Pie

Yield: 1 (9-inch) pie

Crust

2 cups pecans, finely chopped and toasted
5 tablespoons brown sugar, firmly packed

5 tablespoons butter, chilled and cut into small pieces
1 tablespoon light rum

Blend all ingredients well. Press into bottom and sides of a 9-inch pie plate. Freeze for at least 1 hour.

Filling

6 ounces semi-sweet chocolate
½ teaspoon instant coffee powder
4 eggs, room temperature

2 tablespoons light rum
1 teaspoon vanilla extract
1½ cups whipping cream, divided
Chocolate shavings (optional)

Melt chocolate with coffee in top of double boiler over hot water. Remove from heat. Whisk in eggs, rum and vanilla until smooth. Cool for 5 minutes. Whip 1 cup whipping cream until stiff. Gently fold into chocolate mixture. Pour into pie crust. Freeze. Remove from freezer 1 hour before serving. Whip remaining ½ cup cream for top of each slice. Decorate with chocolate shavings, if desired. *Can be frozen up to 3 months.*

Helen Spears

Spanish Lime Pie

Oven: 375° - 8 minutes   **Yield:** 1 (9-inch) pie

Crust

1½ cups graham cracker
        crumbs
1 tablespoon sugar

1 teaspoon cinnamon
6 tablespoons butter, melted

Mix all ingredients. Press into a 9-inch pie plate. Bake at 375° for 8 minutes.

Filling

Rind of 2 limes,
    finely grated
1 cup lime juice
4 eggs, separated

2 (14-ounce) cans sweetened
    condensed milk
Pinch of salt

Mix lime rind and juice. Slightly beat egg yolks. Stir in condensed milk gradually. Add rind and juice. Stir until smooth. Beat egg whites and salt until stiff, but not dry. In 2 or 3 additions, add whites to yolk mixture. Pour as much as crust will hold without running over. Reserve remainder at room temperature. Freeze the pie for about 20 minutes until semi-firm. Pour the remainder of the filling, mounding high in center. Return to freezer immediately. Freeze 4 - 5 hours or until firm.

Cissy Cloud

Kona Ice Cream Pie

Oven: 450° - 4-5 minutes   **Yield:** 1 (9-inch) pie

2 tablespoons instant coffee
        granules
1½ cups whipping cream,
        divided
1 quart + 1 pint vanilla
        ice cream, softened,
        divided

1 (9-inch) pie crust, baked
2 tablespoons Kahlúa
½ cup cashews, chopped
Meringue

Dissolve coffee granules in 1 cup whipping cream. Beat until soft peaks form. Fold into 1 quart vanilla ice cream. Spread about ⅔ of coffee mixture into pie crust. Make a well in center of pie. Place pie and remaining coffee mixture into freezer. Beat remaining ½ cup whipping cream until foamy. Add Kahlúa, beating until soft peaks form. Fold in 1 pint vanilla ice cream. Add cashews; stir gently. Mound mixture over pie. Freeze until firm. Remove pie from freezer. Spread Meringue over filling, sealing to edge of crust. Bake at 450° for 4 - 5 minutes or until browned. Serve immediately.

Meringue

4 egg whites
¼ teaspoon cream of tartar

½ cup sugar

Beat egg whites and cream of tartar until foamy. Gradually add sugar, 1 tablespoon at a time, beating until stiff peaks form.

Judi Whiddon

Vanilla Ice Cream Pie

Yield: 1 (9-inch) pie

1½ cups chocolate chip
    cookies, finely crushed
2 tablespoons sugar
⅓ cup butter, melted

½ cup walnuts, chopped
1½ pints vanilla ice
    cream, softened
¼ cup crème de cacao

Combine cookie crumbs with sugar, butter and walnuts. Blend well. Press mixture into a greased 9-inch pie plate. Chill. Combine ice cream and crème de cacao. Beat until well blended. Spoon ice cream into pie crust. Place in freezer until firm.

Cheryl Ellis

Frosty Mint Ice Cream Pies

Oven: 350° - 25-30 minutes

Yield: 2 (9-inch) pies

Pie Shells

1 (18½-ounce) devil's food,
    dark chocolate or
    chocolate mint cake
    mix
¾ cup ready-to-spread
    chocolate fudge
    frosting supreme

¾ cup water
¼ cup oil

Generously grease bottom, sides and rim of 2 9-inch pie plates or round cake pans. Blend all ingredients with electric mixer at low speed until moistened; beat 2 minutes at highest speed. Spread half of batter (2¼ cups) in bottom of each pan. Bake at 350° for 25-30 minutes. Do not overbake. Cakes will collapse to form shells. Cool completely.

Filling

6 cups (1½ quarts) mint
    chocolate chip
    ice cream

Blend ice cream until smooth; spread evenly in center of each shell leaving ½-inch rim. If desired, heat remaining frosting just until softened. Drop by spoonfuls on top of ice cream; swirl with knife. Freeze at least 2 hours. Store in freezer. Wrap frozen pies airtight to avoid freezer burn.
Vanilla ice cream with peppermint extract and some green food coloring works fine.

Deanie Fincher

Egg Pastry for Fried Pies

Yield: 20-24 pies

3 cups all-purpose flour
1 teaspoon salt
1 cup shortening

1 egg, beaten
4 tablespoons water
1 teaspoon vinegar

Combine flour and salt. Cut in shortening until mixture resembles corn meal. Combine egg and water. Sprinkle over flour mixture. Add vinegar. Stir lightly until mixture forms a ball. Chill 1 hour. Roll out and cut in 5-inch circles. To seal around preferred filling, moisten with water. Fry on both sides until browned. *Turns out like puff pastry.*

Joan Satterfield

Basic Pastry

Yield: 2 (9-inch) pie crusts

2¼ cups all-purpose flour,
    sifted and divided
1 teaspoon salt

¾ cup vegetable shortening
5½ tablespoons cold water

Measure 2 cups sifted flour back into sifter. Add salt; sift into bowl. Add shortening. Cut shortening into flour, using 2 knives or pastry blender, until flour coated particles are the size of a pea. Stir ¼ cup flour into cold water until smooth. Add to shortening mixture, stirring with two-tined fork, until particles stick together. Shape into ball. Chill ½ hour, no longer, before using.

Rebecca Johnston

Rice Parfait

Yield: 4 servings

½ pint whipping cream,
    whipped
1 (16-ounce) can fruit
    cocktail, well drained

⅓ cup cooked rice,
    unsalted

Combine all ingredients. Chill for 2-3 hours.
An easy and unusual dessert. A family tradition for the holidays.

Sylvia Peterson

Combination Trifle

Yield: 12-16 servings

1 angel food cake
1 (16-ounce) jar strawberry
   jam

¾ cup sherry
   Custard
   Topping

Slice cake into ½-inch slices. Place half the slices in a trifle bowl or round casserole dish. Put 1 tablespoon sherry over each slice of cake. Spread with half the jam. Cover with half of the Custard. Make second layer of cake like first layer. Pour another layer of Custard over cake and jam. Chill. Spread Topping over cake and custard a few hours before serving. Refrigerate.
Cake and custard layers can be made the day before.

Custard

⅔ cup sugar
⅛ teaspoon salt
½ cup all-purpose flour
2 eggs, beaten

2 cups milk
1 teaspoon almond extract
½ cup slivered almonds

Mix sugar, salt and flour together; stir in eggs. Slowly add milk, stirring constantly. Cook over low heat, stirring constantly. Remove from heat. Add extract and almonds. Cool.

Topping

10 maraschino cherries,
   chopped
3 tablespoons cherry juice

½ pint whipping cream,
   whipped

Fold cherries and juice into whipped cream.

Florence Cauble

Cheesecake Tarts

Oven: 375° - 12-20 minutes   **Yield:** 2 dozen

24 vanilla wafers
2 (8-ounce) packages cream
   cheese, softened
¾ cup sugar

2 eggs
1 teaspoon vanilla extract
1 (21-ounce) can cherry or
   blueberry pie filling

Place vanilla wafers upside down in cupcake papers. Put in muffin tins. Mix cream cheese, sugar, eggs and vanilla. Spoon onto vanilla wafers, dividing batter equally. Bake at 375° for 12-20 minutes. Cool. Remove from papers. Top with pie filling. Refrigerate.
Keeps well. Better if topping is spooned on before serving each time.

Rita Anderson

Bread Pudding with Lemon Sauce

Oven: 375° - 45 minutes   **Yield:** 4 servings

2 eggs, well beaten
2-3 tablespoons sugar
⅛ teaspoon salt
½ teaspoon cinnmon
½ teaspoon nutmeg

½ teaspoon vanilla extract
2-3 tablespoons raisins
2 cups bread crumbs
1 cup hot milk
Lemon Sauce

Combine eggs and sugar; blend in salt, spices, vanilla, raisins, bread crumbs and milk. Pour into a buttered 9x5-inch loaf pan. Bake at 375° for 45 minutes. Serve with Lemon Sauce.
This recipe doubles easily. Bake in a 9x13-inch baking dish 25-30 minutes. It is a delicious addition to a holiday meal.

Lemon Sauce

1 egg, beaten
1 cup sugar
Juice of 2 lemons

Grated rind of 1 lemon
1 tablespoon margarine

Combine egg, sugar, lemon juice and lemon rind in saucepan over low heat. Cook until thickened, stirring constantly. Add butter; stir until melted.

Joan Satterfield

Amaretto Cheesecake

Oven: 375° - 45-50 minutes   **Yield:** 12 servings
          500° - 5 minutes

Crust

1½ cups graham cracker
    crumbs
2 tablespoons sugar

1 teaspoon cinnamon
¼ cup + 2 tablespoons
    margarine, melted

Combine crumbs, sugar, cinnamon and butter; mix well. Press onto bottom and halfway up sides of 9-inch springform pan. Chill

Filling

3 (8-ounce) packages cream
    cheese, softened
1 cup sugar
4 eggs
⅓ cup + 1 tablespoon
    Amaretto, divided

1 (8-ounce) carton sour cream
1 tablespoon + 1 teaspoon
    sugar
¼ cup almonds, sliced
1 (1.2-ounce) chocolate candy
    bar, grated (optional)

Beat cream cheese until fluffy. Gradually add 1 cup sugar, mixing well. Add eggs, one at a time, beating well after each. Stir in ⅓ cup Amaretto; pour into prepared pan. Bake at 375° for 45-50 minutes or until set. Combine sour cream, 1 tablespoon plus 1 teaspoon sugar and 1 tablespoon Amaretto; stir well. Spoon over cheesecake. Bake at 500° for 5 minutes. Cool to room temperature. Refrigerate for 24-48 hours. (Best when thoroughly chilled.) Garnish with almonds and grated chocolate, if desired.

Linda Hasty

Praline Cheesecake

Oven: 350°   **Yield**: 8-10 servings
   Crust: 10 minutes
   Filling: 50-55 minutes

Crust

1 cup graham cracker crumbs	3 tablespoons butter, melted
3 tablespoons sugar	

Combine crumbs, sugar and butter; press onto bottom of a 9-inch springform pan. Bake at 350° for 10 minutes.

Filling

3 (8-ounce) packages cream cheese, softened	3 eggs
1¼ cups dark brown sugar, firmly packed	1½ teaspoons vanilla extract
	½ cup pecans, chopped
2 tablespoons all-purpose flour	1 tablespoon maple syrup
	Pecan halves

Combine cream cheese, brown sugar and flour, beating until blended. Add eggs, one at a time, beating well after each. Add vanilla and nuts. Pour over crumbs. Bake at 350° for 50-55 minutes. Cool; then chill. Brush with maple syrup. Garnish with pecan halves.
Can be frozen.

Myrna Pruett

Chocolate Chip Cheesecake

Oven: 275° - 2 hours 30 minutes   **Yield**: 12 servings

Crust

2½ cups graham cracker crumbs	½ teaspoon cinnamon
¼ cup sugar	½ cup butter, melted

Combine all ingredients. Press onto bottom and halfway up sides of a 9½-inch springform pan. Chill

Filling

8 ounces semi-sweet chocolate chips	¼ cup all-purpose flour
5 (8-ounce) packages cream cheese, softened	1 teaspoon vanilla extract
	6 eggs
1¾ cups sugar	¼ cup half and half

Chop chocolate chips in a food processor; set aside. Blend together cream cheese, sugar, flour and vanilla until smooth in a processor or with a mixer. Add eggs, one at a time, beating after each. Stir in chocolate and half and half. Pour into shell. Bake at 275° for 2 hours 30 minutes. Cool. Chill overnight covered.

Linda Hasty

Chocolate Marble Cheesecake

Oven: Crust: 400° - 10 minutes
    Filling: 300° - 1 hour

Yield: 16 servings

Crust

- ¾ cup all-purpose flour
- 2 tablespoons sugar
- ¼ teaspoon salt
- ¼ cup butter, softened
- 1 (6-ounce) package semi-sweet chocolate chips, melted, divided

Mix flour, sugar and salt. Cut in butter. Stir in 2 tablespoons melted chocolate. (Set aside remaining chocolate for filling.) Press onto bottom of 9-inch spring-form pan. Bake at 400° for 10 minutes.

Filling

- 3 (8-ounce) packages cream cheese, softened
- 1 cup sugar
- ¼ cup all-purpose flour
- 2 teaspoons vanilla extract
- 6 eggs
- 1 cup sour cream

Beat cream cheese with sugar until smooth. Blend in flour and vanilla. Add eggs, one at a time, beating well. Blend in sour cream. Blend 1¾ cups filling with remaining melted chocolate. Pour remainder of filling over crust. Top with spoonfuls of chocolate mixture. Cut through to marble. Place in oven at 400° immediately reducing to 300°. Bake for 1 hour. Turn off oven. Leave in for an additional 1 hour. Cool completely. Chill overnight.

Carole Haley

Delicious Cheesecake

Oven: Crust: 425° - 10 minutes
    Filling: 325° - 45 mins.-1 hour

Yield: 10-12 servings

Crust

- ⅓ cup butter, melted
- 1½ cups graham cracker crumbs
- ⅓ cup light brown sugar, firmly packed
- ½ teaspoon cinnamon

Combine all ingredients. Press onto bottom of a 9-inch springform pan. Bake at 425° for 10 minutes. Remove pan; reduce oven temperature to 325°.

Filling

- 2 (8-ounce) packages cream cheese, softened
- ¾ cup sugar
- 2 eggs
- 1 teaspoon vanilla extract
- ¼ teaspoon salt

Combine cream cheese, sugar, eggs, vanilla and salt. Blend thoroughly with mixer or with whisk. Pour into crust. Bake at 325° for 45 minutes - 1 hour.

Selene Hendrix

Nugget's Cheesecake

Oven: 325° - 1 hour   **Yield:** 8-10 servings

Crust

6 ounces Zwieback toast, crushed	**2 tablespoons sugar**
½ cup butter, melted	**1 teaspoon cinnamon**

Combine all ingredients for crust. Press onto bottom and on sides of a 9 or 10-inch springform pan. (If you use larger pan, use crust on bottom of pan only.) Chill crust.

Filling

2 (8-ounce) + 1 (3-ounce) packages cream cheese, softened	**2½ tablespoons all-purpose flour**
	Pinch of salt
1½ cups + 3 tablespoons sugar, divided	**7 eggs**
	1 cup sour cream
	Juice of 1 lemon

Beat cream cheese, 1½ cups sugar, flour and salt until smooth. Add 1 egg and 6 egg yolks. Add sour cream and lemon juice. Beat six egg whites until stiff, but not dry; slowly add 3 tablespoons sugar. Fold into cheese mixture. Pour into crust. Bake at 325° for 1 hour or until set. Turn heat off; let cake cool in the oven. Chill until ready to serve.

Nugget Gold

Banana Pudding

Yield: 4-6 servings

½ cup sugar	**1 teaspoon vanilla extract**
2-3 tablespoons all-purpose flour	**1 cup coconut, divided**
2 cups milk	**Vanilla wafers**
2 egg yolks, beaten	**4-5 bananas, sliced**
1 tablespoon margarine	**Meringue**

Mix sugar and flour. Add 1 cup of milk; mix well. Add egg yolks and remaining cup of milk. Cook until thick, stirring constantly. Stir in margarine and vanilla. Add ½ cup coconut. Put a layer of vanilla wafers, bananas, filling and a sprinkling of coconut in a deep dish. Repeat layers. Top with Meringue and sprinkling of coconut. Bake at 400° until browned.
Variation: Can add pineapple on top of last 2 layers.
This is an original recipe.

Meringue

2 egg whites	**¼ teaspoon cream of tartar**
2 tablespoons sugar	

Beat egg whites until foamy; gradually add sugar and cream of tartar. Beat until stiff.

Hazel Hasty

Fresh Coconut Pudding

Yield: 12 servings

1 pint milk
3 tablespoons unflavored
   gelatin
¼ cup cold water
1 cup sugar
1 teaspoon almond extract
2 cups coconut, freshly
   grated

¼ cup almonds, chopped
1 pint whipping cream,
   whipped
¾ cup sherry
Coconut
Red cherries for garnish

Bring milk to a boil. Dissolve gelatin in cold water; add to milk. Add sugar, dissolving well. Cool. Add almond extract, coconut and almonds. Fold into whipped cream. Pour into a mold. Chill until firm. Unmold. Sprinkle generously with additional coconut. Garnish with cherries.

Julia Ellis

Boiled Custard

Yield: 6-8 servings

1 quart milk
4 eggs
1 cup sugar

1 teaspoon vanilla or
   almond extract

Put milk in top of a double boiler over simmering water to get hot. Do not boil. Beat the eggs together with the sugar. Add a small amount of milk to egg mixture; then put all together in the double boiler. Cook, stirring constantly, until mixture coats a spoon. Do not boil. Add extract. Set aside to cool before serving.

Katherine Fincher

Apricot Noodle Pudding

Oven: 350° - 1 hour

Yield: 10-12 servings

9 eggs, beaten
½ cup margarine, melted,
   divided
1 teaspoon vanilla extract
1 (12-ounce) jar apricot
   preserves, divided
4 apples, peeled and
   thinly sliced

1 cup raisins
1 cup sugar
1 teaspoon cinnamon
Lemon juice to taste
1 (12-ounce) package medium
   egg noodles, cooked
   and drained

Mix eggs, ¼ cup margarine, vanilla and ½ jar apricot preserves. Combine apples and raisins with cinnamon, sugar and lemon juice. Grease a 10x10-inch baking dish with remaining margarine. Place ½ noodles on bottom. Cover with apple-raisin mixture. Add remaining noodles. Pour egg mixture over noodles. Bake at 350° for 45 minutes. Remove from oven. Spread remaining apricot preserves over the top. Bake an additional 15 minutes.

Joan Anderson

Lemon Schaum Torte

Oven: 250° - 20 minutes
270° - 40 minutes

Yield: 6-8 servings

4 eggs, separated
½ teaspoon cream of tartar
1½ cups sugar, divided
1 teaspoon cornstarch
1 teaspoon lemon rind,
grated
2 teaspoons lemon juice

½ cup water
Pinch of salt
½ pint whipping cream,
whipped
Almonds or pecans,
finely chopped

Beat egg whites until bubbly. Add cream of tartar. Beat until stiff. Add slowly 1 cup sifted sugar. Beat until stiff and glossy. Pour into a buttered 9-inch square baking pan. Bake at 250° for 20 minutes; then at 270° for 40 minutes. Cool completely. Combine egg yolks, ½ cup sugar, cornstarch, lemon rind, lemon juice, water and salt in a double boiler. Cook until thickened, stirring constantly. Cool. Spread ½ of whipped cream over baked meringue; then spread lemon custard; top with remaining whipped cream. Sprinkle with chopped almonds or pecans. Refrigerate overnight.

Virginia Jones

Strawberries Romanoff

Yield: 4-6 servings

1½ pounds fresh
strawberries, quartered
lengthwise
¼ cup Cointreau, Grand
Marnier, or
Triple Sec

¼ cup sugar
Chantilly Romanoff
3 tablespoons pistachio
nuts, chopped

Combine strawberries and liqueur in large bowl; sprinkle with sugar. Mix gently. Cover with plastic wrap. Refrigerate 3-4 hours, spooning syrup over berries once or twice. One hour before serving, divide berries and syrup among 4-6 sherbet glasses. Refrigerate. Spoon Chantilly Romanoff over berries just before serving. Sprinkle with pistachio nuts.

Chantilly Romanoff

1 cup whipping cream,
well chilled
2 tablespoons Cointreau,
Grand Marnier, or
Triple Sec

½ teaspoon vanilla extract
½ cup sour cream

Beat cream until slightly thickened. Add liqueur and vanilla. Beat until soft peaks form. Fold in sour cream. Beat until mixture is thick. Refrigerate until ready to use.

Wanda Roach

Angel Dessert

Yield: 8-10 servings

1 (12-ounce) package semi-
   sweet chocolate chips
2 tablespoons sugar
5 tablespoons water

3 eggs, separated
1 pint whipping cream,
   whipped
1 large angel food cake

Melt chocolate chips in double boiler with sugar and water; cool. Add beaten egg yolks. Cook 5 minutes; cool again. Beat egg whites until stiff. Fold egg whites and whipped cream into chocolate mixture. Break cake into small pieces. Place ½ of cake in a 9x13-inch pan. Pour ½ of chocolate mixture over cake. Repeat layers. Cover tightly. Freeze until firm. Cut into squares.

Bonnie Massey

Snowball Cake

Yield: 12 servings

2 envelopes unflavored
   gelatin
4 tablespoons cold water
1 cup boiling water
1 (20-ounce) can pineapple
   chunks, undrained
1 cup sugar

½ teaspoon salt
1 tablespoon lemon juice
3 (1.5-ounce) envelopes
   whipped topping mix,
   divided
1 angel food cake

Soften gelatin in cold water. Dissolve in hot water. Add pineapple and juice, sugar, salt and lemon juice; mix well. Chill until partially set. Beat 2 envelopes of whipped topping mix, according to package directions, until very stiff. Fold into gelatin mixture. Break cake into small pieces. Line a colander or bowl with plastic wrap. Layer cake and gelatin mixture. Chill overnight. Unmold. Whip remaining envelope of whipped topping mix, according to package directions. Frost the cake. Refrigerate.
87 calories per serving.

Betty McDaniel

Bananas Foster I

Yield: 2 servings

1 cup brown sugar
Juice of 1 lemon
1 teaspoon cinnamon
Creme de banana liqueur

Orange liqueur
1 large banana, sliced
Vanilla ice cream

Melt brown sugar, stirring for 1-2 minutes, in a large frying pan. Slice lemon in half; wrap each in cheesecloth; squeeze juice of both into pan. Heat, stirring for 2 minutes. Add cinnamon and sliced banana. Add 1 pan length Creme de banana and 1 pan length orange liqueur, stirring constantly. Flame. Pour over ice cream. Serve immediately.

Nugget Gold

Bananas Foster II

Yield: 6 servings

2 tablespoons butter
4 tablespoons brown sugar
2 bananas, quartered
Pinch of cinnamon

1 tablespoon banana liqueur
1 ounce rum or brandy
Vanilla ice cream

Mix butter and brown sugar in saucepan. Cook over medium heat until caramelized. Add bananas; cook until tender. Add cinnamon and liqueur; stir. Add rum or brandy to top of mixture. Do not stir. Light with match. Spoon over ice cream while flaming.

This is from Brennan's Restaurant in New Orleans.

Rebecca Johnston

Blueberry Dessert

Oven: 350° · 10-15 minutes

Yield: 10-12 servings

First Layer

1½ cups self-rising flour
1 cup nuts, chopped

2 tablespoons sugar
¾ cup margarine, melted

Combine all ingredients. Press into a 9x13-inch baking dish. Bake at 350° for 10-15 minutes. Cool.

Second Layer

1 (8-ounce) package cream
cheese, softened
1 cup confectioners' sugar

1 (10-ounce) carton frozen
whipped topping

Combine all ingredients. Spread on crust.

Third Layer

2 cups blueberries
1 cup sugar
½ cup water, divided

2 tablespoons cornstarch
1 (8-ounce) can crushed
pineapple, drained

Combine blueberries, sugar and ¼ cup water. Bring to a boil over medium heat. Mix remaining ¼ cup water and cornstarch. Add to blueberries, stirring until thick. Cool. Stir in pineapple. Spread on cream cheese layer.

Fourth Layer

1 (10-ounce) carton frozen
whipped topping, thawed

1 cup nuts, chopped

Spread whipped topping over blueberry mixture. Sprinkle with nuts. Chill.

Tammie Curtis

Lemon Lush

Oven: 350° - 15 minutes

Yield: 8-10 servings

First Layer

1 cup all-purpose flour
1½ cups pecans, chopped

½ cup margarine, softened
1 tablespoon sugar

Combine all ingredients. Press into an 11x13-inch baking dish. Bake at 350° for 15 minutes. Cool.

Second Layer

1 (8-ounce) package cream cheese
1 cup frozen whipped topping

1 cup confectioners' sugar

Blend all ingredients. Pour over baked crust.

Third Layer

2 (3½-ounce) packages lemon instant pudding

3 cups milk

Mix pudding and milk until thickened. Pour over cream cheese layer.

Fourth Layer

1 cup frozen whipped topping, thawed

1 cup coconut
1 cup pecans, chopped

Spread whipped topping over pudding. Sprinkle coconut and pecans over top. Chill overnight.
Chocolate, vanilla or butterscotch instant pudding may be substituted.

Marie Moore

Fruit Pizza

Oven: 350° - 12-15 minutes

Yield: 10 servings

1 (17-ounce) package refrigerated sugar cookies
1 (8-ounce) package cream cheese
½ cup sugar
1 teaspoon vanilla extract

1 (11-ounce) can mandarin oranges, drained
Assorted sliced fruit - bananas, strawberries, kiwi fruit
¼ cup fruit marmalade
2 teaspoons hot water

Slice cookie dough ⅛-inch thick. Arrange on round pizza sheet so that they touch. Bake at 350° for 12-15 minutes. Cool. Cream together the cream cheese, sugar and vanilla. Spread cream cheese mixture over cookie crust. Arrange fruit over the cheese. Dilute the marmalade with the hot water; spread over fruit as a glaze. Cover; refrigerate for at least 4 hours before serving.
To enhance fresh fruit taste delete marmalade. A beautiful dish! Wonderful for summer parties.

Christi Kook

Yum Yum

Yield: 6-8 servings

2½ cups graham cracker
   crumbs
½ cup butter, melted
1 (8-ounce) package cream
   cheese, softened
¾ cup sugar

2 (1.5-ounce) envelopes non-
   dairy whipped topping
1 cup milk
1 teaspoon vanilla extract
2 (21-ounce) cans cherry
   pie filling

Mix crumbs and butter; reserve some for topping. Press onto bottom and sides of a 9x13-inch dish. Cream together cream cheese and sugar. Whip topping, milk and vanilla. Fold cream cheese mixture into whipped topping. Place half of mixture in crust. Spread pie filling over mixture. Top with remaining cream mixture. Sprinkle crumbs. Chill overnight.

Jeanette Samples

Special Peach Cobbler

Oven: 350° - 1 hour

Yield: 8-10 servings

8 cups fresh peaches,
   sliced
⅓ cup all-purpose flour
2 cups sugar
1 teaspoon cinnamon

1 cup water
½ cup butter or margarine,
   melted
1 teaspoon almond extract
Basic Pastry (page 247)

Dredge peaches in flour; add next 5 ingredients; mix well. Pour into lightly greased 13x9-inch baking dish. Prepare Basic Pastry. Roll out into ½-inch thickness. Cut into ½-inch strips. Arrange in lattice fashion over peaches. Bake at 350° for 1 hour.
To save time, use a refrigerated pie crust. Roll out and cut into strips.

Rebecca Johnston

Sweet Potato Cobbler

Oven: 350° - 30 minutes

Yield: 6-8 servings

2 cups sweet potatoes,
   sliced
1 cup sugar
½ teaspoon salt

2 cups water
Basic Pastry (page 247)
2 tablespoons butter
Sugar

Combine potatoes, sugar, salt and water in saucepan. Boil for 5 minutes. Cover bottom and sides of deep casserole dish with pie dough. Pour potato mixture over pie dough. Cut up small strips (approximately 1 cup) of pie dough; drop into potato mixture. Cut butter over pie mixture. Cover potato mixture with large pie crust. Cut dots of butter over top of pie crust. Sprinkle top of crust with sugar. Bake at 350° for 30 minutes.

Gladys Stephens

Sweet Potato Cobbler Pie

Oven: 350° - 1 hour

3 large sweet potatoes,
  peeled and sliced,
  divided
Water
1 teaspoon salt, divided
2 cups sugar, divided
1 teaspoon vanilla extract,
  divided

1 teaspoon lemon extract,
  divided
½ cup butter, divided
Dash of nutmeg
Favorite biscuit recipe

Cook potatoes in water to cover until barely done. Drain; reserve water for later use in pie. Place ½ of the potatoes in a 9x4-inch deep baking dish. Sprinkle with ½ teaspoon salt, 1 cup sugar, ½ teaspoon vanilla and lemon extracts and nutmeg. Dot with ½ of the butter. Completely cover with water from the potatoes. Cover with ½ biscuit dough rolled to fit the pan. Repeat with another layer of remaining ingredients. Cover with potato water. Bake at 350° for 1 hour. Rub butter on top crust. Serve immediately.
This is an old-fashioned family recipe.

Kate Roach

Apple Dumplings with Caramel Sauce

Oven: 350° - 30-45 minutes   **Yield:** 6-8 servings

2 tablespoons butter
¼ cup shortening
4 tablespoons milk
4 cups all-purpose flour
¼ teaspoon baking powder

½ teaspoon salt
6-8 apples, peeled and cored
Sugar
Cinnamon
Caramel Sauce

Cream butter and shortening. Add milk, flour, baking powder and salt. Mix well. Roll out dough and cut into rounds or squares. Place one apple in center of cut pastry pieces. Sprinkle with sugar and cinnamon. Pinch pastry up over apples. Place in a greased baking dish. Pour Caramel Sauce over dumplings. Bake at 350° for 30-45 minutes.
Red or Golden Delicious apples are best for this recipe.

Caramel Sauce

2 cups brown sugar,
  firmly packed
2 cups water

½ cup butter or margarine
Lemon juice

Combine sugar, water, butter and lemon juice. Stir mixture over medium heat until it comes to a boil.

Ann Hopkins

Apple Crisp

Oven: 375° - 1 hour   **Yield:** 8 servings

6 **large or 8 medium apples,**   ½ **cup butter, softened**
    peeled and sliced   1 **cup all-purpose flour**
1 **cup sugar**   1 **cup nuts, chopped**
1 **teaspoon cinnamon**   **Vanilla ice cream**
½ **cup brown sugar,**   **(optional)**
    firmly packed

Place apples in a buttered 2-quart baking dish. Combine sugar and cinnamon; sprinkle over apples. Cream brown sugar and butter. Add flour gradually; mix until smooth. Add nuts. Pat mixture in a thin crust over apples. Bake at 375° for 1 hour. Serve warm with vanilla ice cream, if desired.

Frances Gober

Applescotch Crisp

Oven: 350° - 45 minutes   **Yield:** 6-8 servings

4 **cups apples, peeled**   ⅔ **cup all-purpose flour**
    and sliced or   ½ **cup rolled oats**
    2 (20-ounce) cans   ½ **cup nuts, chopped**
    pie-sliced apples,   ¼ **cup sugar**
    drained   ½ **teaspoon salt**
½ **cup brown sugar,**   1 **teaspoon cinnamon**
    firmly packed   1 **(3⅝-ounce) package**
1 **tablespoon all-**   **butterscotch or vanilla**
    purpose flour   **pudding (not instant)**
¼ **cup milk**   ¼ **cup butter, melted**
½ **cup water**

Combine apples, brown sugar, 1 tablespoon flour, milk and water. Pour into a greased 9-inch square pan. Combine ⅔ cup flour, oats, nuts, sugar, salt, cinnamon, pudding mix and butter until crumbly. Sprinkle mixture over apples. Bake at 350° for 45 minutes.

Julia Dennis

Cran-Apple Cobbler

Oven: 400° - 30-35 minutes   **Yield:** 6-8 servings

3 **cups apples, peeled**   ¾ **cup sugar**
    and sliced   ½ **teaspoon cinnamon**
2 **cups cranberries, chopped**   ½ **cup mayonnaise**
¾ **cup light corn syrup**   ½ **cup nuts, chopped**
1 **cup all-purpose flour,**
    unsifted

Combine apples, cranberries and corn syrup. Mix well. Place in a greased 8-inch square baking dish. Stir together flour, sugar and cinnamon. Cut in mayonnaise until mixture resembles coarse crumbs; add nuts. Sprinkle over fruit. Bake at 400° for 30-35 minutes or until lightly brown. Serve warm.

Betty Little

Tosca Apples

Oven: 375° - 15-20 minutes   **Yield:** 8 servings

8 tart apples
½ cup unsalted butter
6 heaping tablespoons sugar
¾ cup slivered almonds

2 tablespoons milk
2 tablespoons all-purpose
   flour
Whipped cream

Grease a shallow baking pan. Peel and core the apples; cut into halves. Place close together in pan with cut side up. Melt butter. Add remaining ingredients, except whipped cream. Cook about 2 minutes until well blended. Spread over the apples. Bake at 375° for 15-20 minutes. Apples should be tender when pierced with a toothpick. Serve either warm, lukewarm or cold with whipped cream.
Can be served without whipped cream as a side dish.

Joan Anderson

Sour Cream Apple Squares

Oven: 350° - 25-35 minutes   **Yield:** 12-15 servings

2 cups all-purpose flour
2 cups brown sugar,
   firmly packed
½ cup margarine, softened
1 cup pecans, chopped
2 teaspoons cinnamon
1 teaspoon baking soda

½ teaspoon salt
1 cup sour cream
1 teaspoon vanilla extract
1 egg
2 cups apples, peeled
   and finely chopped

Combine flour, brown sugar and margarine. Blend at low speed until crumbly. Stir in nuts. Place 2¾ cups of crumb mixture into an ungreased 13x9-inch pan. Add cinnamon, soda, salt, sour cream, vanilla and egg to remaining crumb mixture. Blend well. Stir in apples. Spoon evenly over crumb layer in pan. Bake at 350° for 25-35 minutes or until toothpick inserted comes out clean. Cut into squares.

Wanda Roach

Apple Surprise

Oven: 350° - 1 hour   **Yield:** 8 servings

1 (21½-ounce) can prepared
   apple pie filling (can
   substitute fresh apples)
1 (16-ounce) can applesauce
1 box butter cake mix
Nuts, chopped (optional)

Cinnamon to taste
Nutmeg to taste
¾ cup margarine
Vanilla ice cream or
   whipped topping
   (optional)

Layer ingredients in the order listed in a 9x11-inch baking pan. Dot with margarine. Bake at 350° about 1 hour or until top is browned and crisp. Serve with vanilla ice cream or whipped topping, if desired.
Easy, quick and good!

Linda Hasty

Pumpkin Tart

Oven: 350° - 20 minutes   **Yield:** 8 servings

Crust

24 graham crackers, crushed   ½ cup butter
⅓ cup sugar

Mix all ingredients; press into a 9x13-inch pan.

First Layer

2 eggs, beaten   1 (8-ounce) package cream
¾ cup sugar   cheese, softened

Mix all ingredients; pour over crust. Bake 350° for 20 minutes.

Second Layer

2 cups pumpkin   1 envelope unflavored
3 eggs, separated   gelatin
¾ cup sugar, divided   ¼ cup cold water
½ cup milk   Whipped cream
½ teaspoon salt   Nuts, chopped
1 teaspoon cinnamon

Cook pumpkin, egg yolks, ½ cup sugar, milk, salt and cinnamon until it thickens. Remove from heat. Dissolve gelatin in cold water; add to pumpkin mixture. Let cool. Beat egg whites and ¼ cup sugar until stiff; fold into pumpkin mixture. Pour over baked crust. Chill until firm. Top with whipped cream; sprinkle with nuts. Refrigerate.

Lillian Thomason

Ma Rae's Hot Fudge Pudding

Oven: 350° - 40-45 minutes   **Yield:** 6-8 servings

1 cup all-purpose flour,   2 tablespoons shortening
   sifted   1 cup nuts, chopped
½ teaspoon baking soda   1 cup brown sugar
¼ teaspoon salt   1¾ cups boiling water
¾ cup sugar   Vanilla ice cream or
6 tablespoons cocoa,   frozen whipped topping
   divided   (optional)
2 tablespoons vinegar and
   milk to make ½ cup

Sift together flour, baking soda, salt, sugar and 2 tablespoons cocoa. Add milk, vinegar, shortening and nuts to sifted mixture. Stir until well blended. Turn into a greased 8-inch square pan which is at least 2 inches deep. Mix brown sugar and 4 tablespoons cocoa together; sprinkle over batter. Pour boiling water carefully over all. Bake at 350° for 40-45 minutes. (Bottom will rise to top and top will become pudding bottom.) Serve with vanilla ice cream or frozen whipped topping, if desired.
Great dessert for chocoholics!

Deborah Fincher

Chocolate Fondue Marveilleuse

Yield: 4 cups

1 (12-ounce) package semi-
　　sweet chocolate chips
2 (14-ounce) cans sweetened
　　condensed milk

Pinch of salt
Vanilla, almond or brandy
　　extract to taste

Mix the chocolate, milk, salt and extract in a fondue pot. Place over burner. Heat, stirring frequently, until chocolate is melted. Keep warm. Dip any of the following into chocolate:

marshmallows
cherries
banana slices
pineapple chunks
angel food cake chunks

strawberries
apple slices
doughnut pieces
pound cake chunks
grapes

Ollie White

Fudge Cupcakes

Oven: 325° - 30 minutes

Yield: 2 dozen

1¾ cups sugar
1 cup all-purpose flour
4 eggs
4 (1-ounce) squares semi-
　　sweet chocolate

1 cup margarine
1½ cups pecans, chopped
1 teaspoon vanilla extract

Combine sugar, flour and eggs; blend by hand, but do not beat. Melt chocolate and margarine in saucepan. Stir in nuts. Combine sugar mixture, chocolate mixture and vanilla. Blend, but do not beat. Pour into paper-lined muffin tins. Bake at 325° for 30 minutes.
Can glaze with a simple chocolate icing.

Pat Rodgers

Ultra-Rich Chocolate Sauce

Yield: 10-12 servings

½ cup margarine
1 (6-ounce) package semi-
　　sweet chocolate chips
½ teaspoon salt
1 (13-ounce) can evaporated
　　milk

3 cups sugar
2 tablespoons sherry
2 tablespoons coffee liqueur

Melt margarine and chocolate chips over low heat. Add salt. Stir in evaporated milk. Add sugar, 1 cup at a time, stirring until completely dissolved. Stir in sherry and coffee liqueur. Serve warm on cake or ice cream. Store in refrigerator. Can be reheated for later use.
Makes a neat Christmas, birthday, Valentine's Day gift.

Deborah Fincher

Mile High Strawberry Pie

Oven: 350° - 20 minutes   **Yield:** 12 servings

1 cup all-purpose flour
¼ cup light brown sugar
½ cup nuts, chopped
½ cup margarine, melted
2 egg whites
1 tablespoon lemon juice
1 cup sugar

1 (10-ounce) package frozen
   strawberries, thawed
1 cup whipping cream,
   whipped
Strawberries (optional)
Mint leaves (optional)

Combine first 4 ingredients until crumbly. Spread on cookie sheet. Bake at 350° for 20 minutes. Stir occasionally to brown evenly. Press ⅔ mixture in a 9x13-inch baking dish. Reserve the rest for topping. Combine egg whites, lemon juice, sugar and strawberries. Beat at high speed for 15-20 minutes. Fold in whipped cream. Spread on crust. Put in freezer for several hours. To serve, garnish with remaining crumbs. Cut into squares. Top each square with a strawberry and mint leaves, if desired.
A light, pretty dessert.

Susan Roach
Jackson, Georgia

Tortoni

Yield: 12 servings

3 eggs, separated
¼ cup water
¾ cup sugar
Dash of salt
¼ cup whole blanched
   almonds
1¾ teaspoons almond
   extract, divided

1½ cups heavy cream,
   whipped
¾ teaspoon vanilla extract
12 maraschino cherries
12 (2½-inch) paper baking
   cups

Place egg whites in a bowl. Let stand to room temperature. Refrigerate yolks. Mix water and sugar in a 1-quart saucepan; stir over low heat to dissolve. Boil, uncovered, without stirring to 236°F on a candy thermometer. (Syrup spins 2-inch thread when dropped from spoon.) Beat whites with salt just until soft peaks form. Pour hot syrup in thin stream over whites, beating constantly until very stiff peaks form. Refrigerate, covered, for 30 minutes. Place blanched almonds in shallow baking pan. Bake at 350° for 8-10 minutes or until lightly toasted. Chop almonds finely or grind in electric blender. Turn into small bowl. Stir in 1½ teaspoons almond extract; set aside. Beat cream with ¼ teaspoon almond extract and vanilla until quite stiff; fold into egg white mixture until well combined. Spoon into 12 paper-lined muffin pan cups. Sprinkle with almond mixture; top with cherry. Cover with foil. Freeze until firm.
Can be frozen up to 1 month.

Ollie White

Peppermint Stick Ice Cream

Yield: 2 quarts

¾ cup sugar
½ cup light corn syrup
1 teaspoon vanilla extract
⅛ teaspoon salt

2 cups heavy cream
1 cup light cream
½ cup peppermint candy, crushed

Stir together sugar, corn syrup, vanilla and salt. Add heavy and light cream, stirring until sugar dissolves. Freeze in a 2-quart ice cream freezer. Add peppermint candy after about 15 minutes of freezing (when it is mushy). Continue freezing.

Debbie Perry

Peach Ice Cream

Yield: 1 gallon

2 (13-ounce) cans evaporated milk
3 cups sugar
1 (12-ounce) can apricot nectar

1 dozen peaches, peeled, sliced and mashed
Milk

Combine all ingredients, stirring until sugar is dissolved. Pour in ice cream freezer. Fill up to freezer capacity (fill line) with whole milk. Freeze as usual.

Julia Dennis

Vanilla Ice Cream

Yield: 1 gallon

1 (3½-ounce) package instant vanilla pudding
1 (13-ounce) can evaporated milk
1 (14-ounce) can sweetened condensed milk

2 eggs, beaten
¾ cup sugar
4 cups milk
1 pint whipping cream
Dash of salt
1 teaspoon vanilla extract

Mix the pudding, evaporated milk and sweetened condensed milk. Add the remaining ingredients, blending well. Pour into ice cream freezer. Freeze. *Keeps well in refrigerator freezer after freezing; stays soft.*

Ruth Gramling

Sliced Lemon Ice Cream

Yield: 2 quarts

5 or 6 lemons, according
   to sizes

2 cups sugar, divided
6 cups half and half

Slice one lemon paper thin. (The food processor can get 42 slices if thinnest disc is used with very light pressure.) Cut each slice crossways in half. Squeeze the juice from the remaining lemons. Combine juice, lemon slices and 1 cup sugar. Refrigerate for several hours. Add remaining cup of sugar to half and half. Put into a freezer bowl (mechanical freezer - or a large metal mixing bowl.) Stir until sugar dissolves in cream. Put in freezer until it thickens. Pour lemon mixture into thickened half and half; freeze. (Can be covered and stirred several times in a refrigerator freezer compartment, but does better in a mechanical freezer, if possible.)

Sara Jones

Chocolate Sherry Cream Bars

Oven: 350° - 25 minutes

Yield: 5 dozen

2½ ounces baking chocolate
1 cup margarine
2 cups sugar
4 eggs

2 cups all-purpose flour
½ teaspoon salt
1 teaspoon vanilla extract

Melt chocolate and margarine in top of double boiler over hot water. Cool slightly. Beat eggs until light. Gradually cream in sugar. Add remaining ingredients. Beat 1 minute. Pour into greased and floured 10x14-inch pan. Bake at 350° for 25 minutes. Cool.

Filling

½ cup margarine
4 cups confectioners'
   sugar, measured after
   sifting

¼ cup cream
¼ cup sherry
1 cup nuts, chopped

Beat butter and sugar while gradually adding cream and sherry. Mixture should be light and fluffy. Add nuts. Spread over the first layer. Chill.

Topping

1 (6-ounce) package semi-
   sweet chocolate chips

4 tablespoons margarine,
   melted
4 tablespoons water

Melt chocolate and butter with water in top of double boiler over hot water. Mix well. Dribble over filling. Chill until firm. Cut into 1x2-inch bars. Store in refrigerator.

Grace Hyatt

Brownies

Oven: 350° - 35 minutes   **Yield:** 2 dozen

½ cup butter
½ cup margarine
2 cups sugar
4 tablespoons cocoa
4 eggs

½ teaspoon salt
1½ cups all-purpose flour
2 teaspoons vanilla extract
1 cup nuts, chopped
Frosting (optional)

Melt butter and margarine. Add remaining ingredients in order given. Pour into a greased and floured 9x13-inch pan. Bake at 350° about 35 minutes. Do not overbake. Remove. Cool. Frost, if desired. Cut into squares.

Linda Merrell

Crème de Menthe Brownies

Oven: 350° - 20-25 minutes   **Yield:** 2½-3 dozen

First Layer

1 cup sugar
½ cup butter, softened
4 eggs, beaten
1 cup all-purpose flour

1 teaspoon salt
1 (16-ounce) can chocolate
   syrup
1 teaspoon vanilla extract

Cream sugar and butter. Add eggs and remaining ingredients. Blend well. Pour into a greased 13x9-inch baking dish. Bake at 350° for 20-25 minutes. Cool completely.

Second Layer

2 cups confectioners'
   sugar
½ cup butter, softened

2 tablespoons green Creme
   de Menthe

Mix all ingredients. Pour over cooled cake layer.

Glaze

1 (6-ounce) package semi-
   sweet chocolate chips

6 tablespoons butter

Melt chocolate chips and butter. Cool until able to spread easily. Spread over brownies. Chill. Cut into squares.
Sinfully rich! This makes an elegant dessert if made in a jelly roll pan.

Cissy Cloud

Apple-Orange Brownies

Oven: 350° - 15 minutes

6 tablespoons butter
   or margarine
1 cup dark brown sugar,
   firmly packed
½ cup applesauce
1 teaspoon orange peel,
   grated
1 egg, beaten

1 teaspoon vanilla extract
1¼ cups all-purpose flour,
   sifted
1 teaspoon baking powder
½ teaspoon salt
¼ teaspoon baking soda
½ cup walnuts, chopped
Orange Glaze

Combine butter and brown sugar in saucepan. Cook until melted, stirring constantly. Beat in applesauce, orange peel, egg and vanilla. Sift flour, baking powder, salt and soda. Stir into applesauce mixture. Add walnuts. Spread in a greased 15½x10½-inch pan. Bake at 350° for 15 minutes. While warm, top with Orange Glaze.

Orange Glaze

1½ cups confectioners'
   sugar, sifted
½ teaspoon vanilla extract

Dash of salt
2 tablespoons orange juice

Combine all ingredients, mixing well.

Emma Ridenhour

Oatmeal Bars

Oven: 350°
  Crust - 10 minutes
  Filling - 15-20 minutes

Yield: 2 dozen

1 cup + 3 tablespoons
   all-purpose flour, divided
1 cup rolled oats
¾ cup brown sugar,
   firmly packed
½ teaspoon baking soda
¼ teaspoon salt

¾ cup butter, melted
1 (6-ounce) package semi-
   sweet chocolate chips
½ cup pecans, chopped
¾ cup caramel ice cream
   topping

Combine 1 cup flour, oats, brown sugar, soda, salt and butter. Blend well at low speed with mixer to form crumbs. Press half of crumbs in bottom of a greased 11x7-inch pan. Bake at 350° for 10 minutes. Remove from oven. Sprinkle with chocolate chips and pecans. Blend caramel topping and 3 tablespoons flour; pour over chocolate and pecans to cover. Sprinkle with remaining crumbs. Bake at 350° for 15-20 minutes or until bars are golden brown. Chill 2 hours. Cut into bars.

Frances Gober

Mocha Creme Bars

Oven: 350° - 30 minutes   **Yield:** 2½ dozen

1 cup butter, softened
2 cups sugar
4 eggs
3 teaspoons vanilla extract
½ teaspoon salt

1¾ cups all-purpose flour
1 cup pecans, chopped
2 (1-ounce) squares
   unsweetened chocolate,
   melted
Mocha Creme Frosting

Cream butter and sugar until light and fluffy. Add eggs, vanilla and salt; mix well. Stir in flour. Divide batter in half. Add nuts to ½ of mixture. Mix well and spread this half evenly over bottom of a 13x9-inch pan. Blend chocolate into remaining half; spread evenly over the layer already in the pan. Bake at 350° for 30 minutes. Cool. Frost with Mocha Creme.

Mocha Creme Frosting

½ teaspoon instant coffee
   granules
1 tablespoon hot water
½ cup butter, softened
1 tablespoon cocoa

2 cups confectioners'
   sugar
1 egg yolk
½ teaspoon vanilla extract
Dash of salt

Dissolve coffee in hot water. Cream butter, cocoa, sugar and coffee mixture until smooth. Add remaining ingredients. Beat until light and fluffy.

Cathie Bass

Coconut Pecan Squares

Oven: 350°   **Yield:** 1-1½ dozen
Crust - 20 minutes
Filling - 20 minutes

½ cup margarine, softened
½ cup dark brown sugar,
   packed
1 cup + 2 tablespoons sifted
   all-purpose flour, divided
2 eggs, beaten until
   frothy

1 cup light brown sugar
½ cup shredded coconut
1 cup nuts, chopped
1 teaspoon vanilla extract
Pinch of salt
Confectioners' sugar

Cream margarine and dark brown sugar. Add 1 cup flour; mix well. Press into a greased 8-inch square pan, spreading evenly into corners. Bake at 350° for 20 minutes. Beat eggs. Gradually add sugar and beat until thick. Toss coconut with 2 tablespoons flour. Add remainder of ingredients except confectioners' sugar. Mix well. Spread over baked crust. Bake at 350° for 20 minutes more or until browned. Sprinkle with confectioners' sugar when cool. Cut into squares.

Betty Barrett

Graham Cracker Bars

Yield: 20 squares

¾ cup butter
1 cup sugar
½ cup evaporated milk
1 egg, beaten in milk
1 cup graham cracker
  crumbs

1 cup flaked coconut
1 cup pecans, chopped
1 (14-ounce) box honey
  graham crackers
Frosting

Combine butter, sugar, evaporated milk and egg. Cook over low heat until thickened. Stir in graham cracker crumbs, coconut and pecans. Line a greased 10x15-inch pan with graham cracker squares. Pour filling on top of crackers. Place another layer of graham cracker squares over filling. Spread Frosting over squares. Chill overnight. Cut into squares. Store in refrigerator.

Frosting

½ cup butter, softened
2 cups confectioners'
  sugar

2 or 3 tablespoons
  evaporated milk

Beat all ingredients to spreading consistency.

Pam Gaddis

Cream Cheese-Almond Squares

Oven: 300° - 1 hour 10 minutes   **Yield:** 2½ dozen

½ cup butter or
  margarine, softened
1 cup + 2 teaspoons
  sugar, divided
2 tablespoons milk
1½ teaspoons grated lemon
  rind, divided
1⅓ cups all-purpose flour
2 (8-ounce) packages cream
  cheese, softened

1 egg, slightly beaten
1 cup almonds, chopped
  and toasted
1 cup sifted confectioners'
  sugar
1 tablespoon water
1 teaspoon cinnamon
Toasted sliced almonds
  (optional)

Combine butter, 2 teaspoons sugar, milk and ½ teaspoon lemon rind; beat until light and fluffy. Add flour; mix well. Press mixture into the bottom of a greased 9-inch square baking pan; set aside. Combine cream cheese, 1 cup sugar, 1 teaspoon lemon rind and egg; beat until smooth. Stir in almonds. Pour mixture over layer in pan. Bake at 300° for 1 hour 10 minutes or until set. Combine confectioners' sugar, water and cinnamon; mix well. Spread over hot mixture; let cool. Chill 3 to 4 hours; cut into squares. Garnish with toasted sliced almonds, if desired.
Great for parties and cocktail buffets.

Martha Nichols

Cheesecake Squares

Oven: 350°
   Crust - 25 minutes
   Filling, Topping - 25 minutes

Yield: 3 dozen

Crust

1¼ cups all-purpose flour
½ cup butter or
   margarine, softened
¼ cup sugar

1 egg
½ teaspoon vanilla extract

Mix flour and butter until crumbly. Add sugar, egg and vanilla. Mix until well-blended. Place on flat surface. Knead into a ball. Wrap in waxed paper. Chill for 40-50 minutes. Press dough into bottom of a greased 8-inch square pan. Bake at 350° for 25 minutes. Remove from oven, leaving oven on.

Cheese Filling

1 (8-ounce) package cream
   cheese, softened
¼ cup sugar
1 egg

2 tablespoons sour cream
1 tablespoon lemon juice
½ teaspoon vanilla extract

Beat cream cheese until smooth. Add remaining ingredients; mix well. Pour over crust.

Nut Topping

¼ cup brown sugar,
   firmly packed
2 tablespoons all-purpose
   flour
1 tablespoon butter,
   softened

¼ teaspoon cinnamon
½ cup nuts, chopped

Mix all ingredients until crumbly. Sprinkle over filling. Bake at 350° for 25 minutes. Cool. Cut into squares.
Assembled bars can be frozen.

Myrna Pruett

Triplets

Oven: 350° - 10-15 minutes   **Yield:** 6-7 dozen

1 cup brown sugar,
    firmly packed
1 cup sugar
1 cup shortening

2 eggs
2½ cups all-purpose flour
1 teaspoon salt
1 teaspoon baking soda

Cream sugars, shortening and eggs. Combine flour, salt and soda. Blend well. Add to creamed mixture, mixing well. Divide dough into three parts. Combine with each of the following variations.

Chocolate Crinkles

⅓ cup semi-sweet
    chocolate chips

½ cup confectioners'
    sugar

Melt chocolate chips over hot water; add to one part of the dough. Shape into 1-inch balls; roll in confectioners' sugar. Place on greased cookie sheet. Bake at 350° for 15 minutes.

Cherry Almond Drops

½ cup cut-up candied
    cherries, drained well
½ cup flaked coconut
    or shredded coconut

½ teaspoon almond extract
½ cup slivered almonds

Add cherries, nuts, coconut and almond extract to one part of the above dough. Drop by teaspoonfuls on greased cookie sheet. Bake at 350° for 10 minutes.

Date Nut Chews

½ cup dates, cut up   ½ cup nuts, chopped

Add dates and nuts to one part of the above dough. Shape into 1-inch balls. Place on greased cookie sheet. Bake at 350° for 15 minutes.

Virginia Spears

Cream Cheese Bars

Oven: 350° - 30 minutes   **Yield:** 2 dozen

1 box yellow cake mix
½ cup butter, melted
3 eggs, divided
1 teaspoon vanilla extract

1 (8-ounce) package cream
    cheese, softened
1 (16-ounce) box
    confectioners' sugar

Mix cake mix, butter and 1 egg. Press into a greased 9x13-inch baking dish. In a blender or processor, mix 2 eggs, vanilla, cream cheese and confectioners' sugar. Pour over crust. Bake at 350° for 30 minutes. Cool completely. Cut into bars.
Very quick and easy.

Charlotte Greene

Lemon Bars

Oven: 350°   Yield: 1 dozen
　　Crust - 20 minutes
　　Filling - 25 minutes

1　cup + 2 tablespoons all-purpose flour, divided	2　eggs, slightly beaten
½　cup butter	1　cup sugar
¼　cup confectioners' sugar	¼　teaspoon salt
	3　tablespoons lemon juice
	½　teaspoon baking powder

Cream 1 cup flour, butter and confectioners' sugar. Press mixture into a greased 8 or 9-inch square pan. Bake at 350° for 20 minutes. Cool. Mix eggs, sugar, salt and lemon juice. Add 2 tablespoons flour and baking powder. Mix. Pour over cool crust. Bake at 350° for 25 minutes. Sprinkle with additional confectioners' sugar while hot. Chill in refrigerator for several hours or overnight. Cut into bars.

Jane Wofford

Cherry Balls

Yield: 2 dozen

2　tablespoons cocoa	1　cup pecans, chopped
1　cup confectioners' sugar	2　(6-ounce) bottles maraschino cherries with stems
1　cup bourbon	Cocoa and confectioners' sugar for dredging
2　tablespoons light corn syrup	
2½　cups vanilla wafers, crushed	

Sift cocoa and sugar together. Combine bourbon and syrup. Stir into sugar mixture. Add wafers and pecans; mix thoroughly. Roll mixture around a cherry and dredge with sugar mixed with a small amount of cocoa. Arrange on serving dish with stems up.
Stem on cherry makes this an ideal party treat, and they're very easy - no baking!

Sue Cannon

Caramel Bars

Oven: 350° - 30 minutes   Yield: 4 dozen

1　cup margarine, melted	2　teaspoons baking powder
1　(16-ounce) box light brown sugar	1　teaspoon salt
2　eggs	1　cup nuts, chopped
2　cups all-purpose flour	1　teaspoon vanilla extract

Cream butter, brown sugar and eggs. Add flour, baking powder, salt, nuts and vanilla to creamed mixture, beating well. Pour into a greased 13x9-inch pan. Bake at 350° for 30 minutes. Let cool in pan. Cut into squares.
Freezes well.

Ann Benzel

Pineapple Preserves Cookies

Oven: 375° - 10 minutes   **Yield:** 5 dozen

1 cup sugar
¾ cup margarine, softened
1 egg
2¼ cups all-purpose flour

1 teaspoon baking soda
½ teaspoon salt
Pineapple or apricot
  preserves

Cream sugar and margarine until light and fluffy; add egg, beating well. Combine flour, soda and salt. Add to creamed mixture, mixing well. Stir in ¼ cup preserves. Shape dough into walnut-sized balls on cookie sheet. Make a slight indentation in each cookie. Spoon a small amount of preserves in each indentation. Bake at 375° for 10 minutes.

Joan Satterfield

Lizzie's Fruit Cake Cookies

Oven: 325° - 15 minutes   **Yield:** 4 dozen

1 pound chopped candied
  cherries
1 pound chopped candied
  pineapple
1 pound raisins
½ cup whiskey
1 cup butter, softened
¾ cup brown sugar,
  firmly packed

2 eggs
2 cups all-purpose flour
½ teaspoon baking soda
1½ tablespoons milk
1 teaspoon cinnamon
1 teaspoon allspice
1 teaspoon cloves
1 teaspoon nutmeg
3 cups nuts, chopped

Combine cherries, pineapple and raisins. Soak overnight in whiskey. Cream butter and sugar; add eggs, beating after each. Sift dry ingredients; add to creamed mixture along with milk. Fold in fruit and nuts. Drop by teaspoonfuls onto greased baking sheet. Bake at 325° for 15 minutes.

Lila Stevens

Mom's Date Pinwheel Cookies

Oven: 350° - 10-15 minutes   **Yield:** 4 dozen

½ cup butter
½ cup brown sugar,
  firmly packed
1 cup sugar, divided
1 egg, unbeaten
1 teaspoon vanilla extract

2 cups all-purpose flour
¼ teaspoon salt
¼ teaspoon baking soda
7¼ ounces dates, chopped
1 cup nuts, chopped
½ cup water

Cream butter, brown sugar and ½ cup sugar. Add egg and vanilla. Sift together flour, salt and soda. Add to creamed mixture. Chill for 2 to 3 hours. Combine dates, nuts, ½ cup sugar and water. Simmer for 5 minutes; cool. Roll dough into a rectangle. Spread with filling. Roll up as a jelly roll. Chill dough. Slice cookies. Bake at 350° for 10-15 minutes.

Pat Stewart

Chocolate Crinkles

Oven: 350° - 15 minutes   Yield: 4 dozen

½ cup shortening
1⅔ cups sugar
2 teaspoons vanilla extract
2 eggs
2 (1-ounce) squares
    unsweetened chocolate,
    melted and cooled
2 cups all-purpose flour

2 teaspoons baking powder
½ teaspoon salt
⅓ cup milk
½ cup walnuts or pecans,
    chopped (optional)
Sifted confectioners'
    sugar

Cream shortening, sugar and vanilla. Beat in eggs, then chocolate. Add dry ingredients alternately with milk. Stir in nuts. Chill 3 hours. Form into 1-inch balls. Roll in confectioners' sugar. Place on a greased cookie sheet. Bake at 350° about 15 minutes. Cool slightly. Remove from pan.

Deborah Smith

Benne Seed Cookies

Oven: 325° - 20 minutes   Yield: 2 dozen

⅓ cup butter, softened
¾ cup light brown sugar,
    firmly packed
1 egg
¾ cup all-purpose flour

¼ cup benne seeds
    (sesame seeds), toasted
½ teaspoon vanilla extract
⅛ teaspoon baking powder

Cream the butter and sugar together; mix with the remaining ingredients in the order given. Drop with a teaspoon onto waxed paper-lined cookie sheet. Place about 2 inches apart, allowing plenty of room for spreading. Bake at 325° for 20 minutes or until light brown.

Carolyn Weaver

Gingerbread Cookies

Oven: 375° - 6 minutes   Yield: 2 dozen

4 cups all-purpose flour
1 tablespoon baking soda
½ teaspoon salt
2 teaspoons ginger
½ teaspoon cinnamon

½ cup butter
1 cup dark brown sugar
1 cup molasses
1½ tablespoons milk

Sift together flour, baking soda, salt and spices. Heat butter, sugar and molasses over low heat until butter is melted and sugar dissolved. Cool mixture. Add flour mixture and enough milk to make a firm dough. Wrap in waxed paper. Chill 1 hour. Roll out dough to ¼-inch thickness. Cut out shapes. Place on greased cookie sheet. If desired, add decorations. Bake at 375° for 6 minutes. *Makes great Gingerbread Men.*

Jean Gober Hunter
Roswell, Georgia

Butter Drops

Oven: 350° - 12-15 minutes   **Yield:** 6 dozen

1½ cups butter
1½ cups sugar
3 egg yolks

2 teaspoons vanilla extract
3½ cups all-purpose flour
   Quince or Guava jelly

Cream butter and sugar; add egg yolks. Mix in flour and vanilla, blending well. Roll into little balls. Dip finger in flour and make a hole in each one. Fill with a firm jelly such as quince or guava. Bake at 350° for 12-15 minutes or until light brown.

Margaret McFather

Ice Box Cookies

Oven: 350° - 10 minutes   **Yield:** 5 dozen

3½ cups all-purpose flour
 1 teaspoon baking soda
 ½ teaspoon salt
 1 cup butter or
   margarine

2 cups brown sugar,
   firmly packed
1 cup pecans, chopped
2 eggs

Sift flour, soda and salt. Mix the firm butter and flour together until it looks like crumbs. Add brown sugar, then nuts. Beat eggs together until light; mix into a dough which will be rather firm. Knead until smooth. Make into a round roll the size desired. Wrap in waxed paper. Place in freezer overnight. Slice cookies; place on baking sheet. Bake at 350° for 10 minutes or until light brown.
Rolls may be kept indefinitely in the freezer and cooked as needed if properly wrapped.

Ruth Denney

One Cup Cookies

Oven: 350° - 10-12 minutes   **Yield:** 3-4 dozen

  1 cup sugar
  1 cup brown sugar,
    firmly packed
  1 cup margarine, softened
  1 cup vegetable oil
  1 egg
3½ cups all-purpose flour
  1 teaspoon cream of
    tartar
  1 teaspoon baking soda

1 teaspoon salt
1 cup rolled oats
1 cup oven-toasted rice
   cereal
1 cup flaked coconut
1 cup semi-sweet
   chocolate chips
1 cup pecans, chopped

Cream sugars, margarine, oil and egg. Sift together flour, cream of tartar, soda and salt; add to creamed mixture. Beat until well blended. Add oats, rice cereal, coconut, chocolate chips and pecans. Drop by teaspoonfuls onto a greased cookie sheet. Bake at 350° for 10-12 minutes.
These freeze well.

Madelin Phelps

Old-Fashioned Oatmeal Cookies

Oven: 400° - 8-10 minutes   **Yield:** 6½ dozen

1 cup raisins	2½ cups self-rising flour
1 cup water	1 teaspoon cinnamon
¾ cup shortening	½ teaspoon cloves
1½ cups sugar	2 cups rolled oats
2 eggs, beaten	½ cup nuts, chopped
1 teaspoon vanilla extract	

Simmer raisins and water over medium heat until raisins are plump, about 15 minutes. Drain raisins, reserving liquid; add enough water to liquid to equal ½ cup. Mix thoroughly the shortening, sugar, eggs and vanilla. Stir in reserved liquid. Blend in flour, cinnamon, cloves, oats and nuts. Drop dough by rounded teaspoonfuls, about 2 inches apart, onto an ungreased baking sheet. Bake at 400° for 8-10 minutes or until light brown.

Barbara Gentry

Peanut Butter-Oatmeal Cookies

Oven: 350° - 8-10 minutes   **Yield:** 5 dozen

1 cup soft shortening	2 cups all-purpose flour, sifted
1 cup brown sugar, firmly packed	2 teaspoons baking soda
¾ cup sugar	½ teaspoon salt
2 eggs	1 cup rolled oats
1 cup creamy peanut butter	

Beat shortening and sugars together until creamy. Add eggs and peanut butter; mix well. Sift together flour, soda and salt. Add to creamed mixture, mixing well. Stir in oats. Shape dough to form 1-inch balls. Place on ungreased cookie sheets. With tines of fork, press to make crisscrosses on each cookie. Bake at 350° for 8-10 minutes.
Kids love to roll into balls and press.

Joy Owen

Sandies

Oven: 325° · 25 minutes   Yield: 7½ dozen

1 cup butter or
   margarine, softened
⅓ cup sugar
2 teaspoons water
2 teaspoons vanilla extract

2 cups all-purpose flour,
   sifted
1 cup pecans, chopped
   Confectioners' sugar

Cream butter and sugar. Add water and vanilla. Mix well. Add flour and pecans.
Chill 3-4 hours. Shape into small balls. Place on an ungreased cookie sheet.
Bake at 325° for 25 minutes. Cool slightly. Roll in confectioners' sugar.

Jackie Swords

Sugar Cookies I

Oven: 300° · 10 minutes   Yield: 3 dozen

1 cup shortening or ½ cup
   shortening and ½ cup
   butter
1 cup sugar
1 egg, slightly beaten

1 teaspoon vanilla extract
2½ cups self-rising flour
   Milk
   Sugar

Cream shortening with sugar. Add egg, vanilla, flour and a little milk. Mix
thoroughly. Chill 2 to 3 hours. Roll out on a floured surface. Cut out using
favorite designs. Sprinkle with sugar. Place on a greased cookie sheet. Bake at
300° for 10 minutes.

Pat Stewart

Sugar Cookies II

Oven: 375° · 20 minutes   Yield: 2 dozen

2 cups all-purpose flour
½ teaspoon baking soda
½ teaspoon salt
½ cup shortening
1 cup sugar

1 egg, separated
½ teaspoon vanilla extract
½ cup buttermilk or
   sour milk
   Sugar

Sift together flour, soda and salt. Beat shortening, sugar and egg yolk until fluffy.
Mix in flour alternately with buttermilk. Stir in vanilla. Beat egg white until stiff.
Fold into creamed mixture. Drop by tablespoons onto a greased cookie sheet.
Sprinkle with sugar. Bake at 375° for 20 minutes.
*This is my great-grandmother's recipe. They are large, old-fashioned soft
cookies.*

Pat Gold

Granny Anderson's Peanut Butter Cookies

Oven: 350° - 8-10 minutes   Yield: 6 dozen

1 cup brown sugar,
   firmly packed
1 cup sugar
1 cup peanut butter

1 cup shortening
2 eggs
2¼ cups self-rising flour
1 teaspoon baking soda

Mix all ingredients thoroughly. Pinch off into balls. Place on ungreased cookie sheet. Flatten with a floured fork. Bake at 350° for 8-10 minutes for chewy cookies. For crunchy cookies, bake longer.

Patty Mann

Snickerdoodles

Oven: 400° - 8-10 minutes   Yield: 5 dozen

1 cup shortening
1½ cups sugar
2 eggs
1 teaspoon vanilla extract
2¾ cups all-purpose flour,
   sifted

½ teaspoon salt
1 teaspoon baking soda
2 teaspoons cream of
   tartar
2 tablespoons sugar
1 tablespoon cinnamon

Cream shortening, sugar, eggs and vanilla. Sift together flour, salt, soda and cream of tartar. Add to creamed mixture. Roll into walnut-sized balls. Roll in mixture of sugar and cinnamon. Place 2 inches apart on an ungreased baking sheet. Bake at 400° for 8-10 minutes until lightly browned but still soft.

Cindy Holcomb

Millionaires

Yield: 2 dozen

1 (14-ounce) package caramels
1 tablespoon water
2 cups pecan halves

⅛ pound paraffin
1 (6-ounce) package semi-
   sweet chocolate chips

Melt caramels and water in double boiler; stir in pecans. Drop by teaspoons on buttered pan. Refrigerate until firm. Melt paraffin and chocolate chips in double boiler. Dip caramel mixture into chocolate. Place on waxed paper to cool.

Ollie White

Italian Cream Candy

Yield: 7 pounds

6¾ cups sugar
1½ pints Carnation
    evaporated milk
    (no substitute)

1 pint light corn syrup
1 teaspoon vanilla extract
3 pounds English walnuts,
    shelled and chopped

Boil sugar, milk and syrup until it forms a soft ball in water. Cool. Add vanilla; beat to a stiff paste. Add nuts; beat until glossy finish turns dull. (Proper beating is the secret of this candy.) Pour out and spread on large sheet of heavy foil. Cut into 1-inch squares.
Heavenly; worth the effort.

Jackie Swords

Coconut Bonbons

Yield: 120 balls

½ cup butter or
    margarine
2 (3½-ounce) cans flaked
    coconut
1 (14-ounce) can sweetened
    condensed milk

3 cups pecans, chopped
2 (16-ounce) boxes
    confectioners' sugar
½ pound paraffin
2 (12-ounce) packages semi-
    sweet chocolate chips

Melt butter. Add coconut, milk, sugar and pecans. Mix well. Butter hands and roll candy into small balls. Place on cookie sheet which has been covered with waxed paper. Chill 30 minutes. Melt paraffin over low heat in a double boiler. Add chocolate chips; stir until smooth. Cover. Put toothpicks into balls; dip into chocolate mixture. Return to waxed paper to cool. Remove picks before chocolate hardens. Store in an airtight container in refrigerator.
Makes an excellent holiday gift.

Dorothy Densmore

Reeses Peanut Butter Squares

Yield: 36 squares

1½ cups graham cracker
    crumbs
1 cup butter, melted,
    divided
1 (16-ounce) box
    confectioners' sugar

1½ cups peanut butter
1 (6-ounce) package semi-
    sweet chocolate chips

Stir together crumbs, ¾ cup melted butter, sugar and peanut butter. Line a 13x9-inch pan with waxed paper. Pat mixture firmly into lined pan. Melt chocolate pieces and ¼ cup butter over low heat; spread over peanut butter mixture. Cool in refrigerator. When ready to cut, lift out of pan by waxed paper.
Variation: Crunchy peanut butter may be substituted.

Susan Roach
Jackson, Georgia

Toffee Butter Crunch

1 cup butter	1 cup slivered almonds,
1⅓ cups sugar	toasted and finely chopped
1 tablespoon light corn	2 (8-ounce) milk chocolate
syrup	bars, melted
3 tablespoons water	

Melt butter, sugar, syrup and water in a large heavy saucepan. Cook over medium heat, stirring occasionally, until hard crack stage (300° on candy thermometer) is reached. Quickly stir in almonds. Spread in a well-greased 13x9-inch pan. Cool. Refrigeration speeds cooling. Turn out onto waxed paper. Spread with half the chocolate. (If desired, sprinkle with an additional ½ cup finely chopped almonds.) Put in refrigerator to cool. Turn candy over, spread with remaining chocolate. Cool. Break into pieces. Store in an airtight container.

Makes a great gift.

Nancy Rushton

Rum Balls

Yield: 120 (1-inch) balls

2 pounds confectioners'	2 cups nuts, chopped
sugar	½ cup light rum or bourbon
1 cup margarine or butter,	1 (12-ounce) package semi-
softened	sweet chocolate chips
½ (14-ounce) can sweetened	¼ pound paraffin
condensed milk	

Mix sugar, margarine, milk, nuts and rum. Shape into 1-inch balls. Refrigerate at least 2 hours. Melt chocolate and paraffin in a double boiler. Cool until luke-warm. Dip balls in chocolate. Place on waxed paper to cool. Store in airtight container in refrigerator.

Margaret McFather

Divinity

Yield: 4 dozen

2⅔ cups sugar	2 egg whites
⅔ cup light corn syrup	1 teaspoon vanilla extract
½ cup water	⅔ cup nuts, chopped

Heat sugar, corn syrup and water in 2-quart saucepan over low heat, stirring constantly, until sugar is dissolved. Cook, without stirring, to 260° on candy thermometer or until small amount of mixture dropped into very cold water forms a hard ball. Remove from heat. Beat egg whites until stiff peaks form; continue beating while pouring hot syrup in a thin stream into egg whites. Add vanilla; beat until mixture holds its shape and becomes slightly dull (mixture may become too stiff for mixer). Fold in nuts. Drop mixture from tip of buttered spoon onto waxed paper. Store in an airtight container.

Jeanette Black

Katie's After Dinner Mints

Yield: 150 mints

1 egg white
1 tablespoon cream
1 teaspoon vanilla extract
3 drops peppermint or
½ teaspoon peppermint
extract

Food coloring
1 (16-ounce) box
confectioners' sugar
1 tablespoon butter

Combine egg white, cream, vanilla, peppermint and food coloring. Mix well. Add sugar all at once; mix well. Add butter (and additional sugar if needed to make firm). Shape in small balls. Arrange on waxed paper and press with a fork dipped in confectioners' sugar. Let stand overnight to form crust. Then pack in tins with waxed paper between layers.
Can be frozen.

Carolyn Jones

Chinese Noodles

Yield: 30

1 (6-ounce) package
butterscotch morsels
1 (5-ounce) can Chinese
noodles

1 (6½-ounce) can salted
peanuts

Melt morsels in top of double boiler. Stir in nuts and noodles. Drop by teaspoonfuls onto waxed paper.

Patty Mann

"El Magnifique Fudge"

Yield: 3 pounds

4½ cups sugar
1 (13-ounce) can evaporated
milk
½ cup margarine or butter
4 (4½-ounce) chocolate bars
1 (12-ounce) package semi-
sweet chocolate chips

1 pint marshmallow cream
2 cups walnuts or pecans,
chopped
1 teaspoon vanilla extract
1 tablespoon Frangelica
liqueur (optional)

Combine sugar, milk, margarine; boil 8 minutes, stirring constantly. Remove from heat and add chocolate bars and chocolate chips. Beat well. Add marshmallow cream, nuts and vanilla (and liqueur); beat until cool. Pour onto flat surface and press out to cut into squares.

Deborah Fincher

Chocolate Fudge

Yield: 1 pound

2 cups sugar
2 tablespoons light corn
   syrup
4 tablespoons cocoa
¾ cup milk

2 tablespoons butter
⅛ teaspoon salt
1 teaspoon vanilla extract
¾ cup pecans, chopped

Combine sugar, syrup, cocoa, milk and butter. Cook over medium heat until mixture forms a soft ball. Set in cold water for 15 minutes. Add salt, vanilla and nuts. Beat until the color lightens. Pour into a greased 8-inch square pan to harden. Cut into squares.

Jane Wofford

White Fudge

Yield: 1½ pounds

2 cups sugar
½ cup sour cream
⅓ cup light corn
   syrup
2 tablespoons butter

¼ teaspoon salt
2 teaspoons vanilla extract
¼ cup candied cherries,
   quartered
1 cup nuts, chopped

Combine sugar, sour cream, corn syrup, butter and salt in saucepan. Slowly bring to a boil, stirring until sugar dissolves. Without stirring, boil until candy thermometer registers 236° (or until a small amount dropped in cold water forms a soft ball). Turn off heat and let stand 15 minutes (do not stir). Add vanilla. Beat until mixture begins to lose its gloss, about 8 minutes. Stir in cherries and nuts. Quickly pour into a buttered 9-inch square pan. Cool; cut into squares.

Janice Ingram

Rocky Road Fudge

Yield: 2 pounds

1½ cups miniature
   marshmallows, divided
6 squares semi-sweet
   chocolate
½ cup butter or margarine

2 cups sugar
⅔ cup evaporated milk
1 cup walnuts, chopped
1 teaspoon vanilla extract

Freeze ½ cup marshmallows until firm. Place chocolate and butter in large bowl. Combine sugar, 1 cup marshmallows and evaporated milk in heavy saucepan. Bring to boil over medium heat; boil for 5 minutes, stirring constantly. Pour over chocolate and butter; blend well until mixture begins to thicken. Stir in walnuts, vanilla and frozen marshmallows; pour into lightly greased 8-inch square pan. Chill until firm. Cut into squares.

Jeanette Black

Peanut Brittle

1½ cups sugar
2 tablespoons water
2 cups raw peanuts

½ cup light corn syrup
1½ teaspoons soda

Mix sugar, water, peanuts and syrup in skillet. Cook at moderate boil (350°) for 10 minutes or until syrup is golden tan. Stir in soda. Pour out on greased foil and spread thinly. Cool and break into serving pieces.

Patty Mann

Peanut Butter Balls

Yield: 60 (1-inch) balls

1 (12-ounce) jar peanut butter
1 (16-ounce) box confectioners' sugar

1⅓ sticks butter
¼ pound paraffin
1 (12-ounce) package semi-sweet chocolate chips

Mix peanut butter and sugar. Melt butter and pour evenly over peanut butter mixture. Mix well. Shape into balls about 1-inch thick. Put toothpick into each ball and place in freezer for 30 minutes. Melt paraffin and chocolate chips in top of double boiler. Remove balls from freezer and dip in chocolate mixture. Place on waxed paper to cool.
These freeze well and keep well in refrigerator.

Audrey Turner

Candied Orange Peel

3 oranges
9 cups water, divided

3½ cups sugar, divided

Cut peel of each orange into 4 sections with a sharp knife. Remove peel carefully with fingers. Scrape white membrane from peel with a spoon. Cut peel lengthwise into strips ¼-inch wide. Heat peel and 8 cups water to boiling in a 3-quart saucepan; reduce heat. Simmer, uncovered, 30 minutes; drain. Repeat simmering process. Heat 2 cups sugar and 1 cup water to boiling in 2-quart saucepan, stirring constantly, until sugar dissolves. Add peel. Simmer, uncovered, stirring occasionally for 45 minutes. Drain in strainer. Roll peel in 1½ cups sugar. Spread on waxed paper to dry.

Jeanette Black

Microwave

Spicy Meat Loaf

Yield: 6 servings

2 eggs, beaten
¾ cup milk
⅔ cup fine dry
  bread crumbs
2 onions, finely chopped
1 teaspoon salt

½ teaspoon chili powder
Dash of pepper
1½ pounds ground beef
¼ cup hot-style catsup
1 tablespoon brown sugar
½ teaspoon dry mustard

Combine eggs, milk, bread crumbs, onion, salt, chili powder and pepper. Add beef; mix well. Shape into a loaf in a 10x6-inch baking dish. Cook, covered, at MEDIUM HIGH for 20-22 minutes, giving dish a half turn once. Drain off excess fat. Combine catsup, brown sugar and dry mustard; spoon on top meat. Cook, uncovered, at MEDIUM HIGH for 1½-2 minutes. Let stand 5 minutes before serving.
Easy and good. Works well in food processor.

Margaret Logan

Oriental Meat Loaf

Yield: 6 servings

1½ pounds ground beef
½ cup fine, dry
  bread crumbs
½ cup rolled oats
2 eggs, beaten
½ cup onion, finely
  chopped
½ cup green pepper,
  finely chopped
⅓ cup water chestnuts,
  finely chopped
  (optional)

5 tablespoons catsup,
  divided
3 tablespoons soy sauce,
  divided
½ teaspoon salt
¼ teaspoon pepper
1 tablespoon brown sugar
½ teaspoon dry mustard

Combine ground beef, bread crumbs, oats, eggs, onion, green pepper, water chestnuts, 3 tablespoons catsup, 2 tablespoons soy sauce, salt and pepper; mix well. Shape into a 10x5-inch slightly rounded loaf in a 12x8-inch baking dish. Cover with waxed paper. Microwave at HIGH for 14-18 minutes or until firm to touch, giving dish a half turn after 7 minutes. Drain off excess drippings. Combine 2 tablespoons catsup, 1 tablespoon soy sauce, brown sugar and dry mustard; spoon over meat loaf. Microwave at MEDIUM HIGH for 1½-2 minutes. Let stand 5 minutes before serving.
Sauce really makes the dish.

Ollie White

Corned Beef and Cabbage Supper

Yield: 4 servings

1 medium onion, thinly
   sliced
2 medium potatoes, thinly
   sliced
¼ cup water
¾ teaspoon salt
¼ teaspoon pepper

½ pound Deli corned
   beef or roast, sliced
½ head cabbage, cut
   into thick slices
¼ cup butter or margarine,
   melted

Layer onions and potatoes in a greased 3-quart baking dish; add water, salt and pepper. Heat, covered, on HIGH 7-8 minutes. Add corned beef and cabbage; pour butter over cabbage. Heat, covered, at HIGH for 10-11 minutes until cabbage is tender. Stir once. Let stand, covered, 3-5 minutes before serving. *Men love it. Great winter supper.*

Helen Spears

Tacos

Yield: 6 servings

1 pound ground beef
½ cup onion, chopped
1 clove garlic, minced
¾ teaspoon salt
1 teaspoon chili powder
   Onion rings
12 fried and shaped taco
    shells

2 tomatoes, chopped
3 cups lettuce, finely
   shredded
2 cups Cheddar cheese,
   shredded
   Canned Mexican hot sauce
   or enchilada or taco
   sauce

Crumble beef into 1½-quart baking dish; add chopped onion, garlic, salt and chili powder. Cook, uncovered, at HIGH for 5 minutes, stirring 3 times. Drain off excess fat. Garnish with onion rings. To serve, spoon meat mixture into taco shells; top with tomato, lettuce and cheese. Pass sauce. *Easy and good.*

Christi Kook

Turkey Divan

Yield: 6 servings

2 (10-ounce) packages frozen chopped broccoli
2 tablespoons margarine
3 tablespoons all-purpose flour
½ teaspoon salt
2 cups milk

½ cup natural Swiss cheese, shredded
2 cups cooked turkey or chicken, cut into bite-sized pieces
¼ cup Parmesan cheese, grated

Place broccoli in 10x6-inch baking dish. Cook, uncovered, at HIGH for 10 minutes, breaking up and stirring twice. Drain well. Cover; set aside. Place margarine in a 4-cup glass measure. Cook, uncovered, at HIGH for 30 seconds. Blend in flour and salt. Add milk all at once. Cook, uncovered, at HIGH for 1¼ minutes. Stir. Cook at HIGH for 4½-5 minutes, stirring after each minute. Stir in Swiss cheese until melted. Place turkey over broccoli. Pour in sauce on top. Sprinkle with Parmesan cheese. Cook, covered, at MEDIUM HIGH for 5-8 minutes or until hot.
May do ahead. Easy.

Margaret Logan

Divine Chicken

Yield: 2-4 servings

¾ cup fine dry bread crumbs
⅔ cup Parmesan cheese, grated
4 tablespoons parsley, minced
¼ teaspoon pepper
1 cup butter or margarine, melted

1 clove garlic, crushed (or equivalent garlic powder)
2 teaspoons salt
4 chicken breasts, skinned and boned
6 tablespoons lemon juice
Dash of paprika

Blend bread crumbs, Parmesan cheese, parsley and pepper. Combine butter and garlic with salt. Dip chicken into butter then into bread crumb mixture, coating thoroughly. Roll each piece into firm rolls; secure with wooden toothpicks. Arrange in a 12x8-inch baking dish. Sprinkle with lemon juice; drizzle remaining butter over chicken. Cover with waxed paper. Microwave at MEDIUM HIGH for 12-15 minutes. Let stand 3-4 minutes before serving. Sprinkle with paprika to serve.
Easy and good.

Martha Nichols

Chicken Cacciatore

Yield: 4-6 servings

1 (2½-3 pound) chicken, cut
    into serving pieces
1 (15-ounce) can tomato sauce
1 (4¼-ounce) jar sliced
    mushrooms, drained
½ cup onions, chopped
1 tablespoon sugar
    (optional)

1 teaspoon oregano
1 teaspoon salt
½ teaspoon garlic, finely
    chopped
¼ teaspoon pepper

Arrange chicken, meatier portions toward edge of dish, in a 2-quart baking dish. Combine remaining ingredients; pour over chicken. Cover with waxed paper. Set power select at HIGH for 18-20 minutes. Rearrange chicken pieces once. Chicken should be tender. Let stand, covered, 7 minutes.
Serve with spaghetti.

Ollie White

Easy Barbecue Chicken

Yield: 6 servings

6 chicken breasts or
    assorted pieces
½ (18-ounce) bottle Kraft
    barbecue sauce
1 teaspoon dried green
    onion
1 teaspoon oregano
1 teaspoon garlic powder
2 tablespoons brown sugar
    or honey

2 tablespoons vinegar
¼ cup catsup
2 tablespoons lemon juice
    Dash of Worcestershire
    Dash of hot sauce
    Dash of dry mustard
    Salt and pepper to taste

Place chicken in shallow microwave dish with cover. Cook on HIGH for 4 minutes. Turn chicken. Cook additional 4 minutes. Combine remaining ingredients, blending well. Brush chicken with barbecue sauce. Cook on grill. Continue brushing with sauce while cooking. Do not overcook. Serve immediately.

Richard Kook

Ginger Orange Chicken

Yield: 4-6 servings

1 (2½-pound) fryer, cut up
1 teaspoon salt
¼ teaspoon paprika
⅓ cup frozen orange juice
concentrate, thawed
⅓ cup water
2 tablespoons brown sugar

2 tablespoons snipped parsley
2 teaspoons soy sauce
½ teaspoon ginger
1 tablespoon cornstarch
1 tablespoon cold water
Cooked rice

Arrange chicken in 12x7½-inch baking dish. Sprinkle with salt and paprika. Combine orange concentrate, water, brown sugar, parsley, soy sauce and ginger; pour over chicken. Cook, covered, at MEDIUM HIGH for 20 minutes or until tender. Remove chicken to platter. Cover; keep warm. Skim off fat from pan juices. Blend cornstarch and water. Add to pan juices. Cook at HIGH for 3½ minutes until mixture thickens and bubbles, stirring after each minute. Spoon sauce over chicken before serving. Serve with rice.

Margaret Logan

Roux in Microwave

Yield: 4 cups

⅔ cup vegetable oil
⅔ cup all-purpose flour
2 cups onion, chopped
1 cup celery, chopped
½ cup green pepper,
chopped

4 cloves garlic, minced
¼ cup parsley, chopped
¼ cup green onion tops,
sliced
¼ cup water
(approximately)

Mix oil and flour in 4-cup glass measure. Microwave, uncovered, on HIGH for 6 minutes. Roux will be a light brown and will need to cook 30 seconds - 1 minute longer. Stir every 30 seconds until browned. Stir in onion, celery and green pepper. Sauté on HIGH for 3 minutes. Add garlic, parsley and green onion to Roux. Sauté 2 minutes (3¾ cups now); pour off excess oil. Add water to make 4 cups.
Can be frozen.

Joan Anderson

Sweet Potato Pone

½ cup butter
2 (16-ounce) cans sweet
    potatoes or yams,
    drained
1 egg
½ cup milk
2 tablespoons brown sugar

2 tablespoons molasses
½ teaspoon cinnamon
¼ teaspoon nutmeg
    Dash of cloves
½ cup miniature
    marshmallows (optional)

Set power select at HIGH. Heat butter in a 1½-quart baking dish 1-1½ minutes or until melted. Put butter, potatoes, egg, milk, sugar, molasses, cinnamon, nutmeg and cloves in medium bowl; mash until smooth. Spread into baking dish; cover with plastic wrap. Heat for 8-9 minutes on HIGH or until heated through.

Judy Bishop

Acorn Squash Stuffed with Apples

Yield: 2 servings

1 acorn squash
2 tablespoons butter
⅛ teaspoon salt
3 tablespoons port or sherry
1 medium tart apple,
    cored and cubed

¼ cup dark raisins
¼ teaspoon cinnamon
2 tablespoons dark brown
    sugar

Pierce whole squash through center in several places with metal skewers. Put in microwave oven on paper towel. Microwave on HIGH 4 minutes; turn squash over. Microwave on HIGH 2-4 minutes more or until soft to the touch. Let stand 5 minutes. Cut in half; remove seeds. Put butter into baking dish with squash, cut side up. Mix remaining ingredients in small bowl. Put half of the mixture into each squash. Cover with waxed paper. Microwave on HIGH 2-4 minutes until apples are tender.

Deanie Fincher

Stuffed Zucchini

Yield: 4 servings

2 medium zucchini
½ cup cooked rice
¼ cup onion, chopped
¼ cup green pepper,
    chopped

½ teaspoon salt
¼ teaspoon basil
1 small tomato, peeled,
    seeded and chopped

Cut zucchini in half lengthwise. Scrape out pulp, leaving a ¼-inch shell. Chop pulp. Combine with rice, onion, green pepper, salt and basil. Place zucchini shells into an 8x8-inch baking dish. Mound ¼ of vegetable mixture into each shell. Top with tomato. Cover with waxed paper. Microwave on HIGH 5-7 minutes, or until shells are tender; rotating dish half turn after 3 minutes.

Cookbook Committee

Potato Onion Casserole

Yield: 5 servings

6 medium potatoes, thinly
   sliced
2 medium onions, thinly
   sliced

½ cup margarine, cut
   into pieces
Salt and pepper to taste

Layer potatoes and onions in a baking dish. Put margarine over the top. Add salt and pepper to taste. Cover. Microwave on HIGH 15 minutes. Stop microwave; stir casserole. Cover again. Bake 15 minutes more.

Linda Schwamlein

Baked Vidalia Onions

Vidalia onions
Butter, cut into pieces
Salt and pepper to taste

Peel onions and slightly hollow out top of each. Place in baking dish; cover with plastic wrap. Microwave on HIGH about 3 minutes. Place pat of butter on top of each onion; season well with salt and pepper. Microwave on HIGH until tender. Timing will depend on number and size of onions.
Variation: Top each onion with 1 slice Velveeta cheese and garlic powder. Microwave on HIGH 1-3 minutes or until melted.

Elly Hobgood

Garden Vegetable Casserole

Yield: 4 servings

2 small yellow summer
   squash, sliced
1 medium zucchini, sliced
1 small white onion, sliced
1 tomato, sliced

2 tablespoons Parmesan
   cheese, grated
½ teaspoon seasoned salt
½ teaspoon basil
½ teaspoon thyme

Place all sliced vegetables in baking dish. Mix all other ingredients. Toss lightly with vegetables. Cover; microwave on HIGH for 8-10 minutes.
May be cooked in conventional oven for 20-25 minutes at 350°.

Lila Stevens

Better Baked Beans

Yield: 6 servings

3 slices bacon, diced
½ cup green pepper or
    onion, chopped
2 (16-ounce) cans pork and
    beans
¼ cup molasses

¼ cup catsup
1 tablespoon prepared
    mustard
½ teaspoon Worcestershire
    Dash of hot pepper sauce

Set power selection at HIGH. Heat bacon and green pepper in a 1½-quart baking dish 3-4 minutes or until bacon is crisp. Stir in remaining ingredients; heat, covered with waxed paper, 3-4 minutes at HIGH or until mixture is bubbly. Set power selection at MEDIUM-LOW. Heat, covered with waxed paper, for 10-12 minutes.

Judy Bishop

Fast Fixin' Chocolate Fudge

Yield: 3 pounds

2 (16-ounce) boxes
    confectioners' sugar
1 cup cocoa
½ cup milk

1 cup butter or margarine
1½ cups nuts, chopped
    (optional)
2 tablespoons vanilla extract

Set power select at HIGH. Mix sugar and cocoa in a microwave bowl. Add butter and milk (do not stir). Heat 4½-6 minutes, or until butter is melted; add nuts and vanilla, stirring until smooth. Spread into well-greased 9-inch square baking dish. Chill until firm. Cut into squares.
So easy to satisfy that late night sweet tooth.

Ollie White

S'More Pudding

Yield: 6-8 servings

2 (3¾-ounce) packages vanilla
    pudding mix
3 cups milk
1 cup sour cream

¼ cup graham cracker
    crumbs
    Marshmallows (optional)
    Chocolate syrup (optional)

Combine pudding and milk in a 1½-quart bowl. Cook, uncovered, on HIGH for 8-9 minutes, stirring 3 times. Cool. Fold in sour cream. Spoon into 6-8 sherbet dishes. Sprinkle with graham cracker crumbs. Chill. Top with a marshmallow and drizzle with chocolate syrup, if desired.

Joan Anderson

Apple Pie

Yield: 6 servings

Pastry for 1 (9-inch)
2 crust pie
¾ cup sugar
2 tablespoons all-
purpose flour

1 teaspoon cinnamon
⅛ teaspoon nutmeg
¼ teaspoon salt
5-6 apples, peeled, cored
and sliced ¼-inch thick

Bake bottom crust on HIGH power for 4-6 minutes. Combine sugar, flour, cinnamon, nutmeg and salt; mix with apples. Heap into bottom crust. Top with second crust. Flute edges and vent. Cook at HIGH power for 8-10 minutes until apples are tender.
For brown crust, place finished pie in conventional oven under broiler until golden.

Joan McFather

Melba Cheesecake Pie

Yield: 8 servings

¼ cup margarine
1¼ cups graham cracker
crumbs
⅓ cup + 2 tablespoons sugar,
divided
1 (16-ounce) can sliced
peaches, drained

1 (8-ounce) package cream
cheese
½ cup sour cream
1 egg
½ teaspoon almond extract
⅓ cup raspberry jam

Microwave margarine in glass 9-inch pie plate for ½-1 minute on HIGH or until melted. Mix in crumbs and 2 tablespoons sugar; press onto bottom and sides of pie plate. Microwave on HIGH 1½-2 minutes. Arrange peaches on crust. Microwave cream cheese in glass mixing bowl 1 minute on MEDIUM, or until soft. Blend in remaining ⅓ cup sugar, sour cream, egg and almond extract; pour over peaches. Microwave on HIGH 3½-4½ minutes or until edges are set, rotating once. Cool. Spoon jam onto pie; spread to cover. Refrigerate until served.
Easy. Very rich cheesecake in 6 minutes.

Margaret Logan

Hearty Chicken Chowder

Yield: 8 servings

1 (10-ounce) package frozen
   baby lima beans
½ cup onion, chopped
½ cup celery, sliced
¼ teaspoon salt
1 cup water
1 (10¾-ounce) can cream
   of chicken soup
1 (16-ounce) can tomatoes,
   cut up

2 cups loose-pack frozen
   hash browns
1½ cups cooked chicken,
   chopped
¼ teaspoon poultry
   seasoning
¼ teaspoon garlic salt
½ cup natural Cheddar
   cheese, shredded

Combine lima beans, onion, celery, salt and water in a 3-quart bowl. Cook covered, at HIGH for 20 minutes, or until beans are tender, stirring twice. Stir in soup, tomatoes, hash browns, chicken, poultry seasoning and garlic salt. Cook, uncovered, at MEDIUM for 15 minutes, stirring once or twice. To serve, ladle into bowls and sprinkle cheese on top. Add water if it becomes too thick.

Cookbook Committee

Coquille St. Jacques

Yield: 6 servings

1 pound sea scallops
¼ cup white wine
2 tablespoons margarine
   or butter
1 tablespoon dried onion
   flakes
2 tablespoons all-purpose
   flour
   Dash of white pepper
¾ cup light cream or milk

1 (2½-ounce) jar sliced
   mushrooms, drained
⅓ cup Swiss cheese,
   shredded
⅓ cup Cheddar cheese,
   shredded
   (or use all Cheddar)
¼ cup buttered bread crumbs
   Parsley flakes

Set power select at MEDIUM. Place scallops in a round baking dish; pour wine over scallops; heat, covered, 5-6 minutes or until scallops are tender, stirring once. Drain liquid; reserve ¼ cup. Let scallops stand, covered. Heat butter and onion flakes 45-60 seconds; stir in flour and pepper; gradually add cream and reserved liquid, stirring until smooth. Heat for 3-3½ minutes or until mixture is thick, stirring twice. Stir in mushrooms and cheeses. Add scallops. Top with bread crumbs and parsley. Return to microwave for 2 minutes on HIGH to melt cheese.

Very rich. For conventional cooking you may need more wine.

Ollie White

Refrigerator Sweet Roll Dough

Yield: 24 rolls or
2 coffee cakes

3½-4 cups all-purpose flour,
    divided
  1 package active dry yeast
  1 cup milk

½ cup sugar
⅓ cup shortening
½ teaspoon salt
2 eggs

Combine 2 cups flour and yeast in a large mixing bowl. Combine milk, sugar, shortening and salt in a 4-cup glass measure. Heat, uncovered, at HIGH for 1½-1¾ minutes, just until mixture is warm and shortening starts to melt (115°-120°F). Add to dry mixture in bowl; add eggs. Beat at low speed on mixer for 30 seconds, scraping bowl constantly. Beat 3 minutes at high speed. By hand, stir in enough of the remaining all-purpose flour to make moderately stiff dough. Turn out on lightly floured surface; knead until smooth and elastic, 5-8 minutes. Shape into a ball. Place in a greased bowl; turn once to grease surface. Cover and refrigerate 2 hours or up to 5 days. Use for making cinnamon or orange rolls, coffee cakes or other sweet rolls.

Margaret Logan

Cinnamon or Orange Rolls

Yield: 12 rolls

½ basic recipe
    "Refrigerator Sweet
    Roll Dough"
2 tablespoons margarine,
    softened
2 tablespoons sugar

½ teaspoon cinnamon or
  ¾ teaspoon grated orange
  peel
½ cup pecans, chopped
  Confectioners' Sugar
  Icing

Roll out chilled dough on floured surface to 12x8-inch rectangle. Spread with margarine. Combine sugar and cinnamon (orange peel); sprinkle evenly over margarine. Sprinkle with nuts. Roll up, starting with long side; seal seams. Slice into 12 rolls. Place each roll, cut side down, in a greased 8x1½-inch round glass baking dish. Fill a 4-cup glass measure with 3 cups water. Heat at HIGH for 7-8 minutes until boiling. Place dish of dough in oven with water; heat at LOW for 7 minutes. Bake in conventional oven at 375° for 20-25 minutes. Remove from dish; cool on rack. Drizzle with Confectioners' Sugar Icing.

Confectioners' Sugar Icing

½ cup sifted
    confectioners' sugar
¼ teaspoon vanilla extract

2-3 teaspoons milk

Combine sugar and vanilla. Stir in enough milk to make drizzling consistency. (For orange rolls, substitute 2-3 teaspoons orange juice for the milk.)

Margaret Logan

Biscuit Breakfast Ring

Yield: 5 servings

⅓ cup dark brown
    sugar, firmly packed
3 tablespoons butter or
    margarine

1 tablespoon water
⅓ cup nuts, chopped
10 refrigerator biscuits

Combine sugar, butter and water in a 1½-quart baking dish. Cook 1 minute on HIGH. Stir in nuts. Cut each biscuit into fourths. Stir into sugar mixture, coating each piece. If using round dish, place a custard cup or glass in center. Cook on HIGH for 3 minutes. Turn dish quarter turn every 30 seconds. Let stand 2 minutes. Invert onto platter. Serve immediately.

Frances Gober

Honey Whole Wheat Bread

Yield: 2 loaves

2 packages active dry
    yeast
3 cups whole wheat flour
⅓ cup honey
1 tablespoon salt

¼ cup shortening
2¼ cups water
2¾-3 cups all-purpose
    flour

Combine yeast and the whole wheat flour in large mixing bowl. Combine honey, salt, shortening and water in a 4-cup glass measure. Heat, uncovered, at HIGH for 2 minutes, until warm and shortening begins to melt (115°-120°). Add to dry mixture in mixing bowl. Beat at low speed for 30 seconds, scraping bowl constantly. Beat 3 minutes at HIGH speed. Stir in enough flour to make a moderately stiff dough. Turn onto floured surface; knead until smooth and elastic, 8-10 minutes. Place in greased bowl; turn once to grease surface. Fill a 4-cup glass measure with 3 cups water; heat, uncovered, at HIGH for 7-8 minutes, until boiling. Place bowl of dough in microwave oven with water. Heat, uncovered, at LOW for 15 minutes. Punch down; divide in half. Shape each into a loaf; place in 2 greased 8¼x4½-inch glass loaf dishes. Brush tops lightly with a little melted butter; sprinkle top with whole wheat flour. Heat 3 cups water in 4-cup glass measure at HIGH for 7-8 minutes, until boiling. Place loaf dishes in oven with water; heat, uncovered, at LOW for 7 minutes. Bake in conventional oven at 375° for 40-45 minutes. Cool on rack.
Microwave really speeds up bread making process!

Margaret Logan

Children in the Kitchen

Pizza Crackers

1 box Rye Crisp Bread
   Crackers
1 (8-ounce) can tomato
   sauce

1 (8-ounce) package
   Mozzarella cheese,
   grated

Place crackers on a cookie sheet. Spread 1 teaspoon of tomato sauce on each cracker. Sprinkle grated cheese on top. Bake until cheese is bubbly. The "crisp bread" softens to be just like real pizza crust.

Laura Spears
Age 8

Peanut Butter Log

Yield: 1 (10-inch) log

½ cup peanut butter
2 tablespoons honey
2½ tablespoons nonfat
   dry milk

½ cup raisins
   Shredded coconut
   (optional)

Blend peanut butter and honey. Work in as much powdered milk as you need to make the mixture easy to handle and fairly stiff. Pick up the mixture and knead in the raisins distributing them evenly. Roll into a 10-inch long log, 1 inch thick. Roll log in coconut, if desired. Chill. Slice or pull apart.

Rand Bagwell
Age 7

Cookie Monster's Own Cookies

½ cup peanut butter
½ cup confectioners' sugar
¼ cup nonfat dry milk
1 tablespoon + 2 teaspoons
   water

½ cup semi-sweet
   chocolate chips
⅛ cup nuts, chopped
⅛ cup graham cracker
   crumbs

Mix peanut butter, confectioners' sugar, dry milk and water in a large bowl. Add chocolate chips and nuts; mix. Roll into balls. Roll balls in graham cracker crumbs. Store covered in refrigerator.
An easy, fun, no-cook recipe.

Lauren Hasty
Age 7

Lemon Pie

1 (6-ounce) can frozen
    lemonade concentrate
1 (14-ounce) can sweetened
    condensed milk

1 (4-ounce) carton frozen
    whipped topping
1 (9-inch) graham cracker
    crust

Stir lemonade into milk in a bowl, mixing well. Pour into crust. Chill for 3-4 hours. Top with frozen whipped topping.
Easy enough for even small children. Deliciously rich grown up taste.

Heather Kook
Age 8

Raggedy Ann Salad

Yield: 1 serving

Body: Peach half
Arms and legs: Small celery sticks
Head: Half a hard-cooked egg
Eyes, nose, buttons and shoes: Raisins
Mouth: Slice of cherry
Hair: Grated yellow cheese
Skirt: Ruffled leaf lettuce

Walker and Betsy Cloud
Ages 6 and 3

Easy Peanut Butter Balls

1 cup peanut butter
1 cup light corn syrup

1¼ cups nonfat dry milk
1¼ cups confectioners' sugar

Mix all ingredients together. Roll into 1-inch balls. Roll balls in additional confectioners' sugar or sprinkles.

Meg, Fran, Lori and David Haley
Ages 10, 8, 8, and 5

Saturday Sandwich

Oven: 350° - 10 minutes   Yield: 4-6 servings

**6 slices of white (or
    choice of) bread
1 (16-ounce) can pork and
    beans**

**6 hot dogs, sliced
6 slices American cheese**

Place bread slices on baking sheet. Spoon a covering of baked beans over bread. Place hot dog slices on top of beans. Add a slice of cheese to each sandwich. Bake at 350° for 10 minutes or until warm and cheese melts.

*John Anderson
Age 15*

Cheese Biscuits

Oven: 450° - 8-10 minutes   **Yield:** 1 dozen

**2 cups Bisquick mix
⅔ cup milk**

**1 cup Cheddar cheese,
    grated**

Mix all ingredients together into soft dough. Beat hard by hand about 30 seconds. Drop by tablespoons onto an ungreased cookie sheet. Bake at 450° for 8-10 minutes.

*Kate McFather
Age 9*

Animal Cookies

**Confectioners' sugar
Water
Food coloring
Animal crackers**

Spoon confectioners' sugar into small bowl. Add enough water to make easy to spread. Add a few drops of food coloring. Spread over small animal crackers and eat.

*Megan Buchanan
Age 5*

Honey Yummies

½ cup peanut butter
½ cup confectioners' sugar
½ cup raisins

½ cup oven toasted
  rice cereal
½ cup honey

Put all ingredients together in a big bowl. Mix well with spoon. Make into small balls. Put balls on waxed paper.

Josh Spears
Age 7

Oreo Treats

1 (16-ounce) package Oreo
  cookies, crushed
½ gallon vanilla ice
  cream, softened

1 (12-ounce) carton frozen
  whipped topping, thawed
Maraschino cherries

Combine cookie crumbs, ice cream and whipped topping. Spoon into dessert glasses; top with a cherry. Cover with plastic wrap. Freeze until firm.

Grant Gober
Age 6

Easy Hot Chocolate Mix

1 (8-quart) box powdered milk
1 (16-ounce) box instant
  chocolate drink mix

1 (6-ounce) jar non-dairy
  creamer
1½ cups confectioners' sugar

Mix all ingredients together in an airtight container. Use two heaping table-spoons per cup of boiling water for instant hot chocolate.
Great gift in decorated jar for Christmas.

Heather Kook
Age 8

S'Mores

Yield: 1 serving

2 graham crackers
4 squares milk chocolate
 candy bar

1 large marshmallow or
 6 small marshmallows

Place one graham cracker on paper towel. Top with chocolate squares, then marshmallow. Microwave, uncovered, at HIGH for 15 seconds. Top with second cracker. Let stand 1 minute before serving. (2 or 3 s'mores: 20 seconds; 4 s'mores: 25 seconds.)

Theron Gober
Age 12

Fudgesicles

1 (3½-ounce) box instant
 chocolate pudding

½ cup evaporated milk

Make instant pudding according to package directions. Add evaporated milk. Pour into ice cube tray. Use plastic spoons, knives or popsicle sticks for handles. Freeze until solid.

Christopher Bishop
Age 8

Very Berry Punch

2 quarts gingerale
3 (46-ounce) cans of apple
 juice or fruit punch

1 (10-ounce) package frozen
 strawberries

Mix gingerale and juice or punch in a big bowl. Add frozen strawberries. Serve in paper cups.

Josh Spears
Age 7

Yahoos

1½ cups ground sunflower
 seeds
1 cup pitted dates, chopped

¼ cup honey

Grind seeds in blender to a fine powder. Mix dates with 1 cup of seed powder. Add honey; blend until well mixed. Shape into 1-inch balls. Coat with remaining ground seeds.

Megan Bagwell
Age 6

Chocolate-Chip P'nut Butter Cup Cookies

Oven: 350° - 10-12 minutes   **Yield:** 2½ dozen

1 (16-ounce) roll Pillsbury
   chocolate chip cookies
1 (9-ounce) box Reece's
   peanut butter cups

Miniature muffin paper
   cups

Cut chocolate chip cookies in ¾-inch slices; then cut into ¼-inch pieces. Unwrap Reece's peanut butter cups. Use paper cups to line miniature muffin tins. Place ¼ of cookie slice into middle of paper cups. Bake cookies at 350° for 10-12 minutes. Remove from oven and immediately put Reece's peanut butter cup in the middle. Allow to cool for 1 hour or put in freezer for 15 minutes before removing from tins.
Very easy and surprisingly good.

Jay and Shannon Benzel
Ages 12 and 13

Roasted Pumpkin Seeds

Oven: 250° - 1 hour 30 minutes

2 cups pumpkin seeds,
   separated from pulp
   but not washed

2 tablespoons vegetable
   oil
1½ teaspoons salt

Spread seeds on paper towel to dry. Combine seeds, oil and salt; spread on baking sheet. Bake at 250° for 1 hour 30 minutes.

Stuart and Jennifer Hobgood
Ages 11 and 13

Fruit Flavor Pops

Yield: 8 or 9 large pops

1 (3-ounce) package gelatin,
   any flavor
½ cup sugar
2 cups boiling water

2 cups cold water
8 wooden spoons or
   popsicle sticks

Dissolve gelatin and sugar in boiling water. Add cold water. Pour into paper cups or pop molds. Freeze until almost firm, about 2 hours. Insert wooden spoons or popsicle sticks. Freeze until firm, at least 8 hours or overnight.

Jennifer Fincher
Age 11

Orange Sherbet

1 (20-ounce) can crushed
   pineapple, drained
2 (14-ounce) cans sweetened
   condensed milk

60 ounces of Orange Crush
   or similar orange soda
   pop

Combine all ingredients. Pour into an ice cream freezer to freeze.

Laura and Mandy Ridenhour
Ages 11 and 7

Purple Cow

Yield: 2 servings

1½ cups milk
 3 tablespoons grape juice
   concentrate, thawed

Vanilla ice cream

Place milk, grape juice and 2 scoops vanilla ice cream in blender; blend until smooth. Pour into 2 12-ounce glasses. Top with scoop of vanilla ice cream. *Easy, fun sodas for kids.*

Bryan Roach
Age 8

Candy Cane Cookies

Oven: 375° - 8-10 minutes

Yield: 2½ dozen

½ cup soft shortening
½ cup sifted confectioners'
   sugar
2 tablespoons egg, slightly
   beaten
1¼ cups all-purpose flour,
   sifted

½ teaspoon salt
½ teaspoon almond extract
½ teaspoon vanilla extract
¼ teaspoon red food coloring

Blend shortening, sugar and egg thoroughly. Mix in flour, salt and extracts. Divide dough in half. Tint half the dough with red food coloring. Leave the other portion plain. Roll small piece of plain dough between palms to a 6-inch length. Roll a small piece of red dough in same manner to same length. Twist together. Shape to resemble a cane. Bake on lightly greased cookie sheet at 375° for 8-10 minutes.
Lots of fun for children to make.

Chad, Jason and Tiffany White
Ages 13, 11 and 7

Homemade Toothpaste

1 teaspoon salt
1 teaspoon peppermint or
  spearmint extract

4 teaspoons baking soda

Mix all ingredients. Pour into a small plastic bag and close tightly.

Jeffrey Adams
Age 7

Homemade Play Dough

Yield: 1 large ball

1 cup all-purpose flour
½ cup salt
2 teaspoons cream of tartar
1 cup water

2 tablespoons vegetable
  oil
Food coloring

Combine flour, salt and cream of tartar in a saucepan. Mix water, oil and food coloring. Gradually stir into dry ingredients. Cook over medium heat, stirring constantly, until a ball forms. Remove and knead for 5 minutes. Store in an airtight bag or container.

Cookbook Committee

Chocolate Chip Pizza

Oven: 375° - 15 minutes

Yield: 10-15 servings

½ cup sugar
½ cup brown sugar,
  firmly packed
½ cup margarine,
  softened
½ cup peanut butter
½ teaspoon vanilla extract

1 egg
1½ cups all-purpose flour
1 (6-ounce) package semi-
  sweet chocolate chips
2 cups miniature
  marshmallows

Combine first 6 ingredients. Blend well. Add flour; stir until soft dough forms. Press dough evenly over 12-inch pizza pan, forming rim around edge. Bake at 375° for 10 minutes. Remove from oven. Sprinkle with chocolate chips; top with marshmallows. Bake for 5 minutes more or until marshmallows are brown. Cool. Cut into wedges.

Nathan and Ann Johnston
Ages 5 and 3

Cherokee Entertains

Cherokee Entertains

Our cookbook would not be complete without a sampling of the special, warm hospitality extended by hostesses in Cherokee County. Following are several menus which have proved successful for various occasions. An especially good variety of dinner menus submitted by the supper clubs in this area are included.

Supper clubs have become a popular way to entertain friends and experiment with new recipes. The format and composition of a supper club may be as varied as the imagination of its members. Usually, the host couple plans the menu, prepares the entree, provides the beverage and assigns the remaining members a dish to prepare to complete the menu. Supper clubs in Cherokee County are organized in various ways. One of the more unusual supper clubs consists of 36 couples, all members of the same church. The club is divided into groups of four couples. After each couple serves as host, the entire club is regrouped allowing each couple to entertain and to be entertained by every other couple. In another example, five regular couples meet monthly and the host invites an additional couple. Another supper club of seven couples meets every other month and plans their menus around a selected theme.

Whether you choose to select menus in their entirety or just to spark an idea of your own, we hope they bring you as much pleasure as they do these hostesses when "Cherokee Entertains."

Dinner for a Special Occasion

Hot Crab Triangles*

Fake Clam Dip*

Stuffed Pork Tenderloin*

Curried Lima Beans*

Steamed Carrots

Mixed Green Salad

Dinner Rolls

Amaretto Cheesecake*

*Recipes found in index.

Little Bit of Italy

Antipasto*

Lasagna*

Tossed Green Salad

French Bread

Tortoni*

After School Get-Together

Pizza Crackers*

Hot Dogs

Potato Chips

Chocolate Chip Pizza*

Very Berry Punch*

*Recipes found in index.

"Hangar Party"

(Party was held in an airport hangar)

Spinach Cheese Puffs*

Cheese and Crackers

Broiled Chicken*

Potato Salad

Three-Week Slaw*

Baked Beans*

Sour Dough Bread

Pound Cake I*

*Recipes found in index.

A Taste of the Orient

Shrimp Toast Appetizers*

Water Chestnuts Wrapped in Bacon

Stir-Fry Beef and Snow Peas*

Cooked Rice

Stir-Fry Broccoli*

Stir-Fry Chinese Cabbage*

Fortune Cookies

Hot Oriental Tea

*Recipes found in index.

Saturday Night Dinner
with Friends

Hot Cheese Canapés*

Pic-A-Pepper Spread*

Rib Roast*

Cauliflower Casserole*

Pineapple Aspic*

Quick Biscuits*

Combination Trifle*

*Recipes found in index.

Wednesday Night
Supper Club Dinner

Frosty Fruit Cup*

Burgundy Beef Tips*

Baked Rice

Baked Stuffed Squash*

Bibb Lettuce and Tomato Salad
with Mustard Dressing*

Garlic French Bread

Lemon Chiffon Pie*

*Recipes found in index.

Hawaiian Luau

Cream Cheese Nut Puffs*

Smoked Ham*

Cantonese Chicken*

Bean Salad*

Fresh Fruit Salad

Banana Cake*

Dessert Extravaganza

Chocolate Marble Cheesecake*

Elegant Lemon Cake Roll*

Blueberry Dessert*

Orange Cream Pie*

Coffee

*Recipes found in index.

Supper Club at its Best

Hot Mushroom Turnovers*

Olive Cheese Balls*

Stuffed Beef Tenderloin*

Potato-Zucchini au Gratin*

Mandarin Orange Salad*

Dinner Rolls

Spanish Lime Pie*

*Recipes found in index.

Christmas Dinner Party

Chutneyed Snow Peas*

Oysters Keithburg*

Beef Wellington*

Swiss Style Green Beans*

Mixed Green Salad
topped with Ceviche

Heavenly Refrigerator Rolls*

Strawberries Romanoff*

*Recipes found in index.

A Greek Dinner

Cheese Puffs*

Greek Appetizer Salad*

Chicken Oregano*

Greek Tomato Pilaf*

Greek Honey Walnut Cake*

Independence Day Cookout

Great Hamburgers*

Pinto Bean Salad*

Marinated Summer Salad*

Corn on the Cob

Peach Ice Cream*

Lemon Bars*

Iced Tea

*Recipes found in index.

Annual Service League Spring Ball

Spiced Apricot Bread
Dainty Sandwiches*

Pimiento Cheese Sandwiches*

Dilled Cucumber & Cream Cheese
Sandwiches*

Tangy-Sweet Meatballs*

Hot Broccoli Dip*

Fresh Fruit Tree

Crab Paté*

Melba's Boursin Cheese Spread*

Caramel Bars*

Crème de Menthe Brownies*

Snickerdoodles*

Mom's Date Pinwheel Cookies*

Country Club Punch*

*Recipes found in index.

Sunday School Progressive/ Christmas Dinner

House No. 1

Mock Champagne Punch*

Jalapeño Cocktail Pie*

Spinach Tarts*

Shrimp Butter*

Marinated Mushrooms*

House No. 2

Pineapple Cheddar Salad*

Deluxe Waldorf Salad*

Asheville Salad*

Iced Tea

*Recipes found in index.

Continued

House No. 3

Spicy Pot Roast*

Mother's Broccoli & Rice Casserole*

Hot Fruit Compote*

Yeast Rolls*

Coffee

Iced Tea

House No. 4

Praline Cheesecake*

Frozen Chocolate Pecan Pie*

Italian Cream Cake*

Coffee

Hot Spiced Tea*

*Recipes found in index.

Southeastern Conference Tailgate Picnic

Pitcher Bloody Marys*

Rumaki*

Pico de Gallo*

Lemon Fried Chicken*

Broccoli Pasta Salad*

Parmesan Cheese & Dill Bread*

Southern Pecan Pie*

*Recipes found in index.

Christmas Open House

Hot Seafood Dip*

Fresh Vegetables
with Honey Curry Dip*

Petite Broccoli Quiches*

Toasted Pecans*

1, 2, 3 Cheese Straws*

Chicken Curry Cream Cheese Ball*

Ham in Petite Biscuits

Shrimp Mold*

Candy Cane Cookies*

Sandies*

Divinity*

Cheescake Squares*

Open Bar

Champagne Punch*

*Recipes found in index.

"Get Acquainted" Cocktail Buffet

Caviar Mold*

Mushrooms in Sherry Sauce*

Wontons*

Turkey in Lettuce Leaves*

Tex Mex Dip*

Chocolate Fondue Marveilleuse*

Cream Cheese-Almond Squares*

Open Bar

24-Hour Punch*

*Recipes found in index.

Brunch For Weekend Guests

Simple Sticky Buns*

Breakfast Casserole*

Garlic Cheese Grits*

Orange Juice

Coffee

On the Court with A L T A **

ALTA Almond Coffee Cake*

Mystery Dip*

Salted Peanuts & M & M's Mixture

Cheese and Crackers

Sugar Cookies I*

Assorted Soft Drinks

*Recipes found in index.
**Atlanta Lawn Tennis Association

Bridal Shower Luncheon

Wine Spritzers*

Super Chicken Salad on Lettuce*

Marinated Broccoli*

Rich's Magnolia Room Fruit Salad*

French Lemon Spirals*

Lemon Schaum Torte*

Iced Tea

Cinnamon Coffee

*Recipes found in index.

Ground Hog Day Celebration

(This unique party is held annually at the Cagle Farm.)

Fresh Fruit Tray

Ham and Cheese Sandwiches*

Smoked Salmon Spread*

Cheddar Cheese Pennies*

Spinach Dip with Variation*

Beef Balls*

Shrimp Mold*

Fried Chicken Livers

Boiled Peanuts

Pickled Okra

Hot Spiced Apple Juice*

*Recipes found in index.

Picnic on the Lake

Shrimp Spread*

Cheese Ball II*

Barbecued Ribs

Green Beans Almondine

Fruit Salad*

Sweet Potato Beignets*

Dinner Rolls

Snowball Cake*

*Recipes found in index.

Kitchen Helpers

Substitutions

Instead of:	Use:
1 cup cake flour	1 cup minus 2 tablespoons all-purpose flour
1 cup self-rising flour	1 cup all-purpose flour plus 1 teaspoon baking powder and ½ teaspoon salt
1 teaspoon baking powder	½ teaspoon cream of tartar plus ¼ teaspoon salt
1 tablespoon cornstarch	2 tablespoons flour or 4 teaspoons quick-cooking tapioca
1 cake compressed yeast	1 package or 2 teaspoons active dry yeast
1 cup whole milk	½ cup evaporated milk plus ½ cup water or 1 cup nonfat dry milk plus 2½ teaspoons butter or margarine
1 cup sour milk or buttermilk	1 tablespoon lemon juice or vinegar plus sweet milk to make 1 cup (let stand 5 minutes before using)
1 whole egg	2 egg yolks plus 1 tablespoon water
2 large eggs	3 small eggs
1 cup yogurt	1 cup buttermilk or sour milk
1 cup commercial sour cream	1 tablespoon lemon juice plus evaporated milk to make 1 cup
1 cup honey	1¼ cups sugar plus ¼ cup liquid or 1 cup molasses
1 cup corn syrup	¾ cup sugar plus ¼ cup water
1 (1-ounce) square unsweetened chocolate	3 tablespoons cocoa plus 1 tablespoon butter or margarine
1 tablespoon fresh snipped herbs	1 teaspoon dried herbs or ¼ teaspoon powdered herbs
1 clove fresh garlic	1 teaspoon garlic salt or ⅛ teaspoon garlic powder
1 small fresh onion	1 tablespoon instant minced onion, rehydrated
1 teaspoon onion powder	2 teaspoons minced onion
1 teaspoon dry mustard	1 tablespoon prepared mustard
1 pound fresh mushrooms	6 ounces canned mushrooms
1 cup tomato juice	½ cup tomato sauce plus ½ cup water
⅛ teaspoon cayenne	8 drops Tabasco
1 cup canned tomatoes	1⅓ cups fresh cut-up tomatoes, simmered 10 minutes

Continued

1 cup catsup or chili sauce	1 cup tomato sauce plus ½ cup sugar and 2 tablespoons vinegar (for use in cooked mixtures)
1 cup skim milk	4 tablespoons nonfat dry milk plus 1 cup water
1 cup light cream	⅞ cup milk plus 3 tablespoons butter
1 cup heavy cream	¾ cup milk plus ⅓ cup butter
1 cup broth	1 bouillon cube or 1 teaspoon powdered broth or 1 envelope powdered broth base, dissolved in 1 cup boiling water
1 tablespoon grated raw ginger	½ teaspoon powdered ginger

Equivalent Measures
"Weights and Measures"

Dash (dry)	Less than ⅛ teaspoon
Dash (liquid)	2-3 drops
3 teaspoons	1 tablespoon
2 tablespoons	⅛ cup or 1 fluid ounce
4 tablespoons	¼ cup or 2 fluid ounces
5⅓ tablespoons	⅓ cup or 4 fluid ounces
8 tablespoons	½ cup
10⅔ tablespoons	⅔ cup
12 tablespoons	¾ cup or 6 fluid ounces
16 tablespoons	1 cup or 8 fluid ounces
1 cup	½ pint or 8 fluid ounces
2 cups	1 pint or 16 fluid ounces
4 cups	1 quart or 32 fluid ounces
4 quarts	1 gallon
8 quarts	1 peck
4 pecks	1 bushel or 32 quarts
1 ounce	28.35 grams or 2 tablespoons
1 gram	0.035 ounces
1 quart	946.4 milliliters
1 liter	1.06 quarts
16 ounces	1 pound
32 ounces	1 quart

Equivalent Amounts
"How Much and How Many"

Butter, Cheese, Cream, Eggs

2 tablespoons butter	1 ounce
1 pound American cheese, shredded	4 cups
¼ pound Bleu cheese, crumbled	1 cup
1 cup whipping cream	2 cups whipped
8-10 egg whites	1 cup
12-14 egg yolks	1 cup

Chocolate

1 square unsweetened	1 ounce
4 cups cocoa	1 pound
6 ounces semi-sweet pieces	1 cup

Crumbs

1 slice bread	½ cup fine crumbs
1½ slices bread	1 cup soft crumbs
28 saltines	1 cup fine crumbs
14 square graham crackers	1 cup fine crumbs
22 vanilla wafers	1 cup fine crumbs

Fruits and Vegetables

Apples, 1 pound	3 medium or 3 cups sliced
Bananas, 1 pound	3 medium, 2½ cups sliced, or 1⅓ cups mashed
Berries, 1 pint	1¾ cups
Lemons	
Juice of 1 lemon	3 tablespoons
Grated rind of 1 lemon	1 tablespoon
Mushrooms, 1 pound	5 cups sliced
Onion, 1 medium chopped	¾ to 1 cup
Oranges	
Juice of 1 orange	⅓ cup
Grated rind of 1 orange	2 tablespoons
Raisins, 1 pound	3 cups, loosely packed
Tomatoes, 1 pound	3 medium

Gelatin

1 envelope, unflavored	1 tablespoon

Nuts

Almonds	
1 pound unshelled	1¼ cups shelled
1 pound shelled	3 cups
Pecans	
1 pound unshelled	2¼ cups shelled
1 pound shelled	4 cups
Walnuts	
1 pound unshelled	2 cups shelled
1 pound shelled	4 cups

Pasta, Rice

Macaroni, Spaghetti
    1 cup, uncooked   2 cups cooked
    1 pound, uncooked   5 cups cooked

Noodles
    1 cup (4 ounces) uncooked   1 cup cooked

Rice
    1 cup converted, uncooked   4 cups cooked
    1 cup long grain, uncooked   3-4 cups cooked

Sugar

Brown, 1 pound   2¼ cups firmly packed
Confectioners', 1 pound   3½ cups, sifted
Granulated, 1 pound   2 cups

Can Sizes

No. 1 or Picnic	=	1¼ cups or 10½-12 ounces
No. 2	=	2½ cups or 20 ounces
No. 2½	=	3½ cups or 29 ounces
No. 3	=	5¾ cups or 46 fluid ounces
No. 10	=	12-13 cups or 6½ to 7 pound 5 ounces (equals 7 No. 303 or 5 No. 2 cans)
No. 300	=	1¾ cups or 14-16 ounces
No. 303	=	2 cups or 20 ounces
6 ounces	=	¾ cup
8 ounces (No. ½)	=	1 cup
12 ounces	=	1½ cups

Oven Chart

Very slow oven	250° - 275°
Slow oven	300° - 325°
Moderate oven	350° - 375°
Hot oven	400° - 425°
Very hot oven	450° - 475°
Extremely hot oven	500° - 525°

Thermometer Readings for Meats

	Temperature of meat
Beef	
Rare	140° or 60° C
Medium	160° or 71° C
Well done	170° or 76° C
Veal	170° or 76° C
Lamb	180° or 81° C
Fresh pork	170° or 76° C
Smoked pork	
Fully cooked	130° or 54° C
Cook-before-eating	160° or 71° C
Poultry	185° or 85° C

Thermometer Readings for Candy and Frosting

	Temperature of syrup
Thread	230°-234°
Soft ball	234°-240°
Firm ball	244°-248°
Hard ball	250°-266°
Soft crack	270°-290°
Hard crack	300°-310°

About the Artist

Brenda Harris Tustian was formally eduacated in fine art at the University of Tennessee in Knoxville, and later concentrated on watercolor painting with instruction under Claude Croney in Sao Paulo, Brazil. Brenda has since studied with a succession of distinguished artists and teachers in the United States, including Edgar Whitney, Rudy de Reyna, Tony Couch, and Zoltan Szabo.

Brenda has displayed her work in various exhibitions around the country, receiving numerous awards. She specializes in custom art work with professional decorators, which has brought her paintings into major corporations. Several of her originals are in the office of Senator Sam Nunn and former U.S. Congressman Ed Jenkins.

Brenda and her husband, Michael, live on a lovely farm in the North Georgia mountains. God's country! This beautiful countryside is a great inspiration for many of her watercolors.

CORPORATE COLLECTORS IN THE UNITED STATES, SOUTH AMERICA, AND EUROPE:

- American Insurance Underwriters
- California Federal
- Coca Cola Company
- Coopers & Lybrand
- Cox Broadcasting
- Days Inns of America
- Dow Chemical
- Emory University Hospital

- Harris Corporation
- Hyatt Hotels Corporation
- IBM
- Kodak
- Miller Brewing Company
- Peachtree Federal Savings & Loan
- Touche Ross
- United Airlines

OAKLEIGH HOUSE * 1579 JULIUS BRIDGE RD.
BALLGROUND, GA 30107

Notes

Notes

Notes

(M) Denotes Microwave   (CE) Denotes Cherokee Entertains

(M) Denotes Microwave   **(CE) Denotes Cherokee Entertains**

(M) Denotes Microwave   **(CE) Denotes Cherokee Entertains**

(M) Denotes Microwave   **(CE) Denotes Cherokee Entertains**

(M) Denotes Microwave   **(CE) Denotes Cherokee Entertains**

(M) Denotes Microwave   **(CE) Denotes Cherokee Entertains**

(M) Denotes Microwave   **(CE) Denotes Cherokee Entertains**

(M) Denotes Microwave   **(CE) Denotes Cherokee Entertains**

(M) Denotes Microwave   **(CE) Denotes Cherokee Entertains**

(M) Denotes Microwave   **(CE) Denotes Cherokee Entertains**

(M) Denotes Microwave   (CE) Denotes Cherokee Entertains

(M) Denotes Microwave   **(CE) Denotes Cherokee Entertains**

(M) Denotes Microwave   **(CE) Denotes Cherokee Entertains**

Cherokee Entertains

Service League of Cherokee County, Ga., Inc.
P.O. Box 1132
Canton, Georgia 30114

Please send _____ copies of **Cherokee Entertains** @ $16.95 each $ _____
Add postage and handling @ $ 1.75 each $ _____
Add gift wrap (if desired)* @ $ 1.00 each $ _____
Georgia residents add 5% sales tax @ $ .85 each $ _____

Ship To:

Name _____

Address _____

City _____ State _____ Zip Code _____

Please make checks payable to: **Cherokee Entertains**

*Gift card to read _____

— —

Cherokee Entertains

Service League of Cherokee County, Ga., Inc.
P.O. Box 1132
Canton, Georgia 30114

Please send _____ copies of **Cherokee Entertains** @ $16.95 each $ _____
Add postage and handling @ $ 1.75 each $ _____
Add gift wrap (if desired)* @ $ 1.00 each $ _____
Georgia residents add 5% sales tax @ $ .85 each $ _____

Ship To:

Name _____

Address _____

City _____ State _____ Zip Code _____

Please make checks payable to: **Cherokee Entertains**

*Gift card to read _____

— —

Cherokee Entertains

Service League of Cherokee County, Ga., Inc.
P.O. Box 1132
Canton, Georgia 30114

Please send _____ copies of **Cherokee Entertains** @ $16.95 each $ _____
Add postage and handling @ $ 1.75 each $ _____
Add gift wrap (if desired)* @ $ 1.00 each $ _____
Georgia residents add 5% sales tax @ $ .85 each $ _____

Ship To:

Name _____

Address _____

City _____ State _____ Zip Code _____

Please make checks payable to: **Cherokee Entertains**

*Gift card to read _____